RUDE
AWAKENINGS

A publication of the
Center for Self-Governance

RUDE

AWAKENINGS

What the Homeless Crisis Tells Us

Richard W. White, Jr.

ICS PRESS
San Francisco, California

© 1992 Richard W. White, Jr.

This book is a publication of the Center for Self-Governance, dedicated to the study of self-governing institutions. The Center is affiliated with the Institute for Contemporary Studies, a nonpartisan, nonprofit public policy research organization. The analyses, conclusions, and opinions expressed in ICS Press publications are those of the authors and not necessarily those of the Institute, or of its officers, directors, or others associated with, or funding, its work.

Inquiries, book orders, and catalog requests should be addressed to ICS Press, 243 Kearny Street, San Francisco, CA 94108. (415) 981-5353. Fax (415) 986-4878. For book orders and catalog requests call toll free in the contiguous United States: **(800) 326-0263.** Distributed to the trade by National Book Network, Lanham, Maryland.

Library of Congress Cataloging-in-Publication Data

White, Richard W. (Richard Weddington)
    Rude awakenings : what the homeless crisis tells us / Richard W. White, Jr.
      p.   cm.
    ''A publication of the Center for Self-Governance.''
    Includes bibliographical references and index.
    ISBN 1-55815-158-3 (alk. paper)
    1. Homelessness—United States. 2. Homelessness—Government policy—United States. 3. Housing policy—United States. 4. United States—Social policy—1980- 5. United States—Social conditions—1980- I. Title.
HV4505.W45   362.5'0973—dc20   91-35588

To my family

Contents

LEADERSHIP

COMMUNITY

APPENDIX

Foreword

RUDE AWAKENINGS performs a vital public service: it tells the truth. Most of the homeless are *not* simply people without homes, as many of their advocates would have us believe. The majority suffer from severe problems that are difficult to treat even under optimal conditions—problems such as substance abuse, serious mental illness, and family breakdown. In other words, homelessness is complex, and this book gives that complexity its due.

On a deeper level, this book offers a disquieting picture of our current political culture. The use of deception to achieve "just" ends is increasingly common in American politics. Social problems are typically exaggerated by a factor of ten or more in an effort to win wider media coverage. Once this attention is achieved, great effort is put into "spinning" the story to prove a point or support an agenda. This book's account of the perpetual attempts to make the homeless seem "just like you and me" might be worth a smile if we weren't talking about real people with very real— and severe—problems. Some advocates candidly admit to simplifying and exaggerating homelessness to gain greater public sympathy. The flaw in their reasoning is that when a problem is portrayed as both enormous and easy to solve, it doesn't ring true, and people easily become disillusioned with the prospect of things ever getting better.

Homelessness is at its core a problem of *governance.* Seeing the homeless as people who have difficulty governing their lives points us toward solutions that cut to the heart of the problem. Finding new and innovative ways to help the homeless can guide us to better ways of governing ourselves.

Robert B. Hawkins, Jr., President
Institute for Contemporary Studies

Preface

I DID NOT KNOW what I would find when I began to explore homelessness. So little reported in the press made sense. I first noticed stories of "millions" of Americans without homes in the early months of Ronald Reagan's presidency, stories that often ascribed the problem to his policies. The effects of governmental action usually take longer than a few months to manifest themselves, so I was skeptical that the new president could have played an important role in any increase in homelessness. And the numbers of homeless claimed—3 million—seemed unlikely, though there was no denying that the heart-wrenching problem of people living in the streets was increasingly visible in the early 1980s.

I had worked for twenty years in the administration of federal antipoverty programs, from the day President Lyndon Johnson declared "unconditional war on poverty" until the day President Reagan closed down the war's flagship agency, where I was employed. In 1960, freshly graduated from the University of California with a degree in sociology, I joined the federal government with answers to poverty and many other social problems. At Berkeley I had been a political activist: a card-carrying member of the Socialist party of Eugene Debs, Norman Thomas, and Michael Harrington and a leader in the peace and civil rights movements. I carried these values through my years as a program official and was sympathetic to those who were sounding alarms about the homeless.

I differed from my colleagues, however, in that I had developed strong reservations about the effectiveness of many government policies and programs for the poor. In twenty years of program administration, scientific truths and moral certainties one after another disappeared like the Cheshire Cat, leaving not a smile but a grimace. I was uncertain of the alternatives, but I had come to suspect that many criticisms of such programs were on the mark—that most were not working, and that some were doing more harm than good. The specter of homelessness in America unquestionably spoke to deep failures of one kind or another, and I became curious about its causes as well as how we would react to the problem.

After a survey of what had been written about the homeless, I arranged interviews with social service workers, program administrators, homeless individuals, journalists, policy analysts, professors, and others with first-hand observations or ideas. Over the period of a year I spoke with scores of people across the country—most in person, the rest by telephone—and read extensively on homelessness and related subjects such as alcoholism, mental illness, and housing policy.

In embarking on a search for the roots of homelessness, I had a hunch that not only might I come to understand more fully this sad, painful condition, but also that it might serve as a lens though which we could better comprehend contemporary life in the United States. Now that I have completed this journey, I can say that it proved to be all this and more. The way the problem of homelessness arose and the manner in which we have responded tell us a great deal—if we listen carefully—about our political culture.

The most important thing I found is that much of the time we do not tell each other the truth, and this failing is poisoning our politics. We have a "community of conscience," as the late Mitch Snyder called it, in which activists—generally the same ones, again and again—take up issues and call the rest of us to account. But often these people engage in what I call "lying for justice." Somehow we justify exaggeration or distortion by telling ourselves that the truth alone would fail to gain the support of those we need to do the right thing.

A few candid interviews, for example, confirmed my suspicions about the numbers of homeless reported by many advocates:

there were perhaps only one-tenth of the millions claimed. I had been working for months, however, before I felt I had a reasonable comprehension of the diversity of the homeless and the beginning of an understanding of their condition. The complexity of what I found again ran counter to what many activists claimed: that homelessness was simply a housing problem.

I also found that simplistic views of homelessness were often perpetuated by people who should know better. Many in academia and the media had no inkling of the impending homeless crisis, but once aroused they leapt to solutions based on a flawed understanding of the problem. "The knowledge necessary to reduce the growing toll of damaged lives is now available," announced Lisbeth Schorr in the 1988 book *Within Our Reach: Breaking the Cycle of Disadvantage.* "The lessons of research and experience combine to explode the myth that nothing works," she wrote. Sociologist James D. Wright proclaimed that it is "good science" to "recognize that homelessness is a remediable condition of the environment." He declared that the failure to undertake large-scale "scientifically justifiable interventions" to "do away with homelessness altogether" results simply from our current political and economic climate. Failure to increase spending for homelessness remedies by, say, $30 billion is due to "a doxology of political faith" in the importance of reducing the budget deficit.[1]

Wright merely conveys the collective public position taken by the community of social scientists, social workers, and public health officials when he says that we know the "root causes" of homelessness but fail to take action. In contrast, Randall K. Filer and Marjorie Honig, professors of economics at the City University of New York, reported in 1990 on a comprehensive survey of literature on homelessness. "If one thing stands out from our survey," they declared, "it is the extent to which we do not know the answers to fundamental questions. . . . We do not know why there has been so much debate and effort devoted to the development of public policy regarding homelessness when there is so little understanding of the underlying issues." This recalls some advice from Senator Daniel Patrick Moynihan: "It is better to trust to social values than it is to supposed social science."[2]

Because Wright—not Filer and Honig, nor Moynihan—speaks for social science orthodoxy, it was Wright who was selected to prepare the concluding article in a symposium analyzing the National Academy of Sciences' Institute of Medicine report on homelessness. In this article, Wright complained that the institute failed to tell all that is scientifically known about homelessness, backing away from the truth because of politics. But after twenty-five years of major bureaucratic interventions, with results that can hardly be termed successful, scientists and policy makers reluctant to undertake massive new programs might be given a bit more respect.

Indeed, we might even listen to what they have to say. Some seriously believe (and their views have not been scientifically disproved) that a major cause of homelessness and other social pathologies has been intervention itself—intervention based on social science to be sure, but which nonetheless has eroded the basic social units of society: first and foremost the family, but also the neighborhood, the school, the church, and even person-to-person commercial relationships such as those between landlord and tenant and between shopkeeper and customer. Contemporary homelessness, these critics believe, results from the convergence of several streams, but swelling each throughout its course to the present has been a combination of academic theory, reformist fervor, economic self-interest (often wearing the cloak of altruism), and government action. What has been most profoundly absent is modesty.

THE PROBLEM WITH MANY of our governmental policies is not what they do directly, but rather their unintended side effects. True, the effects of some policies are, on the whole, positive: federal mortgage insurance and Social Security are among the more time-honored examples; Medicare, Medicaid, and visiting services for seniors living alone are more recent. But in researching this book I have become more aware that government policies are generally undertaken without heed for the fragility of our natural institutions. Many government policies have taken social responsibility away from families, cumulatively eroding their ability to fulfill society's most important task: nurturing children and raising them to be responsible adults. I am struck by the similarity to the way that the natural ecology is affected by man's careless, clumsy intervention: we must pay attention to social ecology as well.

That is not to say we should stand by and do nothing. There are things we can do, and there are reasons to believe that they can help. On the one hand, the homeless problem is not nearly so big as advocates have claimed. On the other hand, the problems of the homeless are far more complex than many would have us believe. Together these facts should lead us to design policies that enable families and individuals to take charge of their own lives. Homelessness has too many forms for unitary, centralized solutions. We should structure our programs so that the "invisible hand" that has been so productive in generating economic wealth for us can work socially as well. Such programs should not simply let citizens sink or swim—we do not do that in the business sector either—but instead help them to govern their own lives. Self-governance depends on the health of our natural institutions, those face-to-face arrangements that arise spontaneously out of our nature as social beings. Though fragile, they also exhibit a remarkable ability to rejuvenate if properly cared for.

Some solutions will cost money, but many important problems primarily need creative leadership. Homelessness offers important opportunities to politicians and other leaders who can achieve much by merely reassigning roles and responsibilities within a program and restructuring the way the money flows. Recommendations for new and revised policies are offered throughout this book. Most originate with others; a few are my own. I am not afraid to advance ideas that will cost money because I am confident that when we are reasonably certain that the ideas will work, we will spend the money, federal deficit or no. True, the history of social policy shows that often we have been very certain we knew what to do, and just as often we have been proved wrong in significant ways. To do better, I recommend that each new program be thoughtfully analyzed and tested "small" before being implemented "large."

If my crystal ball is right, adoption of a fresh set of policies may be helped along by the coalescence of a new political center in America. Liberals who work on the front lines with homeless clients now insist that these clients assume a share of responsibility for their condition, and liberals in our legislatures are moving in the same direction. Conservatives who care about the poor have found this demand for personal responsibility to be a critical element missing from state welfare programs. The liberals and conservatives who share common values should be able to join forces, at least for a time, in an active center, to rebuild our natural institutions.

This book may both please and exasperate many readers. I am staunchly conservative in insisting that rights must be accompanied by responsibility and in calling for measures to restore public order. I also call for the wholesale termination of some major government programs. But with some hesitation I recommend the creation of new programs that could cost as much as the ones being eliminated. And I believe the national government should set standards for states to follow and provide strong leadership. It is not that I believe government should stop governing; it should *govern,* not replace, local, natural institutions.

THE NOTES TO THIS BOOK and the list of interviewees form a partial listing of those to whom I am indebted for help. In particular, I would like to acknowledge my friend of more than thirty years, Robert Pickus, whose idea it was to write the book from the perspective of our political culture; David J. Armor, who has continuously challenged my views on practically everything over the same period; Anna Kondratas and Mark Johnston at the U.S. Department of Housing and Urban Development; Stuart Butler and Carl Horowitz at the Heritage Foundation; Alan Sutherland of Travelers Aid International; E. Fuller Torrey, M.D., of the Public Citizen Health Research Group; Professor Robert Pruger and Professor Emeritus James G. Leiby of the University of California School of Social Welfare; mental health executives Stuart McCullough and Theron O'Connor; Bradley Inman, the syndicated real estate columnist; and the sociologist Alan Berger. These individuals subjected themselves to particularly lengthy interviews and also reviewed and commented on the final manuscript. I would also like to thank Robert W. Davis and Robert B. Hawkins, Jr., my editor and my publisher at the Institute for Contemporary Studies.

The research for this book was assisted by a grant from the Lynde and Harry Bradley Foundation and the writing by a grant from the Earhart Foundation. My wife, Kay (also my friend of more than thirty years), provided the bulk of the funding by going to work each day.

I

Homelessness

1

Lying for Justice

"GOOD EVENING. I'm Ted Koppel, and this is 'Nightline.' One way to reduce the number of homeless Americans is to conduct a government survey and simply declare that there aren't nearly as many as previously thought. . . . This may be just what the Department of Housing and Urban Development has done. . . . The most reliable estimate of the homeless population nationwide, it said, is between 250,000 and 350,000. That was roughly one-tenth of the best previous estimates."[1]

Those words launched ABC's "Nightline" broadcast of May 17, 1984, a program featuring a confrontation between a HUD representative and Mitch Snyder, at the time the nation's foremost advocate for the homeless. Homelessness emerged as a national issue in the early 1980s largely due to advocates' insistent claims that the problem was many times larger than Americans thought. According to Snyder, the homeless numbered 2–3 million, about 1 out of every 100 Americans. HUD's estimates, Snyder said, were nothing but a politically motivated undercount. Once publicized, these claims went largely unquestioned by the media. Here is Snyder explaining on "Nightline" where his estimate came from: "Everybody demanded it, everybody said we want a number. . . . We got on the phone, we made lots of calls, we talked to lots of people, and we said 'Okay, here are some numbers.' They have no meaning, no value."

"Nightline" generally reflects the better side of American broadcast journalism. Ted Koppel's interviewing style is persistent but fair. On this evening, however, his questions were distinctly one-sided; Snyder's curious explanation didn't raise even an eyebrow. Koppel's journalistic skepticism was instead directed toward the government study and the HUD official defending it.

HUD arrived at its estimate of 250,000 to 350,000 homeless by conducting

> over 500 interviews with knowledgeable local observers in a nationally representative sample of sixty metropolitan areas, a national survey of emergency shelter operators, site visits to ten localities across the country, a fifty-state survey of state activities, discussions with representatives of national organizations concerned about the homeless, and a review of available local studies and reports.[2]

Snyder offered no direct refutation of HUD's estimate beyond calling it "tripe." Instead he worried that any figure lower than his would "take some of the power away . . . some of our potential impact . . . and some of the resources that we might have access to, because we're not talking about something that's measured in the millions. . . . And that relaxes everybody's drive to do something about it."

In the weeks following the "Nightline" broadcast, attacks by advocates, members of Congress, and journalists were so strong and so often repeated that the report was widely considered to have been discredited. According to Jay Matthews, writing in the *Washington Post* a year later, HUD took "such a political beating" over the report "that the federal government appears to have given up trying to define the problem."[3] Yet as we will see, HUD's estimates have over time held up quite well.

THE FUROR OVER the 1984 HUD report tells us more about America's politics than it does about the homeless. It suggests that understanding the problem is so difficult not because of the technical challenges of counting the homeless (which are formidable), but rather because our politics has reached such a divided condition that the idea of an objective search for truth is regarded by one side or another as evidence of bad faith. Meanwhile, the real and pressing needs of those who are on the streets become a sideshow to the media spectacle.

Consider the experience of Peter H. Rossi, the eminent University of Massachusetts sociologist, who attempted a rigorous count of the homeless in Chicago the year following the HUD study. Rossi, a former radical, describes his politics today as "a fairly bold pink." "The upsurge of debilitated street people wandering aimlessly across the urban landscape is shocking," he says, "a disgrace to a civilized society."[4] An accurate measurement of homelessness was, in Rossi's words, "a problem highly attractive to a liberal academic such as myself."

Counting the homeless was not only morally worthwhile to Rossi the man but a worthy and interesting challenge to Rossi as one of America's premier sociological methodologists. "Conventional censuses and surveys are premised on the assumption that almost all persons can be reached and queried in their dwellings, a premise that is untenable by definition when dealing with the homeless." To achieve an accurate measure, Rossi used research techniques that were "the photographic negative image" of conventional census surveys,

> selecting an unbiased sample of blocks, sending teams of interviewers (accompanied by off-duty policemen) into each of the selected blocks to search all places to which there was access (including streets, alleys, hallways, basements and roofs of occupied and unoccupied buildings, parked cars and trucks). Interviewing teams conducted their searches between the hours of midnight and 6:00 A.M.—a period in which the separation between the domiciled and the homeless would be at a maximum.[5]

Rossi's research team also performed surveys of Chicago homeless shelters, interviewing scientific samples and extrapolating from them.

Rossi's estimate of the number of homeless in Chicago was 2,344. The survey set off an explosion among Chicago's advocates, who had claimed that there were more than 25,000 homeless in that city. Rossi's count was less than one-tenth what advocates claimed. Stung by the angry criticism and bothered by doubts that he somehow had miscounted, Rossi undertook a second survey six months later, expanding the number of blocks counted and refining his techniques of counting. The second, more precise number was 2,020.

In an article mordantly titled "No Good Applied Social Science Research Goes Unpunished," Rossi described the outrage and recrimination that followed the announcement of his findings.[6] When presenting his report before the Chicago Mayor's Committee on the Homeless, he was greeted by a torrent of criticism. "Those two hours were the longest stretch of personal abuse I have suffered since basic training in the Army during World War II," he writes. "It was particularly galling to have to defend our carefully and responsibly derived estimates against a set of estimates whose empirical footings are located in a filmy cloud of sheer speculation and guesses." Critics accused him of having "sold out to the conservative forces of the Reagan administration" and "having seriously damaged the cause . . . by providing state and local officials with an excuse to dismiss the problem as trivial." At conferences of scholars and social workers to discuss homelessness, he became a "non-person," "shunned by all."[7]

In September 1986 the National Bureau of Economic Research (NBER) published the second systematic national estimate of the homeless (HUD's was the first). The authors, Richard B. Freeman of the London School of Economics and Brian Hall of NBER, reported on interviews with 516 representative homeless persons in New York City, "210 shelter dwellers, 101 heads of homeless families in welfare hotels, and 205 people living in the street." Based on what they learned in these interviews, Freeman and Hall determined that about 2.23 homeless persons are living on the streets for each homeless person sheltered. Their inquiries convinced them that this ratio could be applied nationally. Extrapolating from figures in a published national survey of homeless shelters, they estimated 279,000 homeless at the time HUD had estimated 250,000–350,000.[8] Once again, these numbers were roughly one-tenth what advocates claimed.

The third systematic national study, the first to estimate the number of homeless from actual counts in a scientifically designed sample of several cities, was carried out by the Urban Institute in 1987 under a grant from the U.S. Department of Agriculture. In twenty cities of 100,000 or more, four-hundred providers of services to the homeless were selected randomly—soup kitchens, shelters with meals, and shelters without meals. Then 1,800 homeless individuals from these programs were chosen systematically for interview. In addition, providers and police in the twenty cities were asked "to help locate sites where homeless people congregate—parks, train or bus stations, certain street corners, culverts, or day shelters that did not offer meals." Non-random interviews were conducted with 142 homeless individuals at these sites. The study found that a national total of "about 229,000 homeless persons in cities of 100,000 or more used meals or shelter services at some time during a 7-day period in March 1987."[9] Techniques of estimation led the researchers to calculate a maximum of 550,000 to 600,000 homeless.[10] This constitutes about 1 in 400 Americans.[11]

In spite of all this and more evidence to the contrary, the advocates' inflated figures of millions of homeless have had remarkable penetration and staying power. In the May 25, 1989, *Oakland Tribune*, no less a figure than Robert C. Maynard, editor of the paper, nationally syndicated columnist, and frequent David Brinkley panelist, writes that "millions of homeless now wander our towns and cities." On July 22, 1991, the Cable News Network's "World News" reported that the homeless in America numbered "as many as 3 million." The best example of the persistence of the multimillion figure is in the editor's foreword to the 1989 book *Without Shelter*, whose author is Peter Rossi.[12] To my surprise, and I can only assume to Rossi's, the editor refers without qualification to "nearly three million homeless." Given that Rossi's own editor has not gotten the message that there are not 3 million homeless in the United States, we should not be surprised that on June 30, 1990, the Associated Press reported enactment of a one-cent per pack "smoker's tax" in Chicago to aid that city's "estimated 35,000 homeless." It was as though Rossi had never been there and stirred up such a row.

THE POLITICAL COMMENTATOR George Will speaks of a "culture of mendacity." He says that people are getting tired of being lied to.[13] I hope so, and I believe that "lying for justice" is as bad as lying gets. When someone is trying to sell us soap, elixir, or a used car, it is—in a sense—"just business," and we can be skeptical about such sales pitches in a way that is emotionally simple and straightforward. But when we are subjected to dramatization, distortion, even outright prevarication about human pain and suffering, that is particularly dirty pool. Compared with almost anywhere at almost any time, America is a place where the pursuit of social justice is serious and ongoing. As I see it, we may have more lying than we have injustice, and it is crippling our public life.

Advocates for the homeless have decided that we won't act unless we think there is a crisis that is about to destroy us personally and ruin our families. These advocates feed the press information they know to be distorted, exaggerating the number of homeless by a factor of ten and describing their problem as a housing crisis affecting ordinary Americans simply down on their luck. This kind of cynical manipulation, no better in its own way, or any worse, than information management by many other special interests these days, has been largely successful.

The most important reason, I believe, is because the press trusts advocates more than it does officials, business or government. Ralph Nader, for example, is the most trusted source on consumer issues.[14] But often the press needs no help from advocates at all. In a famous example, CBS News shows a baby actually dying as the camera takes its picture. It is 1968, and the program is a news special called "Hunger in America." Reporter Charles Kuralt looks into the lens and says, "The baby is dying of starvation. He was an American. Now he is dead." In fact, this is a three-months premature child whose parents are not poor. Hunger has nothing to do with this child's death. His mother was in an auto accident, then gave birth prematurely. CBS executive Richard Salant later explained why they handled the story this way. "In that area, at that time, and in that hospital, babies were dying of malnutrition," he claimed.[15]

Other times, those lying for justice are our policitians. "This is crack cocaine," President George Bush proclaims solemnly, holding up a cellophane bag for the television cameras. It was "seized a few days ago in a park across the street from the White House." He is dramatizing the seriousness of the nation's drug problem. In fact, these drugs were seized in Lafayette Park only because federal officials succeeded, at great effort, in getting a dealer who normally works somewhere else in Washington to come across town for the occasion. This teenager had to be given directions to find the place. "Where the [expletive] is the White House?" he is heard asking on a recording secretly taped by federal drug enforcement officials. "Little crack," reports the *Washington Post*, citing local law enforcement officials, "is actually sold around the White House, especially in Lafayette Park." But White House staff thought fixing it up this way would make their point more effectively.[16]

Perceiving this pattern in our contemporary political culture, some officials I have interviewed express anger: we ought to be able to manage our affairs without lying to each other. Yet often there is an ambivalence to their emotional response: they are not at all certain that we are capable of turning our national attention to a problem until it is perceived as a crisis. Even so, the "paradigms" advocates create do lasting damage to our understanding of issues. Rossi observes that such "ruling paradigms" as the notion of millions of homeless are "usually not informed by much, if any, credible research," and that they are "focused more on image and impression management, with the intent not to inform but to persuade." Robert Pruger, a professor of social welfare at Berkeley, says that it is probably a good rule of thumb that advocates exaggerate by a factor of ten.[17] The problem is that "lying for justice" ultimately oversimplifies issues to the point where the real problem becomes almost unrecognizable.

CONSIDER HOMELESSNESS in this light. Advocates would have us believe that the homeless are just like you and me, except that they lack a home. In fact, seven out of ten homeless adults across the country have been institutionalized at one time or another—in a mental hospital, detoxification center, jail five days or more, or prison.[18] A prevalent view among those who study the homeless is that about one-third are seriously mentally ill, one-third substance abusers, and one-third in economic or personal crisis.[19]

The situation is more complicated, however, than dividing it into thirds makes it look. Recent comprehensive studies show that the rate of alcoholism among the homeless is much higher than this, and that drug abuse has risen sharply with the advent of crack cocaine.[20] The mentally ill homeless frequently abuse alcohol or drugs; some reports say that most of them do. Drug abusers often abuse alcohol.[21] Economic or personal crisis includes such matters as unemployment, domestic violence, divorce, eviction, lack of low-cost housing, and refugee or immigrant status. In most areas, this category of homelessness includes mainly female-headed families rather than single individuals. Alcohol abuse, often by both husband and wife, is undoubtedly the leading contributor to domestic violence, with drug abuse rising fast. An important contributor to divorce, job loss, and eviction, substance abuse is likely a strong factor in much homelessness now attributed to economic or personal crisis.

Alcoholism has historically been the leading problem of homeless men, and continues to be. Research consensus on this is growing, according to a March 1991 report published by the National Institute on Alcohol Abuse and Alcoholism (NIAAA). The report, a compendium and analysis of the 1980s literature on substance abuse and related illness among the homeless, concludes that "around two-thirds of the men and a third of the women" have an alcohol problem. This estimate is twice as high as the most commonly reported averages. The reason given for the difference is that NIAAA excludes the less scientifically rigorous studies—which tend to underdiagnose alcohol disorders—from its calculation.[22] Across the three California counties where the Rand Corporation conducted a 1987 study, seven of ten homeless individuals showed "substance abuse disorders": alcohol, 57 percent; drugs, 48 percent; and both, 22 percent.[23] Since crack did not hit the street scene until about five years ago, earlier studies can no longer be used even to approximate the rapidly growing drug problem among the homeless.

Homeless men tend to be single (88 percent according to the Urban Institute), whereas women tend to have families (again, 88 percent).[24] Men show much higher rates of alcoholism and drug abuse, while women—particularly the small number of homeless single females—higher rates of mental illness.[25] In a study conducted by James D. Wright on homelessness and health in New York City, 47 percent of the men were found to be problem drinkers; the rate for women was 16 percent.[26] I believe that alcoholism among female family heads, although less than that of males, is seriously underestimated in these studies.

If the only source of information had been advocates, we might have assumed that the "new homeless" as a group are no longer alcohol abusers like the homeless of past decades. Reports from numerous cities across the country prepared over several years by local chapters of the National Coalition for the Homeless, led by Robert M.Hayes, emphasized the economic causes of the new homelessness and mentioned the role of mental illness.

They said nothing about alcohol or drug abuse, however, until May 1989, when Hayes decided to go public on these problems.

The story behind Hayes's belated decision to acknowledge substance abuse as a major component of homelessness is a classic tale of "spin control." During most of the 1980s, advocates led us to believe that the primary cause of homelessness was a lack of housing. But in a May 1989 interview I did with Hayes—next to the late Mitch Snyder, the nation's most prominent homeless advocate—he told me the time was right to acknowledge the problems of alcohol and drug addiction. My notification came in the form of what might have been casual remarks if they had been made by a less careful person. I remember regretting briefly that I did not work for a daily newspaper: Hayes's revised posture was indeed news.

Within a week of our conversation, I saw my "scoop" on the front page of the *New York Times*. "Drug and alcohol abuse have emerged as a major reason for the homelessness of men, women and families," the story began, "complicating the search for solutions, advocates for the homeless say." These advocates knew this all along; "emerged" means that they decided it was time to let us know. "Advocates like Robert M. Hayes," the article continued, "say that they have shied away from discussing the problem of addiction in the past, in part because they feared that the public would lose its sympathy for the homeless. But 'the bottom line,' he said, 'is that we have to tell the truth.' "[27]

To complain about lying for justice is not to say that all advocates engage in it. One who is tiring of lies is Boona Cheema, director of the largest homeless program in the Oakland-Berkeley area and a member of Hayes's National Coalition for the Homeless. Upon reading Hayes's revelations in her local newspaper, Cheema sent Hayes an angry letter that asked "why we need to tell any lies and hide behind any facade. . . . It's very difficult when the coalition paints the homeless as 'safe, sane, and sober' and the programs are overwhelmed with the opposite."[28]

The mentally ill have become a growing portion of the homeless in recent decades as mental wards have been emptied and the patients sent back to their communities. It is important to understand that these are not simply people who are "out of step" with the rest of society; they have profound diseases that, like other serious physiological conditions, require treatment.

Congress enacted legislation that was supposed to take care of them, but the programs were largely turned to other purposes, leaving many of the mentally ill to fend for themselves. This shameful development is no secret: the most visible homeless—those we see on city streets and in parks—are largely those who suffer from serious mental illness. Recently, advocates have invested great effort in "shattering this myth" that the homeless are all mentally ill. But shattering this myth does nothing to change the fact that one in three homeless *do* suffer from mental illness—second only to substance abuse.

Crime among the homeless has been the advocates' best-kept secret. "One of the most striking characteristics of the homeless population," according to the NBER study, "neglected in much popular discussion, is the frequency of criminal activity."[29] Almost four in ten homeless individuals admit having spent time in jail, with the average among these two years. Randall Filer and Marjorie Honig report from a comprehensive survey of the literature on homelessness that slightly more than 50 percent have spent some time in jail, 24 percent in prison.[30] Boona Cheema tells of a murder that took place in a shelter operated by her agency. The killer, it turned out, had a criminal record. Cheema, when asked why she did not check the client's "priors," replied, albeit with some exaggeration, "If we checked their priors, we wouldn't have any clients."[31] Rossi found that sixteen studies report an average of 42 percent of the homeless with jail or prison time. Excluding women and children from these rates would raise them further, although it is difficult to say how far, as many studies do not say if children are included.[32]

On those occasions when advocates have been forced to admit that large numbers of the homeless are alcoholics or mentally ill, commit crimes, or suffer from other severe conditions, they have sometimes fallen back on the argument that homelessness *caused* these other problems. Large-scale studies contradict this view, but agree that homelessness can worsen any of these problems. Freeman and Hall (NBER) asked the homeless about timing of their stays in jail and report that 61 percent of jail time occurred *before* homelessness, "suggesting that (unsuccessful) crime leads to homelessness."[33] The Institute of Medicine says that major mental illnesses such as schizophrenia and affective disorders (bipolar and major depression) "are unlikely to result from the trauma of homelessness." Nor are "'personality disorders,' deeply ingrained maladaptive behavior patterns that usually begin during childhood or adolescence [and] interfere with a person's capacity to relate to others."[34]

YET ANOTHER EXAMPLE of lying for justice is the attempt by some advocates to portray homelessness as a problem afflicting "typical" American families. "Homelessness among families is merely one further confirmation that the homeless population now mirrors the national population," says Maria Foscarinis of the National Coalition for the Homeless.[35] The truth is that most of the homeless today, as in the past, are single adults, and that the typical homeless family is a never-married mother staying with her children in an inner-city homeless shelter.[36]

The blame for distortion should not be placed solely on the advocates, however; often lawmakers and the media are at least as much at fault. The network news focuses on homeless families with whom the producers think their viewers will identify; television dramas do the same. Homeless advocate Robert Hayes once complained, "I can't tell you how often a congressional committee has called and said, 'We need a witness for a hearing. Can you get us a homeless family: mother, father—father out of work in the past four months from an industrial plant—white?'"[37] Why is the story of a black homeless family any less tragic than that of a white one? The true story of homelessness is sad, complex, and challenging. If anything, distorting and simplifying it reduces its power to move people.

To talk of homeless families is largely to talk of the "underclass." Each year in New York City close to 15,000 babies are born to mothers in their teens, most of them unmarried. Several hundred children born five years earlier to mothers between the ages of ten and fourteen years enter public kindergarten.[38] In New York City, Oakland, and other places with a substantial black underclass, homeless families include many such cases of "babies having babies." The unmarried mother often lives for a time in the home of her own mother or grandmother and then moves out, voluntarily or involuntarily. Often the forced departure is precipitated by alcohol or drug abuse. In the past five years the drug has increasingly been crack cocaine, a highly addictive drug that leads users to steal from their families as well as others to support their habit. Where the problem is substance abuse, often the grandmother assumes responsibility for the children when the mother moves out.

Increasingly, these young mothers, with or without their children, live with other relatives or friends for a while and then move into a homeless shelter. Often with help from social services workers, they find a place to live. Sometimes their children are assigned by the courts to foster homes, or the children are put up for adoption. Frequently the babies suffer from the effects of their mothers' substance abuse during pregnancy. Crack is particularly harmful, and urban hospitals around the country report increasing numbers of infants whose development has been severely impaired in this way.

Homeless families, unlike homeless individuals, usually find a place to stay rather quickly. Nearly all the homeless families enumerated in studies are found in shelters. Rossi found no children in his Chicago street searches.[39] Filer and Honig report from official New York City data that not one family applying for shelter during 1984 or 1985 said they were living on the street. Ninety-four percent reported coming from somewhere other than the streets of New York—about 62 percent had been living with relatives or friends, 26 percent had been living in their own apartment, 6 percent were from outside the city, and 6 percent answered "other."[40] Rita Schwartz, an executive at the Port Authority of New York and New Jersey, was awarded a six-month research sabbatical to travel the United States interviewing homeless persons found in transit facilities. She reports that "families are rarely found in transportation centers."[41]

Most families are apparently able to find somewhere to stay, if not with relatives or friends, then in a homeless shelter. After a month or so in the shelter, they find an apartment or are assisted into public housing. Generally, family shelters have social services staff or arrangements with other agencies to help their clients find housing. Most are already receiving Aid to Families with Dependent Children (AFDC) when they come to the shelter.

The impression is general that homeless families do not have the kinds of problems homeless individuals do—that most homeless families are homeless because rents are too high, while homeless individuals are more often mentally ill or substance abusers. Indeed, the Urban Institute study reports that single homeless adults "had much more troubled histories" than homeless adults in families—mental hospitalization, alcohol or drug institutionalization, jail, or prison. Urban Institute researchers found that only 12 percent of adults in families had been institutionalized for two or more of these problems, compared with 42 percent of single homeless persons.[42] There is no reason to doubt that homeless individuals have a higher rate of mental illness than do homeless family heads. Data for Alameda County, California, covering all individuals and families in shelters during one week of 1989, indicate, however, that roughly 40 percent of female family heads in these shelters have a major drug or alcohol problem.[43] Cheema reports that only about 30 percent of the homeless are simply very poor and have no particular problem with drugs, alcoholism, mental illness, or a criminal history.

Another director of a homeless center told me that 80 percent or more of the mothers in her program have a problem with alcohol or drugs that caused them to lose their previous home. When I asked her if she attended meetings of her counterparts from other areas of California and other states, she said she does and that their experiences are generally similar. I was astonished when ten minutes later she said the homeless are like you and me: few of us have the savings to make more than two mortgage payments if we were to lose our job. One minute she spoke from her experience; the next she gave the party line of homeless advocacy. No wonder there is confusion.

A study done in 1989 for the California legislature found that 63 percent of homeless single mothers in Los Angeles "abuse alcohol or drugs or . . . suffer serious emotional problems."[44] Adults in homeless families are younger than homeless single individuals. The Urban Institute probably found "less troubled histories" in part because the mothers are so young that they have had few years in which to be institutionalized. Another reason is that a mother with small children to take care of is not likely to sign into a treatment center voluntarily; moreover, the police and courts are reluctant to take mothers away from their children.[45]

For a small number among the homeless in any community the immediate problem *is* mainly economic—those, for instance, who find the rent too high for their income. Nearly all these are single-parent families surviving on welfare or more rarely on a low-wage job. In some communities we do find two-parent homeless families; Portland, Oregon, is an example. In that city, homeless families are typically new to the metropolitan area from rural communities where a lumber mill has shut down. Cities like Denver, Tulsa, and Houston may also have many such families as a result of the shutdown of oil production facilities. In Portland, where there are low-income housing and jobs, families, either on their own or with the help of local agencies, frequently church affiliated, soon find a new job and a place to live. This rapid turnover in the homeless population is reflected in figures from the City of Portland that show ten times as many homeless annually as there are in a single night; in most communities this ratio is much lower.[46]

While the set of reasons for homelessness is largely unchanged from city to city, the proportions and the circumstances vary widely. Miami, for example, has greatly more refugees than most cities. In San Antonio, immigration from Mexico keeps the homeless numbers up.[47] New York City and Los Angeles have more families whose welfare income is inadequate to pay the rent on available apartments. Berkeley and San Francisco have more who come to the area to take part in a certain kind of street life.[48]

To say that homeless individuals and families generally have severe personal problems underlying their homelessness and that their homelessness is seldom caused mainly by economic conditions is not to deny the importance of housing. As later chapters show, the low-income housing supply has been shrinking rapidly in the past two decades, particularly single room occupancy (SRO) housing in the central cities. At the same time, smaller families and increasing numbers of individuals not forming families, or postponing families but still setting up independent households, have placed a greater demand on the units remaining. In the past, persons and families with serious problems could more easily find a place that would tolerate them. Or when people found themselves in economic difficulty, they could more readily turn to family and community for help before becoming homeless.

In every city council that discusses homelessness, sooner or later someone raises the concern that if the city provides services, it will become a "magnet" for the homeless. Predictably, liberals deny it, conservatives insist upon it, and the better elected officials struggle valiantly to understand what really happens and to make workable decisions. In fact a city's welcoming attitude toward the homeless will sometimes attract significant numbers of them, and a city's hostility may well discourage them from coming.

Other qualities of the city, however, are probably more important: for instance, good weather, seasonal labor opportunities, the presence of a university street community, relatives or friends in the area, and the amenities that anyone else would find attractive. The magnetism of services for the homeless usually does not extend very far and seldom outside the state. The strongest effect is likely to be on those from smaller cities within the state, particularly from less friendly cities in the same metropolitan area. Seattle has attracted a certain number of migratory single individuals from outside the state because of Washington's relatively generous cash welfare payments.[49] Shifting from cash to an offer of treatment for alcoholism and drug abuse, with controls on cash payments, appears to have slowed the flow.

San Francisco, says Boona Cheema of Berkeley, "is a magnet for everyone." Participants on the homelessness panel at a recent conference in San Francisco on crack cocaine and the black family complained that voluntary homeless—particularly "tourists from Australia"—are displacing involuntary homeless in San Francisco from services. So, it was said, are sons and daughters of wealthy American families, "who decide to be a bum and come to the city to live in an SRO." A panelist argued that interviews for free housing should determine whether the applicant is a vagabond or a legitimate refugee fleeing political repression.[50]

Berkeley has appealed to people who like to hang around the University of California since the uprisings of the 1960s. Tolerance and available services near the campus can increase the city's drawing power, as a communications grapevine exists among university street people around the world. Cheema quotes a city councilman she used to think of as reactionary who claimed that every time Berkeley added a shelter bed, ten new homeless people appeared. "I'm not so sure he was wrong," she says now, "although I objected strenuously to his point of view at the time." The lure of Berkeley's downtown shelters does not extend far, she is careful to point out. It is not like the inherent magnetism of the campus. Added shelter spaces in downtown Berkeley only seem to pull from nearby cities such as Oakland. People from Fremont, only twenty miles to the south, do not want to come to Berkeley "and be with all those crazies." Pearl Pritchard, director of an Oakland shelter, reports that about 20 percent of her clients are from other places in California and have moved in search of work. They come to Oakland because of friends and family. Very few are from outside the state.[51] In Hayward, halfway between Fremont and Berkeley, Gisela Bushey, director of the family homeless shelter, says that in 1988 only two of dozens of families who entered her program came from outside California.[52]

In New York City the problem of shelter supply creating its own demand appears to be more acute. "Benefits of System Luring More Families to Shelters," reads a front-page story from the *New York Times* of September 4, 1991. "The city's shelter system for homeless families has become so livable that hundreds, if not thousands of families who could stay elsewhere are flocking to shelters," the article reports, "so they can move to the top of the list for permanent subsidized housing, city officials say."

One family interviewed had been living with relatives, but decided to move into an apartment in a homeless shelter at a cost to the city of $2,730 a month. The couple could have continued to live with relatives, they said, but they saw the shelter system as a way to improve their lot. Although both parents had held jobs, they are now receiving public assistance and don't plan to work until they are placed in permanent subsidized housing. "I consider this a little vacation," one parent said.

MANY THOUSANDS MORE are homeless in America than ten, twenty, or thirty years ago. We see them on the streets of our cities and in the transportation terminals, the parks, the alleys. In spite of what appears to be a general trend toward increasing numbers of homeless, however, there are hundreds of thousands of them, not millions, a tiny fraction of our population. The numbers are manageable, not overwhelming; our faith in our nation should not be undermined.

Several persons I interviewed expressed concern that exaggeration of the numbers by advocates would lead us to throw our hands in the air and declare the problem too big to deal with: there would just not be enough money. Those activists whose main agenda is a fundamental indictment of our system would be perfectly happy with such a response. They want the problem to appear enormous and insoluble—insoluble, that is, except by abolishing our basic institutions and replacing them with something else. But it is in the interest of those who want to improve the situation to understand its true dimensions.

Modest though the overall problem is in size, however, it comprises many different elements, as most advocates now acknowledge. Such a complex problem cannot be solved by some mass admission of guilt, to be followed by hastily considered laws and appropriations. We need to understand who is homeless and why, how this situation came about, what is being done about it, and what helps and what does not.

Although the voluntary sector is growing larger and more capable, many insist that it is overextended and underfunded and will need massive infusions of new resources to tackle social problems effectively, as federal government resources are constricted. As a long-time human services official in the federal and the voluntary sector, I have some observations. First, the voluntary sector should not take over functions the federal government has been performing, but find different ways to help people overcome dependency through self-reliance. Then the numbers of homeless should decline. Second, if we change the incentives in some of our federal policies and programs, the voluntary sector will not find it has so many displaced individuals and families in need of its help in the first place. Third, if government policy begins to put tools in the hands of people to solve their own problems—to become self-governing—instead of paying them not to, the voluntary sector will have even less to do. Fourth, it really does cost only a fraction of the amount to take care of most social problems outside the governmental system as it does either directly or through federal grant making. Fifth, in spite of the first four, solving homelessness will, as voluntary sector representatives maintain, require increased resources. I believe, though, that when we have agreed on what is needed, the money will come.

We need to recognize that our expanded individual freedoms and the enlarged activities of our central government have come at the expense of family and community. We have valued those individual freedoms above our ties to family, friends, and place: now our society is beginning to unravel. Homelessness, though an extreme and improbable result for most of us, is an outward sign of our increasing vulnerability as individuals with weakened ties. As society comes apart, homelessness increases.

Many people are trying to repair the fabric of their communities, but much more needs to be done. Perhaps homelessness can be a focus for our finding our way back—or forward—to a more mutually supportive society. But first we must tell each other the truth.

2

"We Have Met the Enemy. . ."

MOST OF THE HOMELESS we see in our downtown business districts, parks, and other public places are seriously mentally ill. Ten years ago it would have been unnecessary to point this out because it was obvious. Since that time, however, advocates have invested great effort in persuading us otherwise, trying to have us believe that the homeless are just like the rest of us, only without housing.

I say "most of the homeless we see" because although fewer than half the U. S. homeless are seriously mentally ill, these are the most visible homeless. The others congregate elsewhere. Alcoholic and drug-abusing homeless confine themselves, or are confined by the police, usually to downtown skid-row areas. Families homeless because of temporary economic misfortune are concentrated in a few cities, where they are generally placed in special shelters and provided job assistance outside of public view. Chronic welfare families that have fallen into homelessness exist mainly in certain larger cities—more than half may be in New York City alone—and they too are sheltered. The mentally ill homeless are commonly seen in downtown business districts, transportation terminals, and other places ordinary Americans frequent routinely.

E. Fuller Torrey and Sidney Wolfe have estimated that there are about 2 million seriously mentally ill individuals in the United States. About 150,000—around 7.5 percent of the total—

21

are living on the streets and in public shelters, a small proportion of the seriously mentally ill but about a third of the homeless. Torrey has estimated the numbers of these mentally ill in each living situation: 800,000 with their own family, 200,000 by themselves, 300,000 in nursing homes, 300,000 in foster and group homes, 200,000 in hospitals, 26,000 in jail, and 150,000 in public shelters or on the streets.[1]

"Serious mental illness" covers the diseases of the brain that profoundly distort an individual's perception of himself and external reality. Principally these are the various kinds of schizophrenia and manic-depressive psychosis, also called bipolar disorder. These physical brain diseases impair mental processes, markedly limiting social functioning, including work skills. In an unmedicated state, the individual is likely to see and hear things and persons that are not there, dramatically misconstrue what is going on, or entertain grandiose delusions of persecution. Even under medication, the mentally ill's ability to generalize something learned in one situation to another is commonly impaired—for instance, learning to shop in a particular supermarket does not enable one to shop in another supermarket. The ability to handle stress is also likely to be very limited.

As a brain disease, serious mental illness is comparable to other diseases such as epilepsy, muscular dystrophy, and multiple sclerosis—except that these affect primarily physical rather than mental functioning. These are all biological diseases that we do not know either how to prevent or how to cure: we know only something about how to manage them. Some argue that environmental conditions and events may influence their onset, severity, and the way particular symptoms are manifested, but few any longer believe that schizophrenia and bipolar disorder are illnesses that could "happen to any of us" if life got too stressful. During the heyday of Sigmund Freud, many thought that these diseases resulted from bad parenting, but not anymore. Psychotics are not neurotics who have slipped over some indistinct boundary line; they are certainly not "people like you and me" who just got some bad breaks. No one suggests any volitional component in the onset of schizophrenia or bipolar disorder. The seriously mentally ill population varies directly with the whole population. So far nothing we do either enlarges this number or shrinks it.

Many homeless individuals are among the hundreds of thousands of Americans discharged from mental hospitals since the early 1960s, when a national consensus was reached that the mentally ill would be better off outside, and Congress appropriated money for community mental health centers to help take care of them. The younger mentally ill on the streets and in homeless shelters have not been "deinstitutionalized." In earlier times they would have been in institutions, but they became mentally ill after deinstitutionalization had begun. The federal government pays for hundreds of community mental health centers and Congress has allocated billions of dollars to subsidize the education of psychiatrists, psychologists, and social workers to help the mentally ill. But these federal programs have gone astray. The community mental health centers are not serving the seriously mentally ill but rather a different population, and the professionals are treating a different clientele.

These programs have gone off course not through the failure of political or economic commitment by the American public but for other reasons. One of these is that the individuals who got control of them had too great a faith in their "scientific" knowledge. "The care of the seriously mentally ill in twentieth century America has been a public disgrace," writes E. Fuller Torrey, M.D., in *Nowhere to Go: The Tragic Odyssey of the Homeless Mentally Ill.* He holds that "professional self-interest has been confused with altruism, official inaction with benevolence, ideology with science, and ignorance with omniscience."[2] Reformers, academics, and officials were convinced they knew the root causes of mental illness, and they turned out to be wrong. A psychiatrist himself, Fuller Torrey tells what happened. The next few pages draw mainly from his fascinating account.

During World War II, thousands of conscientious objectors were assigned to work in state mental hospitals. Many were greatly upset by the conditions they observed in the hospitals and wrote, first to each other, of their outrage. After a time they began to raise the issue publicly; their descriptions of the absymal conditions in the hospitals led to a succession of hearings and investigations, first in Ohio, then across the country. *Life* magazine published a powerful and moving set of pictures. *Reader's Digest* condensed a novel by Mary Jane Ward, *The Snake Pit*, which was made into a successful motion picture.[3]

Meanwhile, the director of the U.S. military draft testified before congressional committees that mental illness had been a leading cause for rejecting potential servicemen in World War II and that almost four in ten disability discharges "were due to mental disease."[4] Not only was the treatment of mental patients inexcusably bad, but also mental illness was much commoner than we had supposed.

In those days the psychoanalytic theories of Sigmund Freud dominated American professional and academic thinking about mental illness. The cause of schizophrenia, Torrey quotes from one standard textbook of the time, was confidently thought to be "a maladapted way of life manifested by one grappling unsuccessfully with environmental stresses and internal difficulties."[5] This view led psychiatric academics and professionals to believe that the way to deal most effectively with the problem of mental illness was through broad community programs of prevention. Although the reform movement focused on the state hospitals and the plight of their inhabitants, the professionals in psychiatry were really interested in changing the conditions in society at large under which personalities developed. They did not know how to cure mental illness; the best they could hope for in a patient, once a psychotic break with reality had occurred, was indefinite "remission." But they thought they knew how to prevent mental illness.

In 1946, the National Institute of Mental Health (NIMH) was created, on paper at least, and in 1948 it received its first authorization of funds from Congress, $6.2 million. As might be expected, those appointed to head NIMH were leaders in psychiatry and held vigorously to its prevailing theories. Since mental illness sprang, they believed, from environmental influences on personality development, they needed a community network of professionals to reach out into the corners of America and undertake programs and activities to foster mental health. They needed, in short, community mental health centers. The first director of NIMH, Dr. Robert H. Felix, thought that one such center per 100,000 of population would be the right formula.

By 1954, writes Torrey, "it was clear that the Congress and the public both viewed the problem of mental illness as serious and neglected." The Mental Health Study Act of 1955 was passed unanimously. It authorized NIMH to appoint a commission to assess the needs of the mentally ill and recommend programs for enactment by Congress. Meanwhile, "a miracle was taking place in state mental hospitals"—new drugs were proving effective in controlling symptoms of schizophrenia. For the first time in nearly 200 years, in-patient counts were declining.[6]

The Joint Commission on Mental Illness and Health was designed to ensure that whatever it recommended would meet as little resistance as possible in Congress. It comprised forty-five individual members and thirty-six participating agencies covering every organized constituency with any possible claim on involvement—not only members of the broader psychiatric community but also personnel officers, educators, and law enforcement. Even the American College of Chest Physicians was represented, allowing, no doubt, for the theory that emotions are matters of the heart. It took nearly five years for this commission to be appointed and staffed, and for its report to be completed.

Because the recommendations would call for more federal spending, the commission delayed release of the report until after the fiscally cautious Republican administration of Dwight Eisenhower had left office. The report, issued shortly after the inauguration of John F. Kennedy in 1961, was called *Action for Mental Health.* First it gave a nod to the plight of those seriously mentally ill:

> Major mental illness is the core problem and unfinished business of the mental health movement, and . . . the intensive treatment of patients with critical and prolonged mental breakdowns should have first call on fully trained members of the mental health professions.[7]

Then it called for the establishment of community mental health clinics—one for each 50,000 in the population—whose stated role was to take the place of public mental hospitals as the principal institutions for treating these patients. Farther down in the report language was provided to allow the proposed centers to work with a broader population:

> People who are emotionally disturbed . . . that is to say, under psychological stress that they cannot tolerate [need] skilled attention and helpful counseling . . . if the development of more serious mental breakdown is to be prevented.[8]

In a subsequent publication, the commission also, in Torrey's words, "tried to do what nobody had yet done," to define mental health. It began by insisting that it was not simply the absence of mental disease. Mental health consisted in:

- the attitudes of the individual toward himself
- the degree to which the individual realizes his potentialities through action
- unification of function in the individual's personality
- the individual's degree of independence of social influences
- how the individual sees the surrounding world
- the individual's ability to take life as it comes and master it[9]

The commission had laid the political groundwork for a large-scale system of community clinics, whose number-one job was ostensibly working with the seriously mentally ill but whose real agenda was helping people under stress to achieve improved mental health—an agenda based on a "scientific" theory that mental illness could be prevented through psychotherapy and related services.

Three new books appeared in that year, 1961, that changed the nature of discussion about mental hospitals and mental illness. The first, by Erving Goffman, a Berkeley sociology professor of mine, was called *Asylums*. Goffman claimed that most of the "psychotic" behavior of patients was "a reaction to the institutional setting," rather than evidence of an illness. In the second book, *The Myth of Mental Illness*, psychoanalyst-historian Thomas Szasz said that mental diseases do not exist except as "labels assigned by society" to express disapproval for unacceptable behavior. In the third, *An Approach to Community Mental Health*, Harvard professor and psychoanalyst Gerald Caplan said that hospitalization was bad, that it was "an important cause of disability" and stated anew in words carrying the Harvard imprimatur old psychoanalytic theories about the initial causes of mental illness lying in the mother-infant relationship.

These books established the dominance in academic and professional circles and among policy makers of three axioms:

- Psychiatric hospitals are bad and should be closed.
- Psychiatric treatment in the community is better because cases can be detected earlier and hospitalization thereby avoided.

- The prevention of mental diseases is the most important activity to which psychiatric professionals can aspire.[10]

According to Torrey, "from that point onward it was all downhill for the mentally ill; the debacle of deinstitutionalization and the tragedies that accompanied it became virtually inevitable."[11] Again a book later made into a motion picture played an important role in changing the outlook of the broader public. It was *One Flew Over the Cuckoo's Nest*, by Ken Kesey.

With the consensus that mental hospitals should be closed, the Kennedy administration decided that community mental health centers would take their place. In a special message to Congress, President Kennedy, whose sister Rosemary suffered from schizophrenia, proposed a nationwide system of community mental health centers, so that "within a decade or two" we could "reduce the number of patients under custodial care by 50 percent or more."[12]

As reported by Torrey, this proposal concerned the seriously mentally ill, not simply those in the general population who were under stress.

> There was almost no evidence that the care of mentally ill persons could be shifted en masse from state hospitals to the community, no evidence that the projected CMHCs either could or would provide care for the patients already being discharged from state hospitals, no evidence that the CMHCs could reduce admissions to the hospitals, and no evidence that the CMHCs could prevent mental illnesses.[13]

Moreover, no pilot projects were proposed to test the feasibility of the idea before funding hundreds of these new community institutions. What we had was a tragic problem, wishful thinking about it—which among academics and professionals took the form of unproven theories—and a head of steam. The law passed Congress easily and was signed by President Kennedy on October 31, 1963.

In twenty-two days President Kennedy was dead, and it was up to President Johnson to implement the new law, which would become one of many Great Society programs. The psychiatrists in charge at NIMH, in Torrey's words, "carrying on the dreams and hopes of a half century of their predecessors beginning with the leaders of the mental hygiene movement," wrote the regulations. As a result, the CMHCs were never set up to do what President Kennedy and Congress had intended. Instead of firm language requiring a working relationship between CMHCs and state mental hospitals, the regulations did not even mention the goal of supplanting the hospitals. Planning for the centers focused on prevention of mental illness through working to change social conditions—according to the NIMH director at the time, Dr. Stanley F. Yolles, to "help the statesman, the politician, and the poor man himself to intervene in this condition of poverty before it creeps into the fiber and style of a man's thought and behavior."[14] NIMH's planning director, Leonard Duhl, M.D., wrote,

> The city . . . is in pain. It has symptoms that cry out for relief. They are the symptoms of anger, violence, poverty, and hopelessness. If the city were a patient, it would seek help. . . . The totality of urban life is the only rational focus for concern with mental illness . . . our problem now embraces all of society and we must examine every aspect of it to determine what is conducive to mental health.[15]

The psychotherapeutic assumptions of the leadership at NIMH fit nicely with the sociological views underlying the new War on Poverty. The signal sent by NIMH to applicants for community mental health center grants was unmistakable: social action aimed at the prevention of mental illness was the objective, not treatment of the mentally ill.

The first centers were opened in 1967, and by 1981 there were almost 800 of them. During the Johnson administration much emphasis was placed on prevention through community change, and under President Nixon the balance shifted toward individual and group psychotherapy. Seldom did significant numbers of patients flow from mental hospitals to the care and support of CMHCs. Most of the centers drew then and still draw from the community around them not the mentally ill but the "worried well"—not "patients" even, but "clients."

Prevention theory and the agenda of the War on Poverty explain how the centers were diverted from the purpose Congress and the public intended. Why they were never made to conform to their purpose is an ordinary story of political institutionalization and bureaucratic inertia. Since they were funded institutions on the local scene, they were readily able to join the network of local health and welfare agencies and the associations that lobby for them in Washington and the state capitals. Many of these agencies referred clients to the centers or accepted referrals from them; others were institutional colleagues that shared a set of assumptions about community needs. Center staff became accustomed to working with nonpsychotic individuals and groups, just as professionals who came to work at the centers did so expecting this sort of clientele. The original reason for CMHCs became increasingly dim and then was lost.

"The exodus of patients from state mental hospitals, which had begun slowly in 1955," writes Torrey, "accelerated to a stampede."[16] Their numbers declined by 197,921 during the 1960s and by another 205,455 during the 1970s. By 1984, 80 percent of the beds that existed in 1955 were gone from these hospitals: only 118,743 of 551,150 remained. Since the CMHCs had virtually no relationship to this exodus, its continuation requires an explanation. The public rationale might be hospital conditions and patients' rights, but the real reason was money—what Torrey calls "a fiscal shell game."[17] Governor Ronald Reagan of California was its most notorious player, but everyone participated. State governments could reduce their expenditures without political penalty by discharging mental patients to local communities because local hospitals and other agencies received their reimbursement not from the states but from the federal government.

The "power of federal money," writes Torrey, "was the real driving force behind deinstitutionalization."[18] In 1963 when the CMHC legislation was enacted, 96 percent of the governmental expenses for the seriously mentally ill were borne by the states. Then the division of fiscal responsibility changed dramatically. First, liberalized federal rules made the mentally ill living in the community eligible for rent, food, and other living costs under Aid to the Disabled. Medicare in 1965 and Medicaid in 1966 paid a large part of the costs for mentally ill patients in local general hospitals and nursing homes but not in state hospitals. The Food Stamps program, enacted in 1966, was also available to the mentally ill.

State officials, when asked who would take care of the discharged patients, pointed to the community health centers. "This was to be the ultimate revenge for state administrators," writes Torrey:

They had been told by federal officials that because they had done such a poor job, state hospitals were to be closed and new CMHCs would take care of the mentally ill. They had been completely bypassed in the funding of CMHCs. Now they would hand the problem over to the CMHCs. Unfortunately the mentally ill paid a high price for this revenge.[19]

Alan Sutherland, a hospital administrator in New York at the time the CMHCs were being set up, tells me that even while patients were being moved out of the state hospitals and into local general hospitals or nursing homes, the federal government was exerting pressure on the state hospitals to clean up their act or lose federal funds. This federal pressure, a continuing bureaucratic response to the "snake pit" and subsequent revelations, influenced a decision in New York and some other states to keep state mental health funds in the state hospitals even while the patients were being sent back to local communities.[20] In a few states, at least some of the money followed the patients. In most, the burden was just shifted from state and local taxes to the newly enacted federal Medicare and Medicaid programs.

By 1985, the federal share of fiscal support for the mentally ill had grown from 2 percent to 38 percent, and state support had declined from 96 percent to 53 percent. In raw numbers, instead of paying $1 billion per year, the federal government was now paying $17.1 billion; corrected for inflation, this was four times as much as in 1963.[21]

Few experts believe in the environmental theory of prevention any longer. Too much has been learned about the organic bases of schizophrenia and bipolar disorder. It was the "scientific" environmental theory that got the psychiatric community behind CMHCs in the first place and that turned it firmly away from working with the seriously mentally ill. Returning the attention of those professionals to where it should be is an effort under way in more and more states and communities. This is part of the solution to homelessness.

WHEN THE DEFINITIVE HISTORY of America in the late twentieth century is written, I believe that it will lay much blame at the feet of our trial lawyers, particularly those dedicated young attorneys who have forgone high incomes to sue on behalf of what they perceive to be the rights of the poor and powerless. A generation of law school graduates has fought to establish the contradictory principles that various classes of individuals are entitled by right to government benefits and that the rest of society has no right to expect them to do anything in return. In the early 1970s, the mentally ill were identified by these lawyers as an overlooked group of the oppressed—first in need of liberation from mental institutions; then with a right to food, shelter, and treatment; later with a right to live outside in public places if they wished; and then with a right to refuse treatment. Nowhere in all this assertion of rights did anyone consider that the seriously mentally ill often cannot form a reasoned opinion and will suffer and perhaps die in misery unless someone else takes charge. These lawyers give no heed to the role of natural institutions in caring for their members. Instead of the family, friends, or caring professionals deciding with—and, where necessary, for—the patient on issues of treatment or confinement, mental patients themselves would make such decisions. Moreover, lawyers would protect their right to this alleged control over their own lives.

In *Madness in the Streets* (1990), Rael Jean Isaac and Virginia C. Armat provide a complete and fascinating narrative of how psychiatry and the law abandoned the mentally ill.[22] Much of their story describes how these devoted attorneys—Isaac and Armat call them the "patient liberation bar"—have striven with great effectiveness and disastrous consequences to protect the rights of the mentally ill from abridgment by the police, psychiatrists, their own parents, and others seen to be acting on behalf of an oppressive system. It serves this bar's ideological biases to believe the writings of Szasz, Goffman, and academics who either deny the existence of mental illness or see it as caused environmentally—by parents who raise their children badly or by other elements of the system against which they are trying to protect their mentally ill clients.

In 1984, the American Psychiatric Association (APA) published the results of an extensive task force study it had carried out on the homeless mentally ill. The report, *The Homeless Mentally Ill*, shows how pressure from these attorneys has vitiated care for the mentally ill: in fact, the adversary system of our courts has displaced the very cooperation among persons and agencies needed to help these unfortunates. The judiciary, says the report, "values an adversary process, not a collaborative one." Moreover, "when facing uncertainty about an individual, medicine increases its supervisory and observational vigilance, whereas the judiciary tends to free the individual."[23]

This approach would be fine if Szasz were right that mental illness is simply a fiction used in the United States to control deviates. But he is tragically wrong.

According to the APA report, over the past fifteen years these lawyers have been increasingly assertive in representing the patients' stated wishes, whether or not their disease enables them to form a reasoned judgment. Citing legal precedents, the APA notes that the law does not require one's attorney to advocate his expressed wishes.[24] In cases of the seriously mentally ill, to do so is frequently in the interest of no one—not the patient, not the people around the patient, and not society at large. While it makes sense for persons with other kinds of disease, for instance, heart patients, to accept or reject treatment, much as this prerogative may frustrate caring medical professionals or family members, it is not the same thing when a mental patient decides. In the words of Isaac and Armat,

> when the diseased organ is the brain, the afflicted individual cannot make the reasoned decisions regarding treatment that a cardiac patient can be expected to make. Nor does heart disease produce the disordered, sometimes dangerous behavior characteristic of mental illness.[25]

Isaac and Armat describe how these lawyers through dedication and skill changed the law, public opinion, and professional practice so that today tens of thousands of mentally ill who otherwise would be in treatment and living lives as normal as possible are instead alienated from families and friends, living in loneliness, fear, and filth and committing violence upon themselves and others. The authors report that studies since deinstitutionalization began show "consistently higher arrest rates for mental patients and higher rates for violent crime." The pattern of findings, they say, "is too consistent for serious challenge."[26] Because of our policies, the rates of violent crime among former patients are several times higher than those for the general population.[27] These problems need not occur, according to Torrey, Isaac and Armat, and many others I have interviewed, if patients were treated in a collaborative system instead of "freed" from coercion in an adversary system. Where appropriate decisions can be made on treatment and confinement and enforced, mental patients need be no more dangerous on the average to themselves or to others than anyone else.

Early on, the goal of the young lawyers was to establish the rights of patients in mental hospitals. A case brought by the Greater Boston Legal Services (GBLS) ensured the right of patients in these hospitals to refuse treatment. A huge potential source of revenue to support the movement was uncovered, as over a million dollars in attorneys' fees was granted to GBLS. One agency funded by the government (the federal Legal Services Corporation) sued another agency funded by the government (the state hospital); the taxpayers paid for both sides of the case and then also paid the legal fees assessed against the losing side.[28]

Going a step further, the New York Civil Liberties Union passed a resolution calling involuntary hospitalization incompatible with the principles of a free society.[29] Around this resolution, attorneys were organized; conferences were held across the country and lawsuits pursued, some of them successfully. The arguments presented were often brilliant: time and again it was demonstrated that psychiatrists were frequently mistaken in their diagnoses, were poor at predicting dangerous behavior, and did not know what really caused mental illness. The fact that families and professionals who care are the only ones who can help a mentally ill person was lost in a sea of forensic logic.

Thanks to a lawsuit filed by the Milwaukee Legal Services, moreover, it was found discriminatory to institutionalize only the mentally ill before actual commission of a crime. In *Lessard* v. *Schmidt* (1972), the Milwaukee Legal Services convinced the court that the state's commitment laws were invalid because they lacked the procedural safeguards of criminal law. What about the argument that the mentally ill might be dangerous to themselves? The answer was, normal people smoke cigarettes without state intervention.[30]

The movement rolled on, financed by government grants and court awards. In *Wyatt* v. *Stickney*, plaintiffs argued that patients, if they were to be confined to a hospital, had thereby a right to treatment. Fair enough, but the hidden agenda was to free the patients from confinement. The trick, pulled successfully, was to get a friendly judge to define the standards for treatment to include staffing ratios and physical amenities so expensive that hospitals could not afford to meet them. "Fearing the precedent of costly improvements that had been set," write Isaac and Armat, "other states accelerated deinstitutionalization after 1972, since it was clearly the cheapest way to achieve improved staff ratios to patients."[31]

Another suit having a major impact in emptying hospitals was brought in the name of an involuntarily committed patient in a Florida state hospital, Kenneth Donaldson. Donaldson, who had rejected all forms of treatment that doctors at the hospital believed might help him, insisted instead on a combination of occupational therapy, ground privileges, and psychotherapy. Failure of the hospital to provide these resulted in a jury decision that treatment had been denied and an assessment of $20,000 against two doctors at the hospital. The effect, note Isaac and Armat, after the *Donaldson* and *Stickney* decisions had worked their way through the appeals process and been upheld by the higher courts, was not to establish a right to treatment, but—as the antipsychiatric mental health bar had hoped—to spur deinstitutionalization.

These and the many other lawsuits brought by the mental health liberation bar contributed to the further decline of the patient population of state hospitals that had begun with the exposés at the end of World War II and been helped along by the availability of effective neuroleptic drugs. After 1974, the availability of federal Supplemental Security Insurance (SSI) to the mentally disabled, in combination with the lawsuits, according to Isaac and Armat, created "a classic 'push and pull' situation." At the same time that legal actions made it impossible to keep many patients needing institutionalization in the hospitals, SSI enabled states by discharging them to pass along the financial burden for their care to the federal government.[32]

Having confirmed the right to treatment for institutionalized mental patients, the lawyers next went to work to establish the right to refuse treatment. They eventually succeeded in making it so difficult, costly, and time consuming to require treatment for mental patients not wanting it that the release of patients from the hospital to streets or shelters, or leaving patients untreated, became relatively attractive alternatives. In some states, a patient need not even refuse treatment to require a court hearing about it; the simple fact that the patient is seen as too psychotic to make a "competent" decision about his own treatment may require court involvement.[33]

The only standard of involuntary civil commitment that has survived this legal onslaught is dangerousness: that if the patient is left unconfined or untreated he constitutes a danger to himself or others. Many times this condition would be difficult to prove even if it were not the subject for an adversary proceeding. But as these matters have evolved, it has been made even more difficult. In 1955, the population of our mental hospitals reached its peak at 559,000. About then, as the introduction of neuroleptic drugs became widespread, a long-term decline in the numbers of patients in these hospitals began. By 1970, when the mental patient liberation bar had reached full swing, the number was still 339,000. After ten years of litigation and agitation, the number had fallen to 130,000—a drop proportionately much greater in a much shorter time.[34] The population living in the streets and parks mushroomed: these are the mentally ill individuals whose families and doctors (if any) cannot require them to accept appropriate treatment or hospitalization even when it is available.

> The mental health liberation bar has established a new, cruel system for the mentally ill. The right to treatment has become the right to no treatment, the right to freedom is the right to deteriorate on the streets and die in back alleys.[35]

These patient advocacy lawyers might be right about the law: the fact that they win so often in court surely raises the presumption that they are. Their efforts, however, have contributed greatly to the misery in the world. Society does not work when it is run on an adversary basis of abstract conceptions of what is right and just; it works only when flesh and blood people can act on their felt, personal commitment to each other and to enduring civilized values.

MENTAL ILLNESS is not necessarily a lifelong condition. According to Torrey and his associates, about a quarter of the individuals with schizophrenia recover from their first or second episode and never get sick again. In many other cases the mentally ill improve spontaneously over time as they get older. Most can be helped to function much better with good psychiatric and rehabilitative services.[36] In a humane system, laws and regulations will be written and interpreted to establish a legal status in between institutional confinement and complete freedom for some classes of patients. Those needing it will be provided medication and other proven therapies, and some will be required to take their medication as a condition of their freedom to live among the rest of us. Hospitalization will be provided when it is needed, and for some this means long-term hospitalization. Such community support services as residential living arrangements and rehabilitative services will also be standard.

At California's Napa State Hospital I talked with Stuart McCullough, director of alcohol, drug, and mental health programs for Contra Costa County, California. His county has an allotment of 94.5 beds in the hospital. McCullough uses most of them for long-term mental patients who cannot be placed in the community either because of the lack of community-based residential facilities for the mentally ill or because they require too much care. There is nowhere else to put them but Napa or one forty-bed locked ward back in Contra Costa County. Absurdly few hospital beds are available compared with the need, says McCullough, reeling off a string of statistics. One of the benefits to mental patients in the hospital setting, McCullough points out, is their being able to look and act bizarre—they cannot help it—without drawing special attention to themselves.

McCullough introduced me to Clay Foreman, Contra Costa County's conservator and guardian for patients at Napa. He has worked with the mentally ill since 1976. In his view, programs are often underfunded, and much of the money being spent is wasted. Administrators commonly eliminate important items and go on spending for lesser things. The system is too complex; no one at a high enough level to straighten it out is close enough to understand its complexities.

Foreman introduced me to some of the patients he knows as their guardian and conservator. One is a black man of 6 feet 4 inches in late middle age. He cannot stand any longer, confined to a wheelchair because of a stroke. He cannot live in the community because he is too big and powerful, what is left of him. He is known to lash out occasionally with his one good arm, which is still strong enough to do quite a bit of damage. His speech is slurred from a lifetime of medication. He can still chuckle when Foreman teases him about the local women. Another is a white man of about thirty years, standing and fidgeting, face somehow gone crooked. He has wet his pants and appears to be unaware of it. Foreman has told me the man had suffered major brain damage in an accident some years ago. The man, boylike, talked to me. I tried to understand his slurred speech; something about wanting to get out, wanting to go to work, being a good worker. Foreman told the man that he will have a hearing before a judge about release but cautioned him that release is unlikely because of his condition. In another ward, I met a black man of about sixty who, Foreman said, has lived in tunnels under the streets of Richmond, California. When Foreman talked with him about homelessness, the man denied that he had been homeless. He had a family and knew where they are, and he did not consider he had been homeless.

All these individuals are chronically mentally ill. They have no chance of any sort of independent life. As far as I can tell, the staff is kind to them. The wards are kept clean and the linen changed. They have people to talk with, television to watch, other activities, and regular meals and showers. They are sheltered, and the heating bills are paid regularly. Life in this hospital would seem to be much better for a great many of the chronically mentally ill than life outside under present conditions.

McCullough and Foreman introduced me to psychiatrist Jim Diodato, who has worked since 1963 in the mental hospitals of four states. Diodato lamented that he spent most of his time on routine patient maintenance activities, because the hospital has so many chronic patients. While the hospital isstaffed as an acute facility, by necessity it functions largely as a custodial institution. There is simply not enough room for acute patients. Essentially, we have no public system of care for the acutely mentally ill: these "higher functioning" individuals most often end up on the streets. At the same time, the skills of Diodato and other highly trained staff are underused. Funds are spent, Diodato said, on useless activities, and they cannot be spent on needed things. Hospital officials should be able to admit that they are really in the business of providing custodial care and organize accordingly.

Since a 1972 federal court ruling (*Lessard* v. *Schmidt*), decisions concerning involuntary commitment have no longer been based on a determination of "the best interests of the patient" but have required "an extreme likelihood that if the person is not confined he will do immediate harm to himself or others."[37] Most mental health professionals and parent groups believe this policy is a misguided application of civil liberties. According to Elliot Badanes, spokesman for the family-based California Alliance for the Mentally Ill, "There are thousands of people who desperately need help and will not accept it except involuntarily."[38] Family advocates are working to reshape this policy.[39]

The psychiatrist and journalist Charles Krauthammer agrees with them on the issue. For the homeless mentally ill, he asks:

> Why should it be necessary to convince a judge that, left alone, they will die? The vast majority won't. It should be enough to convince a judge that left alone they will suffer.
>
> What prevents us from doing this is the misguided and pernicious civil libertarian impulse that holds liberty too sacred to be overridden for anything other than the preservation of life. For the severely mentally ill, however, liberty is not just an empty word but a cruel hoax. Free to do what?
>
> What does freedom mean for a paranoid schizophrenic who is ruled by voices commanded by his persecutors and rattling around in his head?[40]

Some of the opposition to involuntary commitment stems, rightly or misguidedly, from a concern for civil liberties—either for the liberties of the patients themselves or for what might happen unless we "draw the line" firmly where it will protect stigmatized groups. While parent advocacy groups want to change the rules on involuntary commitment, patient groups want to keep the policy strict. Steven Segal, a Berkeley social welfare professor who works closely with patient groups, believes that the "current civil commitment laws are, for the most part, working."[41] Howie Harp, speaking for the California Network of Mental Health Clients, says, "If somebody wants to stay outside and waste away, that's their right."[42] Some do not trust the professional judgment of psychiatrists. Some consider the care system as it now exists in their community inhumane and do not believe it is right to force people into it except perhaps as a last resort.

Others oppose involuntary commitment for reasons other than civil liberties as such: even where the system is adequate, they say, involuntary participation is antitherapeutic. Forcing an angry and alienated psychotic into treatment against his will is likely to make him even angrier and reinforce his feelings of persecution. Leonard Stein argues that to work effectively with patients,

> Staff must believe that the people they are working with are citizens of the community. . . . [and] that patients are indeed free agents able to make decisions and be responsible for their actions. These attitudes influence clinical behavior. Take for example the medication issue. Patients are frequently ambivalent about taking medications. We find we get better compliance if we relate to patients as responsible [individuals] and make them partners in the medication decisions.[43]

In the Dane County, Wisconsin, system where Stein is director of research and training at the community mental health center, a program is run for the mentally ill who refuse to come in for services. The Dane County center, like the Goddard-Riverside Community Center on Manhattan's upper west side, does "assertive outreach." Refusal to come in, says Stein, is considered "part of the illness," so it is treated in the field.[44]

There is another side to this argument. According to columnist Blake Fleetwood, "Public health authorities estimate that between 4 and 8 percent of the population of all societies is dysfunctional because of addiction or mental problems, a percentage that has remained constant throughout recorded history."[45]

Fleetwood is among those who believe that the public has a right to the enjoyment of public spaces set aside and maintained for that purpose. Unrestricted camping, drinking alcohol in public, publicly relieving oneself, aggressive begging, public sex, shouting obscenities, cursing passers-by, lurking threateningly in the bushes, and creating messes are not constitutionally protected. Publicly visible homelessness has increased partly because tolerance of it has increased, argues Fleetwood, and he insists we have a right to enact "quality of life laws" that reasonably

regulate behavior in public places. In refusing institutionalization or treatment, the mentally ill have no more right than
anyone else, and no less under the equal protection clause of
the Fourteenth Amendment, to insist on living on the streets or
in the parks.

It is, however, morally questionable, legally dubious, and
politically difficult to punish people for having nowhere to live.
Practically speaking, the homeless cannot be rounded up and
removed unless decent accommodations are available for them.
But there is no way to provide pleasant accommodations for the
homeless without increasing their numbers: the nicer the accommodations, the more the homeless. Any place so spartan and
strict that large numbers of nonhomeless will not be attracted out
of their present accommodations will inevitably provoke much
complaining by homeless individuals and their advocates that
the conditions are inhumane. Still, by providing spartan and strict
accommodations to everyone we find living on the street, we
could recapture a considerable measure of control over public
spaces currently occupied by the severely alienated mentally ill,
alcoholics, drug addicts, and persons claiming to be economically
homeless. The seriously mentally ill can be offered the same
choice of accommodations as everyone else, but they must behave
according to the rules wherever they choose to go. No agency
is obligated to keep them.

If a mentally ill individual will not or cannot behave in an
acceptable manner in any of the places he chooses, then the only
logical alternative is commitment. We do not have a legal obligation to let anyone live in the park or anywhere else just because
that is what he wants to do. Being mentally ill does not increase
one's civil rights, even if under present legal interpretations it does
not reduce them.

DEINSTITUTIONALIZATION AND DEMOGRAPHIC FACTORS are behind
the increased numbers of mentally ill in our public places over
the past two decades.[46] Deinstitutionalization is evident both in
the discharge of long-term mental patients and in the noninstitu-
tionalization of later generations of mentally ill individuals who
earlier would have been consigned to life in a mental hospital.
Mental illness does not usually manifest itself before adolescence,

the peak years of onset being between the ages of twenty and forty. Babies born in the birth bulge following World War II are now thirty to forty years old. In addition, as many of their children—the "echo of the baby boom"—are reaching adolescence, the population of mentally ill will continue to increase until the first cycle of the baby boom is no longer with us or until we learn something more about prevention or cure.[47]

Three things have happened in the thirty years since it was decided that the seriously mentally ill should be returned to their communities:

- First, the new community institutions and the newly trained professionals intended to replace the mental hospitals and expand community treatment and support pursued another set of interests and largely ignored the seriously mentally ill.

- Second, even though most of the patients left the mental hospitals, in many states most of the financial resources stayed there, leaving the resources for community treatment inadequate.

- Third, the community treatment and support system that came about in this often resource-deprived environment did so largely without effective leadership and emerged as an uncoordinated hodgepodge of special interests.

As a result of these three developments, today there are, as Leonard Stein describes the national situation, "three treatment paradigms." His preferred paradigm is the "comprehensive community-based treatment model," which, he says, "provides continuing treatment in the community and interim treatment of acute episodes in the hospital." The model "most frequently used," he notes, however, "might be called the revolving-door paradigm: short-term hospital treatment followed by inadequate community treatment leading to unstable patient conditions with frequent relapses and readmissions." The third paradigm, according to Stein, "still used in too many cases in this country," is long-term institutional care.[48]

No one advocates the desirability of the revolving-door paradigm. Most who work in the field see the need to move toward comprehensive community treatment, although they are likely to resist specific proposals that affect their interests. Some, most notably Charles Krauthammer, think the betrayal represented by deinstitutionalization has gone on too long and argue for "rebuilding an asylum system," doing it right this time.[49]

The issue of the seriously mentally ill has moral power. The American Psychiatric Association (APA) set up a task force on the homeless mentally ill in the early 1980s, publishing a report and recommendations in 1984. In many respects the report is excellent; indeed, it has been a useful resource in preparing this book. Predictably, though, it does not ask the great majority of the psychiatric community not working with the seriously mentally ill to begin doing so, even part of the time. Instead, it asks for additional "specially trained workers." It does not ask for agencies and institutions to shift priorities within existing funds toward the seriously mentally ill; instead, it asks for "adequate new monies to finance the system we envision."[50]

Will new money really be needed to help the seriously mentally ill? Or is a change in emphasis what is really needed? Professional associations are necessarily loath to criticize their members or to try to change the emphasis of the profession. While such associations often play a socially useful and responsible role in helping to improve professional standards and practice, their main purpose is to advance the power, prestige, and income of the membership. Before they can be of any use in bringing about a change of direction, they have to be made aware that a change of direction is needed. They have to see a constituency for this change within the membership. They have to be persuaded that moving on the issue is feasible. Even then, they are likely to tread rather softly. In this respect the APA is no worse than most professional organizations, or interest groups of any kind, and surely better than many. The APA's example makes a point, however. Once again it demonstrates that Pogo Possum was right when he said, "We have met the enemy and he is us." The members of APA and the other professional associations have it within their power to change the system. More often they embody a powerful inertia that keeps things from changing course.

Rael Jean Isaac and Virginia C. Armat offer a crisp list of six policies whose acceptance and implementation they believe are needed to provide a humane life for the mentally ill. They call these policies "keys to community living for the mentally ill."[51] They are well worth summarizing here:

- The mentally ill need appropriate treatment for their disease. Most commonly, this is a regime of psychotropic medication, but electroconvulsive therapy (ECT) has been both effective and harmless for a great many patients and deserves rehabilitation.

- Hospitalization must be available as needed and for some on a long-term basis.

- A legal status intermediate between confinement to an institution and total freedom in the community must be created for a group of patients who cannot otherwise sustain a satisfactory life in the community. The authors cite forms of guardianship, outpatient commitment, and cash management.

- Community services, including supported residential and rehabilitation programs, must be provided in one integrated system.

- The need for treatment must be restored as a basis both for involuntary commitment and for treatment in the community. Dangerousness needs to be abandoned as the standard.

- Responsibility for treating the mentally ill must rest with the medical profession, not with the lawyers.

The elements of a comprehensive community treatment program for the homeless mentally ill begin with client outreach that is both persistent and patient.[52] Bernie Wohl, director of New York City's Goddard-Riverside Community Center, described its widely admired outreach program, which involves such sophisticated approaches as making peanut butter sandwiches and leaving them in bags on benches in nearby Central Park. When center officials started doing this in 1980, they just left the bags there, and after a while the bags disappeared. Then they began to leave notes in the bags, offering showers, meals, or someone to talk to. After about two weeks of this tactic, the center had attracted about a dozen and a half seriously mentally ill individuals from the park. The center continues to bring new clients into the program through such efforts. Ten years later, though, there are still individuals in Central Park and throughout the city so angry or withdrawn that nothing seems to work.[53]

Case management, the assignment of one person or one team to work continuously with each client and to ensure the mobilization and coordination of all the appropriate services for that client, is widely recognized as an effective response to the administrative challenge of working with multiproblem populations. Case management is indispensable in working with the mentally ill: many are cut off completely from other humans and need to reestablish a connection. A level of trust is required for the mentally ill to accept treatment. Moreover, the services required are so varied and likely to be so dispersed throughout the community as to make it difficult for even a normal individual to negotiate them. To place a duplicate set of these services in each agency working with the mentally ill would drive the cost beyond even what it would be in a hospital setting. The task force on homelessness of the American Psychiatric Association has declared, "The ultimate goal must be to ensure that each chronically mentally ill person in this country has one person—such as a case manager or resource manager—who is responsible for his or her treatment and care."[54]

According to Diane Sonde of the Goddard-Riverside Center, the agency provides these "seriously disaffiliated people" a nonthreatening place to spend time and then works with them as they come to feel more comfortable. Taking a shower makes them feel more human and healthier, she says. For some it is the first time they have looked in a mirror in a long time. Then the staff "starts to barter with them." Several contacts may be needed to get them out of the park and into Goddard: "then the real challenge begins."[55] The case manager's job is to stay in touch and to help the client live as normal a life as possible. Each client has his own limits to how much he can handle and how soon. The case manager engages with the client in a continuous and patient exploration of these limits.

Keeping the client on the proper balance of psychotropic medication is critical and can be very challenging. Too much and the client is a zombie; too little and he may begin to experience again whatever hallucinations and delusions preoccupied him previously. Commonly, mental patients hate their medicine because it dulls and sometimes depresses them, slows them, and has other undesirable side effects. While it suppresses the more bizarre symptoms that disturb them and interfere with their functioning, the medication may do little to restore their normal skills and abilities. When they feel reasonably well, they are likely to imagine that it is safe to stop "taking their meds." Usually the result is rapid resumption of their previous symptoms. In addition to the things the rest of us need, such as food, clothing, and medical care, many of the mentally ill will need twenty-four hour crisis assistance: symptoms may reappear at any time, and medication may have to be changed or adjusted. Drinking or drug abuse can also precipitate a crisis.

Once established on the appropriate regime of medication, though, the seriously mentally ill are capable of varying degrees of independence and responsibility. What they can handle will range from complete dependence in an organized living structure to independent living with only occasional contact. According to Goddard's Sonde, medication management and money management are the two most important supports for the seriously mentally ill. It is important to gain their acceptance by working with them on these matters on a continuing basis.

Housing for the mentally ill must also be geared to the amount of structure and supervision they need. In any community program a range of supportive housing options must be available with "varying degrees of supervision and structure"—not simply affordable apartments, but "therapeutic residences, halfway houses, group homes, supervised apartments, and independent apartments."[56] So they can reach their potential, retraining in daily living skills and occupational rehabilitation are important services for the case manager to oversee. The case manager must also help them manage their relationships in the larger community—with landlords, neighbors, storekeepers, librarians, employers, welfare agencies, and police.

Even under the best conditions, many of the seriously mentally ill still require periodic hospitalization. Good community care keeps this need to a minimum but does not eliminate it entirely. Irene Shifren Levine, of the National Institute of Mental Health, points out that inpatient (hospital) and outpatient (community) systems often operate under separate administrations and budgets. Both for the sake of effective patient care and for the sake of cost reduction, they need to be integrated. She cautions that if all we do is reorganize the outpatient system and fail to link it properly with the hospitals, we will have missed the problem.[57]

The same can be said if we don't improve the hospitals. Because the state hospitals have been under attack for so long, they have deteriorated badly.[58] In many ways, it is reported, they are even worse than before. They need to be accorded their appropriate and essential role and then shaped to carry it out. Working there, like working with the seriously mentally ill in any proper setting, needs to be given a new measure of recognition and respect.

RECENT RESEARCH SHOWS that to maintain a seriously mentally ill individual properly who can be cared for outside an institution costs less than to do so inside. Based on her review of the field, Irene Shifren Levine believes that for the nation as a whole to do things "the right way rather than the wrong way" should cost no more than at present. She does think, however, that "to do the job we really should be doing" would cost "a lot more."[59] Fuller Torrey and others estimate that we are currently spending about $20 billion on programs for the seriously mentally ill.[60] He has argued that no more money than this should be needed. Research reported by Leonard Stein[61] shows that in five widely distanced communities that have adopted Dane County, Wisconsin's model of comprehensive community-based treatment, excellent clinical results are achieved at only about one-fourth the price of long-term institutional care. Furthermore, these studies all show that the cost of this community-based care is about the same as what we are already getting from our present revolving-door system.

Isaac and Armat stress that the Dane County system depends for its success on legal provisions enabling it to require patients living in the community to take their prescribed treatment. The primary cause of the revolving door is the failure of patients to take their medication after leaving the hospital; the patients then wind up back in the hospital or in jail.[62] As we have seen, under various court decisions, many jurisdictions make it difficult or impossible to commit someone to involuntary treatment or confinement unless the person has been proved in court, following the strict procedural requirements of criminal law, to be immediately dangerous to himself or to others. The success of the patient liberation bar in preventing the treatment of the seriously mentally ill and in aggravating what it costs to do so is discouraging. Whatever the theoretical justice of making it extremely difficult to confine or restrain mentally ill individuals or to force them to take medicine, the problems and the financial costs brought about thereby are considerable. Wisconsin has circumvented the problem for now by amending its state law so that a statutory provision authorizing court-ordered protective services, formerly used mainly for such things as in-home services and housekeeping for the infirm, would also authorize the courts to mandate guardians to see that outpatients take their medication. Such guardianships are "limited to consenting to or refusing medication."[63]

Stein's figures show a per patient cost averaging around $9,500 per year in an effective community-based system, $11,000 in the prevalent revolving-door system, and $37,500 in long-term hospital treatment. Using Torrey's approximations of $20 billion spent annually and of 2 million for the total number of seriously mentally ill adults in America, we are now spending about $10,000 each on the average. Since we are spending little or nothing on over 900,000 of these—NIMH says we do not even know where they are[64]—the average spent on the remainder is close to $20,000 each, considerably more than what Stein and other researchers find that top-quality care should cost. Under the revolving-door paradigm, little or no care is alternated with frequent expensive hospital care. A hard-nosed analysis shows that competent, continuous maintenance in the community may actually be cheaper as well as more humane.

In fact, when any system becomes so tangled and ineffective as this one, money may no longer bear a consistent relationship to quality. Since 1986, Fuller Torrey and Sidney Wolfe have conducted an annual survey of mental illness systems in the fifty states. Their biggest surprise when they started doing this was "the lack of any statistical correlation between the quality of inpatient and community services for the seriously mentally ill and the state's per capita mental health expenditures."[65] Based on this observation and the national total of $20 billion spent each year on services for the mentally ill, Torrey has insisted that a Class A system should cost no more than the revolving door to operate.

In the aggregate, I believe that Torrey is generally right: it should cost no more than it does now to reform the system and provide high-quality care in appropriate settings (ordinarily, the least restrictive feasible) for the seriously mentally ill. Things do not happen in the aggregate, however. Most funds for the mentally ill are raised and spent by the states, not by the federal government. The states that have squeezed spending down over the years as they have emptied out the mental hospitals or that have always had low spending will have to increase it; and taxpayers there will have to pay more taxes. States that save money by doing the job more efficiently will not send their leftover tax money to states that have not been spending enough. The savings will be returned to their own taxpayers or, more likely, be spent on something else.

Even in states with a large enough mental health budget to sustain excellent services for the mentally ill, start-up costs may require a bump in the budget. Experience shows that it may cost the equivalent of one year's operating costs to start up a residential living facility.[66] Some of the one-time costs associated with changing a human care system are for recruiting, retraining old staff, training new staff, ending and starting leases, purchasing different kinds of equipment, contracting for planning and evaluation studies, severance pay for employees terminated from discontinued programs, and paying for two programs simultaneously while patients make a transition from one to another. Conversion costs are not massive, can be assimilated over time, and can often be partially borne by one-time grants. Outside evaluation studies of planning, management, and program delivery can also help achieve efficiencies.

Transition expenses should not be a justification for large new appropriations or a barrier to change. In an article in *Hospital and Community Psychiatry*, Thomas Deiker shows how this transition was handled in one state with a minimum of fiscal pain. The method of administrative budgeting was changed so that the state's money followed the patient when he left the hospital. The political and bureaucratic impact was minimal. Hospital staffs, notorious for high turnover anyway, shrank through normal attrition. Workers interested in doing so were moved into community positions without interruption of their employment. No special appropriations were required to pay transition costs.[67]

In Texas, New York, and other states where most of the money stayed in the hospitals when the patients left rather than returning to the taxpayers or paying for other things, more of it will have to be pried loose. Arizona and a few other states spending dramatically less than the national average will probably need to increase their continuing funding many fold. They have the advantage of having less bureaucracy to change and the disadvantage of having to come up with more new money. The most populous state, California, spends less than the average, in spite of higher than average wages and, in its major metropolitan areas, extremely high housing costs, a major expense in community-based care. Torrey and Wolfe, in the 1990 edition of their annual survey, found California, while eighth in per capita income, to be twenty-third in expenditure for the mentally ill, thirty-first in quality of care, and "moving backwards." California, under Governor Reagan, was one of many states that used deinstitutionalization mainly to cut its budget. Corrected for inflation, the amount the state spent on mental hospitals before deinstitutionalization would be about $3 billion in today's dollars. The state's current mental health budget is about $1.2 billion. A great many of the patients living on the back wards of mental hospitals in the days before Medicare and Medicaid were available for nursing home costs were simply elderly people no longer able to care for themselves, with nowhere else to go. Such individuals no longer need to be considered in the budget for the mentally ill. Care for the seriously mentally ill in California can be provided by an appropriate mixture of settings for about half to two-thirds the hospital price. Considering these factors, I have had conversations with California legislative budget analysts who suggest that it would cost an additional $300 million to $600 million annually, or about $10 to $20 per capita more than we are spending at present, to do the job right. These estimates do not take into account savings that might be achieved through the use of vouchers, broadened contracting with private providers, and other potential cost-saving strategies.

It should be noted that in California's decentralized system per capita spending on mental illness varies greatly from county to county. While according to Torrey's figures the statewide per capita expenditure for the mentally ill was $28.88 in 1983, in Orange County, where housing costs are very high, the per capita expenditure was only $8.22.[68] Undoubtedly, in some metropolitan California counties, and in other places in the United States where housing costs are extraordinarily high, provision of a humane community-based mental illness system will require increased appropriations, sometimes a dramatic increase. Not only will spending need to be increased statewide, but also changes will need to be made in how the state apportions funds among the counties.

We have no quick way to solve the homelessness problem. We could, though, set a national goal of ensuring that all the seriously mentally ill homeless have a designated someone (rarely a family member, as the mentally ill homeless usually lack positive family relationships) who knows where they are and takes responsibility for their support and treatment—their case manager. We could go an important step further and designate this someone the mentally ill person's legal guardian or conservator. Taking the process another step, we could give the guardian a voucher for the support and treatment of the patient. Several classes of vouchers could be provided for patients needing greater or lesser amounts of support or treatment, with the voucher for each based on a psychiatrist's application of preset criteria. The guardian would be accountable for purchasing the needed services, public or private, in the open market. One of the two big points of resistance case managers encounter at present is the unresponsiveness of service bureaucracies. Controlling the funds directly should give them what they need to overcome this problem. The other point of resistance is the patient himself. Although the ability to deliver better on promises to the patient will not magically enable him to begin trusting his case manager, it should help. Guardians could associate with one another and negotiate jointly with providers and assist new providers to go into business. The treatment system, then, would become consumer driven. In effect, persons who know and care about each of the seriously mentally ill would run the system within funding and policies established politically. Such a voucher system should be tested in various forms under a variety of conditions, and if successful, would need to be implemented state by state.

IN RECENT YEARS, leadership has begun to emerge from the ranks in the field of mental illness. Fuller Torrey and Leonard Stein are two in a national movement under way to convert the public mental health system over to what it should have become with the enactment of the Community Mental Health Act of 1963. At NIMH and throughout the United States, without any general awareness, greater attention has been turned to providing mental health services to the seriously mentally ill in their communities, to reorganizing resources so this will happen, and to retraining staff. At the national level, this has meant funding research to find out what models work best and disseminating the results. At the state and community levels, leaders are needed who will give support and direction to a long-term public process of learning what is needed and overcoming resistance to change. The problem is complex, and the opportunities for gratifying public service almost limitless.

Because environmental theories of mental illness have lost most of their following, no longer does a major ideological division hinder development of community care of the seriously mentally ill. There is, however, the resistance of entrenched interests—hospitals that want to keep the money, unions of mental health workers and other employees who have contracts that make it very difficult to change what they do, and agencies and professionals who want to continue their present activities. Moreover, the political, administrative, and financial complexity makes it especially difficult to enlist the press in ways that would be helpful.

Conversion is likely to force the executive and the legislature to set new policies and either increase or reapportion funds. Reapportioning is often the more difficult of these two courses of action politically, because money is taken away from specific programs that are likely to fight agressively and determinedly; increasing the total funds, though, affects marginally all the taxpayers in the state. The only passion the increased tax bill is likely to arouse will come from its being one element in a larger discussion of taxing and spending.

Within a state's total budget for mental health, changing the priorities, funding patterns, and channels for the flow of funds brings real pain and dislocation to agencies and clients, just as changing budget priorities does in a family. A community mental health center may, for example, be using CMHA funds effectively to provide useful and appreciated counseling services to troubled low-income parents or to assist a local school to work with predelinquent students. These may appear to be good investments in the prevention of family breakup and crime. To enable existing clients to complete their treatment or find other providers, and programs to phase down properly, conversion should be a sure and steady process, inevitable but reasonably paced. If a program is both demonstrably effective and useful to the community, given a little time it can usually find funds somewhere to continue—sadly, not always. Just as in any business, however, an economic shakeup usually eliminates more of the weak and borderline operations than it does the good ones.

Managing this transition from the revolving door to a comprehensive community care system is a challenge for politicians and administrators at all levels. In their 1987 fifty-state survey, *Care of the Seriously Mentally Ill*, Torrey and Wolfe found that the leadership provided by state mental health administrators, governors, and legislative leaders "is probably the single most important factor in determining the quality of state services for the seriously mentally ill." They determined that grassroots leadership, "the presence of strong consumer groups representing the seriously mentally ill," was another very important ingredient.[69] Where both are present and where confident government officials are able to see the potential of consumer groups to help bring about change and enlist their participation in program planning and review, progress is likely to follow.

Torrey reports in May 1990 that even though many models for the care of the seriously mentally ill have been demonstrated locally to be both effective and economical, the findings are seldom used to improve the system other places. Research and demonstration projects have been funded, monitored to completion, and evaluated. The results have been reported, reviewed, and critiqued. While the findings are often positive, even dramatically so, little or nothing has been changed in other communities as a result. The reason, Torrey says, is "primarily economic," but not in a simple way. The successful program models usually fit no one else's "existing system of economic incentives."[70] When roles and responsibilities are allocated sensibly between the branches and levels of government in this country, our system works. Such is not the case here. As Torrey writes,

> The funding of public services for the mentally ill in the United States is an incredible pastiche of federal, state, and local efforts with no overall coordination. Individual funding strategies are often at odds with each other. Federal dollars, comprising about 40 percent of the total funds, include Medicaid, Medicare, SSI, Social Security Disability Insurance, block grants, and housing programs of various kinds. State and local funds for the seriously mentally ill have come from a variety of departments including mental health, social services, housing, vocational rehabilitation, and corrections. To run a department of mental health at the state or local level, one needs to be primarily an accountant who keeps track of the many sources of funds and what they can be used for.
>
> This chaotic funding system has grown piecemeal since Medicaid and Medicare were established 25 years ago. New programs have been added incrementally with virtually no attempt to fit the funding pieces together into a coherent whole. The system for the mentally ill in the United States is, in short, more thought-disordered than most of the individuals the system is intended to serve.[71]

The transition to better community care, under way in many states for more than a decade, will take several more years even with increasingly good leadership at all levels. There is no good way to do it quickly. When it is completed, a promise to the mentally ill will belatedly have been kept, and life in our public places will be greatly improved. Although we will still see mentally ill individuals there, they will have a place to stay, have something to eat, and people to care for them, most importantly helping them to stay on their medication. Fewer of them will be screaming epithets, muttering to themselves, and hiding out in the bushes; their violent acts should decline.

Under present federal law, it appears that with the passing of many years this transition may happen. Four out of every five states are at least trying to improve their services for the seriously mentally ill. In about half of the states, things are actually getting better, albeit rather slowly in most of these.[72] A federal law was recently enacted to require that each state have a comprehensive plan to implement appropriate care for the mentally ill. The process of changing to such a system is under way in several states; progress is noticeable, though modest year by year, and more in some states and counties than others depending on the leadership. Even where it is good, the achievement of minimally acceptable services is likely to take a very long time in states where services for the mentally ill have been stripped of state funds. Each year the federal government and the state, and, increasingly, representatives of patients and their families will argue over the plan again, and most of the time quality will inch up another notch. No system is yet in place for outside evaluation of how state plans are being implemented. An open public process in each state, and in each county of decentralized states like California, would probably help to speed things up.

We have no excuse for accepting this snail's pace. The main problem in this field is not money or knowledge: it is lack of focused leadership. Statesmen who may be frustrated by the lack of resources to carry out grand projects have an outstanding opportunity to do something great where political power and creative intelligence are the principal resources required. Where the need for more money is critical, and the money is not available, goals need to be set and funds increased a little at a time. Attention needs to be continuous, so that in prosperous years the opportunity to make major increases will not be missed. Now it is time, in Torrey's words, "to reevaluate the economics of the mental health services system."[73] At this writing, the Bush administration has just created a task force on mental health. The secretary of health and human services, the attorney general, the president, and the governors should get involved and give the movement a higher level of political energy. Leadership, in this case, is the main thing needed in most parts of the country.

If the task force does its work well, a White House conference to review and develop plans for implementation of its findings might be the appropriate next step. Subsequently, in states and communities where additional money will be needed, program officials should first be called upon to demonstrate an effective use of existing resources. Before most of them will be able to prove this claim, they will need to enlist large numbers of ordinary citizens in reviewing the system and demanding of the unions, professional associations, and other vested interests that changes be made. Citizens can also help to overcome neighborhood resistance to accepting residential facilities. The press can play an important and positive role in this agenda for building community.

Unfortunately, given the state of our political culture, the first step of the president or a governor will bring forth the usual cries for more money. These officials will be accused of callousness if they urge not more money but better laws, different priorities, and better use of existing funds. These leaders may be correct, but since no one stands up and demands less money, a constant amount, or even moderate increases, they will find themselves on the defensive.

Newspaper and television accounts will show the president or governor defending his budget rather than giving leadership to a movement. After asking "hard questions," the press will not be concerned about what is being done with existing resources to find research answers and to stimulate changes in state and local programs. They will assiduously search out victims both of the old policy that is being changed and of the change that is being undertaken and dramatize their situation. There will be editorials about how we ought to be ashamed of ourselves.

I like to think that the broader public is tiring of this predictable pattern. When Americans become convinced that money is needed and that spending it will solve a problem, we spend it. We have even spent a lot of it that we did not have on problems the money failed to solve. So often, though, money is spent to build new constituencies that ask for more money and then refuse to accept responsibility for the consequences, always explaining that shortfalls or new problems they may have created resulted from not having enough money. A relatively silent majority of the public and increasing numbers of politicians appear to be aware of this pattern and are skeptical of big spending programs. Congress is often criticized for lack of accomplishment. Whatever good it fails to do, or bad it does, it may deserve some credit for all the worthless bills and excessive appropriations *not* passed. In addition to any lack of awareness or commitment of which our representatives might properly be accused or, conversely, excessive commitment to big campaign contributors, they may also have had their critical faculties improved by the deficit. Indeed, some congressmen and senators may have learned from experience or may be listening to quieter constituencies.

Fuller Torrey has requested a pilot program in which some of the states most highly rated in mental illness services would be given block grant authority over 95 percent of all federal funds for individuals with serious mental illness. One of the conditions he would place on the use of such funds is that these states "confront the legal issues of involuntary hospitalization and the use of involuntary treatment programs such as outpatient commitment."[74] He hopes that state governments will address the issue so that a resolution can be achieved. The U.S. Supreme Court, as its composition has changed in recent years, has shown more respect for decisions made by elected officials in the states and local jurisdictions. This situation affords Americans an opportunity to take a greater measure of control over life in their communities. Because litigation is no way to build civic relationships, it should be restored to its former status as a process for times when respectful give-and-take has clearly failed. Civilized peoples cannot determine the conditions of their daily lives in adversarial proceedings: it is time for us to learn again to live together.

3

Lucky to Be Alive

DUTCH SHISLER SAYS he is lucky to be alive. Twenty years ago he almost died of drink. The doctors put him on a "liver shunt," a device that diverts body waste around the liver, allowing the organ time to regenerate itself. Dutch was fortunate—liver shunts don't always work. Now he drives a van around downtown Seattle, picking up drunks and taking them to the detoxification center at Harborview General Hospital, to "detox," as everyone calls it.

Dutch loves his work. He gets 15,000 calls each year, about 50 per work day, over his two-way radio from a dispatcher at 911 headquarters. "Man down at Second and Yesler," says the voice over the radio, and Dutch replies that he will be there in two minutes.

Dutch has already picked up three drunks. He recognizes all three, guessing that he knows about fourteen out of every fifteen people he picks up. He picks up the same people every few days, with one or two new ones each week or so. Some are locals who have completed a slide from home, perhaps family, to the street. Some are from Montana, Idaho, or Minnesota, Dutch says, "attracted to Seattle because of our liberal program." When Dutch invites them into the van, they go willingly or he doesn't take them. If he believes someone who refuses is a threat to himself or to others, he calls for a community services patrol officer to determine whether involuntary commitment to detox is in order. Seldom is such a call necessary. Most go willingly to detox, where they dry out, eat healthy food, sleep in a good bed, and are treated nicely by a staff they know very well. To many, it is something like home. Unless a drunk commits himself for extended treatment, and this is rare, he is back on the street in three days. Dutch is called to pick him up again, maybe that same day, maybe a day or two later. Detox is a revolving door.

At Fourth and Adams we see two men lying on the sidewalk. I help Dutch and his partner, Dennis, get them to the van. One of the men—Dutch calls him by name—is some help with the walking and step climbing, but not a lot. When the van is full, Dutch tells the dispatcher he is on his way to Harborview. The passengers are quiet except when Dutch makes conversation with them. He gets an occasional clear reply but more often confused ones.

"Citizens call 911, police call in, meter maids do," Dutch says. Officials and other concerned citizens are encouraged to call whenever they encounter someone lying down on the sidewalk in daytime. By nightfall, nearly everyone has been picked up. These homeless alcoholics spend forty-eight to seventy-two hours in detox, which has an overflow capacity of 105 beds. In addition, the county has contracted two "sleep-off centers." Sometimes detox is full before 3 P.M.

Dutch says he has been "clean and sober" for over eighteen years, but only two of the ninety people who went through treatment with him are still sober. He believes aftercare is essential for treatment programs. A "twelve-step" program such as Alcoholics Anonymous works for more people than other approaches, he says. It is important for recovering alcoholics to make personal friendships with one another to sustain their commitment to staying sober. Dutch reminisces about himself and "six other guys" in his AA chapter going fishing together at remote Neah Bay, where, he recalls, the smallest thing they caught was a twelve-pound king salmon.

High proportions of U.S. homeless—both men and women—have a serious problem with alcohol or drug abuse. I judge the proportion to be well over half the men and more than a quarter of the women.[1] This estimate applies to single homeless individuals, but somewhat less to adults in homeless families and their older children. The estimate holds for the homeless mentally ill.[2] The Urban Institute found that nationwide 56 percent of the adult homeless have a jail or prison record. More than a quarter have done time in state or federal prison.[3] People commonly acknowedge by now that substance abuse is associated with most of the serious crimes committed in this nation and with more than half the traffic deaths. Substance abuse is arguably America's number-one problem, and it is the number-one factor in homelessness. Mental illness is number two.

The homeless do not divide neatly into economically displaced families, alcohol abusers, narcotics abusers, and the mentally ill. My impression from talking with workers in the field is that most of the homeless mentally ill are also substance abusers and that most who abuse narcotics also abuse alcohol. The typical homeless individual is a "multiple-diagnosis" client.[4]

Advocates for the view that external forces—not decisions by individuals—lead to homelessness sometimes argue that substance abuse is primarily a result, not a cause, of homelessness. They admit that many of the homeless abuse alcohol and drugs but absolve them of fault by saying that these individuals use such substances as "self-medication" to dull their pain. The only published research that I have found on this issue shows, however, that where a pattern of substance abuse exists, it generally precedes homelessness. In Los Angeles's inner city, Paul Koegel and M. Audrey Burnam found that nearly 80 percent of the alcoholics in their sample of homeless adults "reported that their first alcohol symptom occurred before they were first homeless" and that in 57 percent of the cases this occurred at least five years before their first episode of homelessness.[5]

Most care givers I interviewed who work directly with homeless clients supported this view of the direction alcohol and drug abuse take. Research on many issues other than homelessness shows the relationship of alcohol abuse to social dysfunction. Alcohol or drug abuse generally precedes and contributes to job loss, spouse abuse, child abuse, family breakup, crime, prison, and then continues afterward. These other alcohol-related problems often contribute to homelessness. When rent was cheaper and single-occupancy units were plentiful, the results of substance abuse did not as often lead to actual homelessness as they do today: in that sense, homelessness is a housing shortage. The lack of housing, though, is not the principal tragedy; the housing situation is a sad fact that makes the tragedy of substance abuse and the behavior it leads to more visible than it used to be and more serious. With all that said, however, we should also acknowledge that no one doubts that homelessness aggravates any pattern of substance abuse and makes resolving it even more difficult.

SMITH TOWER is a handsome, white forty-two-story building in Seattle, overlooking the original "skid-road," Yesler Way, where until the 1920s logs were dragged downhill on skids and loaded on ships waiting at Puget Sound's docks. Today the logs that gave skid road its name are gone, but the unfortunates associated with the name "skid road," now more commonly "skid row," are still present in numbers. Steve Freng's office is on the tenth floor, where I went to hear the story of the Alcohol and Drug Addiction Treatment Support Act (ADATSA). Freng, the state administrator for alcoholism programs in the Seattle area, said that between 1980 and 1986, Washington State's general assistance case load for alcoholism and drug abuse soared from 1,400 to 6,400. General Assistance-Unemployable (GA-U) had covered mental illness, physical incapacity, and alcohol and substance abuse. A person could show up in town, satisfy the welfare department he was disabled by such a condition, and then be issued a monthly check. It came to be called a "drunk check," because the main use of the funds was widely seen to be getting and staying drunk.

Elected officials, startled by the sudden increase in case load, thought the state's relatively high general assistance payments of $314 per month had made Washington a magnet for drunks and drug users from other states. In hope of correcting this situation, in 1987 the Washington State legislature passed ADATSA. ADATSA marries income assistance to treatment or supervision. Instead of being given a monthly general assistance check of $314, a client is given a choice of undergoing treatment for his addiction or having his welfare payment administered by a "protective payee," an official who pays his rent for him so that he always has a place to live and who may also—under the tighter of two versions of the program being tried—insist on receipts showing that the client is buying food and other necessities with the balance of the check. The client can live wherever he can afford the rent within his $314 general assistance allotment. It is still possible to find places to rent in Seattle—typically a room with a hot plate—for about $180. The client might also choose to pay rent at a recovery (halfway) house.

In the first year of ADATSA, 25 percent of GA-U clients (we should note here that while some GA-U clients are homeless, most are not) dropped off of welfare rather than enter treatment or have their check managed for them. In 1990, California's Alameda County experienced an even more dramatic decline in participation when its Board of Supervisors decided to offer "room and board instead of quick cash" to homeless persons. Applications for homelessness assistance immediately declined by two-thirds, according to welfare officials, and have continued at the lower level for six months at this writing. The total has shrunk from about 300 to fewer than 100 assistance requests per day.[6] The generally liberal *Oakland Tribune* has supported this policy change in a lead editorial, citing reports from "community activists" that while some applicants use cash grants properly, "others spend the money on other things, including drugs."[7]

Most of the 75 percent in Seattle who chose to stay on general assistance and entered the Washington State program decided on treatment rather than the protective payee option. The treatment program, according to Freng, "sets a standard for treatment, a true continuum."[8] Of those entering treatment, 85 percent did so on an outpatient basis; the other 15 percent undertook a more intensive treatment model that was offered—twenty-one days of intensive inpatient treatment, sixty days in a recovery house, and ninety days as an outpatient. All clients who stayed with the program to completion were enrolled in twelve-step or other follow-up activities to maintain the new set of peer relationships developed in ADATSA.

Street alcoholics under ADATSA, like any other enrollee in the program, can choose treatment or simply have their welfare check managed for them by a protective payee, in this instance, a social case worker. Clients who fail treatment are placed in a "protective payee shelter track." They are signed up thirty-five to a case worker. The case worker is a protective payee, so he or she will see the client regularly and can help with other things. The case worker visits them where they live, diagnoses any medical problems, follows through, and insists on receipts for everything. According to Mike Tretton, who runs ADATSA's largest treatment program, this arrangement helps keep them alive but doesn't cure anything. The street population is mostly in the late-chronic stage of alcohol abuse, and the best that can be done for them by administering their general assistance pay-ment is to stabilize them at a lowered rate of alcohol use, make them safer and more comfortable in their own place to live, and keep them out of hospitals and jails.[9]

Some city officials had feared that ADATSA's policy of ending the "drunk check" would aggravate homelessness: people would be on the street with no money at all instead of with money to buy liquor or drugs. Other city officials thought ending the check would reduce street living in Seattle by taking away the magnet they believed was attracting out-of-staters. In fact, because of ADATSA's exclusive connection to general assistance, it did neither. As it turned out, most of Seattle's street drunks are not on general assistance—a temporary relief program—after all. According to Freng, most of Seattle's skid-row inebriates—about 400–500 individuals—have been impaired irretrievably by years of heavy drinking. As permanently disabled, many qualify for federal Supplemental Security Income (SSI). About 20 percent of Seattle's street drunks had enrolled in SSI; another 25 percent were Native Americans living on tribal funds; 10–15 percent more were on veteran pensions. And 25 percent were receiving no government cash benefits. So ADATSA neither aggravated home-lessness noticeably, nor helped it visibly: it had simply missed most of the individuals that it was expected to affect.

What did ADATSA do for the street drunks it did encompass? According to Freng, treatment programs for long-time street drunks are bound to have very low success rates, no matter how well they are designed and administered: the years of abuse have left too much organic damage. ADATSA helped some homeless alcoholics not yet destroyed by heavy drinking to enter treatment and try to deal with their problems. The protective payee element of the program helped them and others still on general assistance but already permanently disabled to get a place to live and keep the rent paid and food in the cupboard. Because it is tied to the state's general assistance program, ADATSA could do nothing at all for the 80 percent of Seattle's street alcoholics on federal assistance programs or not on cash assistance. To bring that about would require changes in these federal programs.

To almost everyone's surprise, ADATSA attracted many new clients to general assistance. They were drawn by the opportunity to get treatment and a stipend at the same time. A "great many," according to Freng, were twenty- to thirty-five-year-olds, "baby-boomers" who had not been living on the street. This group is, says Freng, "a much more functional population than anticipated." Most still have a place to live—on their own or with friends or family. A substantial number were not on welfare of any kind, although they readily qualified for general assistance, and there-fore for ADATSA, for in their current state they were clearly unemployable. They were "poly-drug users mostly—weed, speed, coke . . . and possibly also with learning disabilities." They were strong candidates for homelessness, experiencing what might be seen as their "pre–skid-row phase." They were attracted to ADATSA because "they saw themselves as on the way to oblivion." Women were much more heavily represented—25 percent—than they had been in programs for public inebriates. For some of these individuals, ADATSA was a homelessness prevention program.

Over the first several years of the program, savings were about $20 million less than expected, almost $6 million per year after paying the increased treatment and shelter costs under ADATSA for existing GA-U recipients and absorbing the new ones.[10] While in the short term, the program could be seen as a modest fiscal success, for the longer term lawmakers feared that ADATSA was becoming the equivalent of a "treatment-on-demand" policy, a commitment they were not ready for. Their analysts were pro-jecting that unless intake of these new clients were controlled, GA-U costs under ADATSA would rise to $150 million, almost three times what had been projected for the same period under the old GA-U program. Alcohol treatment services were attract-ing additional people in Seattle, just as free housing did in New York City: supply was creating its own demand.

Had Washington State officials been convinced that "treatment-on-demand" would pay for itself in recovery by alcohol and drug abusers, they might have been willing to commit the money. But there was, and there is, no strong evidence that such a result would follow. So appointed officials moved to hold things down and cut things back, and the legislature enacted an appropriation ceiling at the level of spending that had been pro-jected under the old GA-U program. They also set priorities. Instead of a first-come first-served program that would have resulted in an overwhelming enrollment of unattached males, this arrangement allowed pregnant women and the parents of young children to move to the head of the line and claim at least 40 percent of the openings.

Results from systematic evaluation do not yet exist for ADATSA, but statistics are maintained carefully. They show that about 80 percent of those who enter treatment complete the six-month program, and half of those are employed the day after graduation, although most did not have jobs before entering the program. The most effective approach to treatment, to the surprise of some, has turned out to be outpatient treatment under the intensive supervision version of the protective payee program, with the client living in his own place rather than in barracks.

The framers of the ADATSA legislation, according to Freng, "naively assumed" that to take away a source of funds for the purchase of liquor and drugs and to establish a "continuum of treatment" where before there were only detoxification, a few halfway houses, and no aftercare would make a dramatic and visible difference on the street. Because so few of Seattle's visible inebriates and drug addicts are on GA-U, however, that was not to be the case. The primary social benefit of ADATSA appears to be helping to prevent dependency and homelessness by providing younger, not yet chronic, alcoholics and earlier-stage drug abusers an opportunity to focus on solving their problem. The program also limits the rate at which alcoholics and drug addicts who are on general assistance destroy themselves, and it helps to keep them housed and fed. Although this program may result in fewer street drunks and drug users in the future, it will have little effect on the present homeless population. What would be of help is for the federal government to implement a protective payee program like ADATSA's, so that fewer clients in SSI, SSDI, and other federal welfare programs would be living on the streets.

Thoughtful alcoholism professionals in Seattle and elsewhere frequently express a concern that no matter what they do, no matter how humane or well-intended, no matter how necessary, such programs are likely to facilitate—to "enable," as they say in the trade—the client's self-destructive behavior. In Seattle, Portland, Los Angeles, and many other cities, vans circulate throughout downtown areas to pick up inebriates and take them, generally with their consent, to detoxification centers, instead of—

as it used to be twenty years ago—jail. The detox van makes just about as many calls per year and picks up just about as many drunks from the street as the police did in earlier times. The difference, I am told, is that now they are "patients" spending a few days in detoxification instead of "offenders" being thrown into a drunk tank. Either way, they go right back to the street. The current approach is a more pleasant revolving door but maybe one that enables them to continue their self-destructive behavior more than the previous harsher treatment.

The drivers of the van in Portland are medical technicians and sworn deputy sheriffs. In Portland's "person down" program, if a person cannot stand up, state law permits him to be taken to detox with or without his agreement. He can be held there for up to twenty-four hours. Then, when he is "somewhat dried out," an attempt is made to get him to agree to a five-day treatment program that enrolls him in Alcoholics Anonymous or Narcotics Anonymous, according to Kathy Stout of Portland's Hooper Detoxification Center. Persons completing the five days continue in the twelve-step program as outpatients.[11]

In Seattle, when a person is publicly drunk and either lying down in the wrong place or making trouble, Dutch Shisler is called, and he picks him up and takes him to detox. Detox can legally hold him forty-eight hours involuntarily, providing it can be proved that he is a danger to himself or others. The client is handled kindly, and Dutch says with pride, "This is the best town to be a drunk in. Everyone is committed to treating them humanely." But there is a sad contradiction: more surely than a less-humane program, his van, the detox center, the system, Dutch believes, "humanely" facilitate self-destruction. They make it possible for a person to destroy himself in relative comfort and safety. They make it less likely he will make the decision that he needs to make to survive. Mike Tretton is of like mind. "Personally, I believe the less you do for someone, the better." Even picking people up off the street discourages them from treatment. "I know," Tretton says, "because I have been there."

Marcia Carlisle, who runs the detox center that routes clients to Tretton's treatment program, says, "Our clients 'come home' to detox: we are a 'wet shelter'—they are allowed to come inside when they are drunk. Many of them come to detox for Christmas." (This means, she says, that the likelihood of people becoming a recidivist to detox is much lower if they have a home somewhere.) Detox takes only people who "pass the Breathalyzer test—who are good and drunk." If they are not drunk enough to get in, some go out and drink more. Some drug users now drink just enough to get in because there is not enough room for those who are just on drugs. There are some, she says, who take no responsibility for their drinking because they know Dutch will pick them up and bring them in. "We are at cross-purposes in so many ways," she says. On the one hand, she believes, for kindness as well as cost-consciousness, there should be a day center for drunks to be drunk together instead of hanging out on the street and being hauled into detox. On the other hand, there also needs to be some persuasive consequence for serious misbehavior. Marcia Carlisle doesn't know what to do, Mike Tretton doesn't, Dutch Shisler doesn't. So they keep on keeping on.

In the daily world of substance abuse treatment programs, local officials try everything they can think of. Some ideas are simple and sensible administrative improvements. Carlisle tells me, for instance, that in Vancouver, B.C., officials have staggered the issuance of welfare checks so that everyone does not get a check on the same day. This pattern confuses thieves and drug dealers, evening out the work load of others who have to deal with the immediate negative results of welfare cash infusion— the police, detox, and the rest.

Kathy Stout tells me Hooper Detox is trying an acupuncture program that "does wonders" for the patient during withdrawal from drugs and alcohol. The client sits for forty-five minutes with five needles in each ear. Hooper has the only licensed detox acupuncturist on the West Coast, she says. "It really helps the druggies, calms them down. It also reduces alcohol craving." Many come back every day for the treatment. Some pay; most don't. The Department of Corrections has asked Hooper to set up programs there.

Another example of an innovative program is the Oxford House Movement, which began in Washington, D.C., says Bob Huebner of the National Institute on Alcoholism and Alcohol Abuse (NIAAA). A number of drunks leased a group house and established minimal rules: no booze, no drugs, self-government. The Omnibus Drug Act targets this concept for an appropriation.[12]

Huebner also draws attention to a program in Canada. An entire Indian reservation in British Columbia has gone "dry."[13]

The motto on the reservation is: "The honor of one is the honor of all!" They claim a 90 percent success rate, but Huebner cautions this figure may include only members who have chosen to remain on the reservation under the dry policy.

A final example is Seattle's "wet shelter." Faced with dozens of alcoholic men on its downtown business streets with no intention to go dry, the City of Seattle added to its other services a downtown place for alcoholics to sleep—without rules against drinking, in fact, a minimum of rules of any kind beyond those necessary for health and safety. Two rather interesting things happened. First, it proved necessary several times to restrain the staff from setting standards and to remind them of the policy to let the people live the way they wanted to. Second, a sizable number of the residents decided on their own to change their habits, stopped drinking, and left.[14]

Marcia Carlisle says that about 150 persons are eating up 80 percent of Seattle's resources in mental health, medical emergency, food, shelter, clothing, public housing, intake services, police, and so forth. In most distributions of any sort of behavior, about 20 percent of the people do 80 percent of the good—or the mischief.[15] To grasp the importance of this pattern may be the most important insight one can have in public policy, and in quite a few other fields. "Some of us have a pipe dream," Carlisle says, "of sitting down together, all us officials, and looking at this list of 150 people and figuring out what to do with them." Pursuing this insight in its own agency, Carlisle's detox center is carrying out an experiment with twenty-four of its "most recidivist clients." Two case managers have been assigned a dozen persons each, and "the idea is that they will really spend time with them"—first, to learn how they spend their own time and, second, to give them advice and assistance.[16]

Carlisle says a core of about 50 late-stage alcoholics on any night take up 35 to 40 of detox's 105 beds. About 20 of these don't need to be there at all: they are sober at the moment and waiting to get into a treatment program. They may be waiting for welfare certification so they can get into ADATSA. The remaining 45 beds hold drug addicts, "people with family, say, a job, say, who come once or twice a month," and a few come involuntarily, because they have been determined to be a danger to themselves or others. The two dozen in her experiment are chosen from among the fifty. The goal is to stabilize them on the outside through assigning only a dozen to each case manager. Given the costs of repeatedly reprocessing these individuals, agency staff hope the experiment will demonstrate the feasibility of a practice that is not only better but cheaper.

Mike Tretton cites a study done for Seattle showing that 1,400 individuals cost the state $20 million per year in alcoholism services—ambulances, hospital stays, detoxification, general assistance payments, and other treatments. Reaching in his desk for a hand calculator, Tretton figures the amount at $14,285 per person. "If we can stabilize these individuals," he says, "a lot of these costs will be saved and their lives will be improved."[17] Carlisle is trying her experiment with two dozen of the 1,400.

It may not work. Most experiments in the difficult field of alcoholism don't. More likely, we may not be able to tell for certain whether it worked or not. But it is worth a try on the modest level it is being tried. Moreover, it symbolizes the imagination and thoughtfulness that can be brought to bear on difficult problems when resourceful local administrators are given flexibility.

Complete and permanent abstinence has been the most widely used criterion for treatment success in alcoholism programs. Based on this criterion, treatment of homeless alcoholics seldom succeeds. William Breakey has pointed out that alcoholics living on skid row have achieved a degree of competence in coping with a dangerous, even hostile environment. To leave that environment for another in which their incompetence would be all too apparent is not an attractive prospect. "The prognosis," Breakey writes, "is often extremely poor."[18]

Bob Huebner at NIAAA believes that we need to rethink what we mean by success with this group of clients. When clients reduce their drinking, changing the pattern of their drinking from, say, heavy daily use to an occasional bender, their lives and the lives of their family and friends are significantly improved. Other appropriate program goals short of complete abstinence might be reduced suffering for clients and their associates, more efficient use of human services, and accomplishments other than perfection.

Jean DeMaster, director of Portland, Oregon's largest homeless shelter, the Burnside Project, uses the tougher standard and reports that 55 percent of those who enter her drug and alcohol programs "stay sober" at least six months after completion. They are enrolled in AA programs, but Burnside loses track of them after the six months.[19] Seattle's Mike Tretton has adopted a broader view of success. The way he puts it is that about two-thirds of the clients who enter treatment "do better afterward." No longer is the standard in his program a complete end to alcohol or drug abuse. It is "doing better"—drinking less, getting drunk less often, holding a job more successfully, getting along better with family and friends, and perhaps going on a binge once or twice a year instead of being drunk most of the time. These are more modest objectives, but they are still meaningful ones, Tretton believes.

Marcia Carlisle believes that rates of success for alcohol treatment generally run about 55 to 60 percent—providing the program includes a twelve-step program such as AA, with strong mutual support and follow-up features. She says that programs in existence longer have the better success rates, because they have longer-standing and more effective alumni groups. Substantial numbers of their participants who meet her definition of success "still have a slip or two," but their lives have gone from unmanageable to manageable. "We measure our success," she says, "by the reduction in visits an individual makes to detox," by how much the revolving door is slowed.

Carlisle and others tell me that it is important to have a treatment opportunity available and be able to move the client into it promptly when he is ready to make his decision. She says people have a window of time when they want to stay sober. By the time officials prove that the individual lacks the resources to support himself and get him eligible for public assistance, and therefore for ADATSA, it may be too late. For a Native American, for example, regulations require a search for tribal resources that might support him. If so, he is not eligible for general assistance, therefore not for ADATSA. The client may have a wife with resources who kicked him out years ago without getting divorced. His marital status could make him ineligible until the legal situation is cleared up and he is certified as indigent. By the time he is eligible, his moment of decision may have passed.

Researchers for the Rand Corporation, in a very large study sponsored by NIAAA, reported an even lower rate—about 51 percent "in remission"—among the subpopulation of clients in NIAAA-funded treatment programs of low socioeconomic status and with an unstable family situation. The homeless were not specifically identified in the study, but if there were any they presumably would be at the low end of this subpopulation. The study's definition of "remission" subsumes clients showing lasting improvement and not just complete abstention. Clients in remission include not only long-term abstainers but also persons with no drinking in the past thirty days but some drinking in the past one to five months, and persons who report drinking in the past thirty days that satisfies the authors' definition of "normal drinking."

The Rand team refers to "resumption of normal drinking" as one form of successful treatment outcome. The evidence of their research seems to demonstrate that at least for some years after treatment, some proportion of former, or "recovering," alcoholics can resume controlled drinking.[20] Many who work with alcoholics are deathly afraid of this finding and have treated it with great concern, because they believe it will suggest to some alcoholics who cannot safely take an occasional drink that doing so is all right. Inevitably, many who resume "normal drinking" will, after days, weeks, months, or maybe even years, slip back into a pattern of abuse. It has not been proved conclusively that anyone with a long-term pattern of alcohol abuse can safely drink, but certainly many cannot. If some individuals can, we have no way at present to determine in advance who they are or to tell what they would need to do to ensure that they maintain safe drinking.

IT IS NOT YET PROVED that alcohol treatment "works" as a government policy. I have given examples of the many thoughtful alcohol and drug workers who wonder whether what they are doing is really working or whether they may be functioning as "codependents," enabling abusers to avoid making the firm decision that they need to make and keeping to it. Everything in this field is very loose, always in danger of falling apart: at no time can one say, "He has recovered from alcoholism." He is always "recovering." These workers are right to wonder about what they are doing. They let their advocates demand more money for treatment, and on one level they believe strongly that it is worthwhile. On another, they simply don't know what else to do.

Dressing up what goes on in this field and calling it "treatment" makes it sound very medical and scientific—to the public being asked to pay for it and to clients being asked to believe in it. Most of what goes on in treatment, however, and the best we know how to do, is "talking therapy": a person without formal certification talking to a person who has the certification, or people talking to each other in groups—social interaction. This may be important work, but *treatment* is a rather elevated word for it. No diseased part of the anatomy gets physically and irreversibly removed, as it might in successful surgery. No pill cures the problem or even relieves the important symptoms. The purpose of the effort is to help the client decide to stop drinking (or, in fewer instances, change his drinking pattern), then help the client stick to his decision, and then help the client put his life back together. This is hardly a matter of great science, and yet it gets very complicated because it is difficult to get anyone to make an important decision to change his life and stay with it, let alone someone who is both physically and psychologically addicted to the thing that needs to be changed. The drug makes him feel the best he ever feels. The problem is so ordinary that we don't know how to solve it.

So far, this chapter has avoided three questions whose answers are critical to reaching an informed judgment about the efficacy of alcohol treatment as a policy—that is, whether and under what conditions large-scale funding of such treatment programs can lead to a degree of improvement in the lives of clients that is worth the money and that would not have occurred without the treatment. Billions of dollars have been spent without answering these questions effectively:

- Would the improvement have occurred anyway, with or without treatment?

- How long does the effect of the treatment remain? (How long does the client remain in remission until he needs to be cycled into treatment again?)

- Is a careful match of the form, manner, setting, and other elements of treatment to the client critical to success? And if so, is there a practical way through policy or administration to ensure that treatment is matched to client?

Treatment-on-demand is often called for by advocates. In the great argument about U.S. drug policy, one side demands that the emphasis be shifted from law enforcement and drug education toward treatment, as though treatment would do the job. No one should ever be denied treatment, they insist. Treatment is the only thing that will work, they say, so that is where *most* of the money should go; the 70 percent increase sought by President Bush during his first year in office is not enough. They are now "forcefully" arguing that cocaine addiction (which almost always, they say, is mixed with alcohol or other drugs) can be cured in significant numbers.[21] It is a "myth," they insist, that cocaine addiction—particularly crack addiction—cannot be treated.[22]

They appear to assume that since alcohol treatment works, drug treatment should work too. But until the three questions asked above are answered, we don't even know that alcohol treatment—as a policy—works, let alone treatment for cocaine abuse. Rigorously designed and controlled research into alcohol treatment is not much more than a decade old. No large-scale study has been able both to make sure that clients in treatment are carefully matched with a control group not entering treatment *and* to track these groups for several years. The Rand study comes closest, dividing clients into those who had only an initial contact with an NIAAA treatment program (many of these were involved on their own with Alcoholics Anonymous or other non-NIAAA programs before or during their contact with the NIAAA program, so this is not strictly a nontreatment sample), those with a low amount of treatment, and those with a high amount of treatment. The study findings show only modest bands of difference in drinking behavior among the three groups either at eighteen months or at four years, and there is no way of confidently attributing even this difference to treatment.

Moreover, the study notes that "however much their drinking behavior may have improved after treatment, they did not generally achieve rehabilitation, in the sense of full reintegration into normal social roles."[23]

Among persons who came to formal treatment, alcoholism appears to be a continuing condition for the great majority. . . . [R]emissions are frequent, but are generally intermittent rather than stable. . . . [S]ocial rehabilitation did not occur as frequently as remission. . . . When areas of life other than drinking are examined, only modest improvements in social adjustment are found.[24]

Even among subjects who dramatically reduced their drinking, or stopped altogether, few improved greatly in their social adjustment.

On our measures of social integration and stability, most subjects did not improve substantially after treatment, even when they experienced great reduction in drinking problems per se. . . . [W]hether alternative treatment methods and rehabilitation services might bring about more improvement in psychosocial functioning is an open question, on which further research is needed.[25]

The Rand study and others do appear to demonstrate that treatment results often in the reduced consumption of alcohol, and therefore of various physical symptoms, even if not in a significant reduction in the social and economic problems commonly associated with alcohol abuse. According to the Rand study, those in the sample who were still alive at the end of four years had "experienced a 60- to 80-percent reduction in ethanol intake between admission and the four-year followup." At the time of admission, more than 90 percent had reported "alcohol dependence symptoms" or "serious adverse consequences of drinking;" at the specific time the four-year followup was conducted, almost half the sample was not affected by such problems.[26] However, 81 percent had "had serious drinking problems at one time or another during the four-year period," and many undoubtedly will have them again in the future. About one-seventh of the sample died during the period, more than half of these from alcohol-related causes.[27] The reports by staff and clients in ADATSDA and other well-run local programs and the statistics from these programs commonly seem to show they work. We see a reduction of alcohol intake for many clients. But persons who enter alcohol programs typically do so when they have hit bottom, when they have stopped denying their problem and have decided to do something about it. A large proportion, once they have reached this state of mind, may get better with or without a program. Only the most carefully designed research can control for this possibility.

Further complicating such research is the statistical phenomenon referred to as "regression toward the mean." According to the Rand authors, "a considerable portion" of any "apparent improvement between admission and followup" in their study could have been due to such regression, "the phenomenon by which any group selected because of its extreme condition at one time-point is likely to be less extreme at a later time-point."[28] The study provides strong implicit evidence of this phenomenon in its finding that when the same definitions are carefully applied to the treatment group at eighteen months and at four years, "a nearly identical picture" of drinking behavior emerges at the two points in time.[29] Virtually no improvement or decline occurs for the group as a whole over the latter two-and-a-half years of the four. Some individuals improve and some deteriorate, but those improving are balanced by those deteriorating. The apparent improvement during the first year-and-a-half may have taken place not because of the treatment but because the clients as a group were in the acute phase of their alcohol cycle at the time they entered treatment. Within a year-and-a-half they had completed their regression toward the mean. After that, individual trends cancelled each other out and the group as a whole showed no change.[30]

With so little firm proof that alcohol treatment works generally, should government fund large-scale alcohol treatment? Can drug treatment be effective? The questions about treatment effectiveness are so serious that both of the federal agencies that specialize in alcohol treatment and research—NIAAA and Alcohol, Drug Abuse, and Mental Health Administration (ADAMHA)—fund no treatment programs that do not carry a strong research component.

No large-scale, controlled, long-range study has yet examined the effect of matching treatment to client. The question is whether such matching will increase the band of difference between those undergoing treatment and the control group, particularly after the passage of years—not only in amount of substance abuse but expecially in improved social and economic effectiveness. This issue is the current big question in alcoholism treatment studies. NIAAA has just begun a multiyear research program that focuses on such matching. Not until we have its results, and maybe not then—new questions have a way of arising when good research is carried out—can we know whether known alcohol treatment strategies can work as a policy: that is, can an alcohol program based on some combination of therapies we know be designed and implemented that will lead to an important improvement in the lives of a large number of people—and will the improvement be lasting enough to make the investment worthwhile? Probably no one doubts that alcohol treatment works some of the time for some signficant group of people. But is its provision by government a useful policy? We don't know. The Office of Technology Assessment (OTA), a unit that Congress set up to analyze just such questions as this, tried to answer this one in 1983. After a comprehensive survey and analysis of the research in alcoholism treatment, OTA concluded:

> There is some evidence to support the hypothesis that alcoholism treatment is cost-beneficial. The benefits of alcoholism treatment, even if they fall short of what may be claimed, seem to be in excess of the costs of providing such treatment. It is difficult from the available evidence to determine the relative effectiveness or cost-effectiveness of inpatient v. outpatient treatment; it is also difficult to determine how changing the mix of providers or types of treatment would affect either effectiveness or cost-effectiveness. Because different groups receive different treatments, there is an inherent methodological difficulty in interpreting most of the available research.[31]

Of course, all research to date has been to analyze the effectiveness of treatment strategies that we know about at present. Genetic research could lead to breakthroughs that would result in a completely different kind of treatment. So could chemical research. We could find wholly new ways to deal with alcoholism, maybe even a cure. In the long run the present social therapies may be forgotten completely except by students of medical history.

We know that some clients will get better with a program but not without it. Some will do better without a program that "enables" them to survive without learning to take care of themselves. Some will get better in some programs, not in others, and not without one. And some will not get better no matter what. Some of the clients in this group have already destroyed themselves beyond repair. Some have not yet but cannot or will not keep to their decision to do what is needed to get better. Many will get better for a while, then relapse, and then recover again. Some will improve for a while and then revert permanently, having decided that sobriety is not worth the effort.

According to the Rand study, which did not focus on the homeless, the specific approach to alcohol treatment bears little relationship to client recovery. The crucial variable is not program design, but the client's decision to get better. The client may make that decision before entering treatment or sometime during the program, but the decision itself is what is important. In its 1983 report, OTA published a finding that inpatient care in hospitals costs "significantly more for an equivalent outcome" than out-patient care or care in a nonmedical setting.[32] A major study by Hayashida and associates that hit the front pages in 1989 once again determined treatment to be no more often successful in expensive live-in programs than in less expensive outpatient programs. Such programs can be operated at about one-tenth the cost, a major consideration as costs tripled in the four years 1984–1988 alone.[33]

The Hayashida study, it should be noted, did not focus on the homeless and may inadvertently have screened them out. Outpatient treatment may not work for this group, even if it does for others who have a place to live.[34] The prognosis for inpatient treatment is reportedly more favorable for patients currently under threat, say, of marriage breakup or job loss and less favorable for those who have already lost their marriage or job. Those who have lost their marriage or job, according to a new study from Germany, may "need special treatment preceding long-term inpatient programs.[35] Homeless alcoholics are likely to be in the group that has already lost a marriage or job.

Programs provide a variety of settings, have differing thera-peutic philosophies, and incorporate a wide range of techniques. Some programs provide extensive developmental psychotherapy, some aversion therapy, some family therapy, and some hypnotism or acupuncture. (Acupuncture was not widely practiced in the

United States at the time of the Rand study.) Some programs prescribe a chemical, usually Antabuse, on top of which drinking even a small amount of alcohol makes a person severely uncomfortable, bringing on headaches and nausea, among other things. Some emphasize altered social contexts. A great many incorporate the twelve-step philosophy of Alcoholics Anonymous. No particular program ingredient appears to be important per se to treatment success. It appears that what is critical is the opportunity the program provides for each client to make and keep to his decision.

Another possibility is that inspired treatment, competently administered and well-matched to the client, will have a much higher success rate than no formal treatment—but there may be no practical way to implement inspired, excellent treatment on a large scale. "Rossi's Iron Law" is that "the expected value for any measured effect of a social program is zero."[36] And the better the evaluation is carried out, the closer the result will be to zero. There is no reason to think that alcohol treatment programs are an exception to Rossi's only half-facetious law. One thing that program administrators learn over a number of years and a variety of experiences is that well-run programs tend to work and badly run programs tend not to, regardless of the model. Many of us have experienced both excellent and poor teachers who were rigid authoritarians, and excellent and poor ones who were permissive. We know that teacher quality was more important than pedagogical philosophy. We also know that an important factor was what we brought to the classroom ourselves. The same is true for alcohol treatment.

To arrive at better public policies, we must begin telling what we know—sometimes known as "the truth"—simply and in ways that other people can understand. Along these lines, a specialist at ADAMHA recently interviewed the agency's chief of treatment research on some of the topics discussed here. She forthrightly asked John Allen, Ph.D., the basic question:

Ann Bradley: Until these improvements in evaluation methodology have been widely applied in treatment outcome research, how do we know that alcoholism treatment works?

Dr. Allen: We know from studies of general medical expenditures by alcoholics and their families that these expenditures are reduced substantially following alcoholism treatment. In addition, we know from a 1979 Office of Technology Assessment study that the benefits derived from treating alcoholics offset costs to the general health care system.

On an altogether different level, we know that recovery from alcoholism is a long-term process that requires a substantial investment on the part of the patient, the patient's family, the treatment system, and the alcoholic's larger environment. We see returns on that investment daily, in the lives of the millions of recovering alcoholics in this country.

I think no one would argue for abandoning treatment because it is less than perfect, or for abandoning treatment research because we have yet to measure outcome perfectly. Our investment in building a body of information to guide alcoholism treatment should be no less than the investment of the recovering people and the recovering families that treatment has served.[37]

In other words, it looks as if alcoholism treatment works, Allen is saying, but we do not really know that it does. We know that taking care of the clients' medical needs during treatment means they do not have to be taken care of under other budgets. We have learned a lot about what alcoholism and recovery are like: we need to keep the faith. But we do not know whether alcoholism treatment works.

Researchers and professionals working in the field are learning to define success more modestly than before. For the alcoholism of homeless people, in Marcia Carlisle's words, "Hope is measured in smaller terms and a longer time than I ever believed possible." Seeing alcoholism as a disease, Steve Freng says, "We can humanely manage it, but we can't cure it."

All of this is doubly true of another substance that the homeless abuse, crack cocaine, and it feeds a sense of desperation among those who see its effect in the inner city. On public television's "MacNeil/Lehrer News Hour," Cecil Williams, pastor of the Glide Memorial Methodist Church in San Francisco's Tenderloin district, argues that the seller of drugs should be seen as an injured personality.[38] In sharp contrast, Steve Freng sees the seller as an invading enemy: crack in a project, he says, poisons a neighborhood or a house. Gangs whose purpose is to sell crack are seeking new territory: "Crips" and "Bloods," for example, have moved to Hilltop in Tacoma, Washington, from Los Angeles. Typically, such crack dealers find a single mother with an apartment and move in. Pushed out of Los Angeles by police and other gangs, they are invading other cities. They are mostly Hispanics and blacks, Freng says. And these groups are not growing passive, but extremely aggressive. Speaking in 1989, he foresees the larger society taking on a siege mentality, as such enormous amounts of money and weapons are involved. "[Former drug czar] Bill Bennett is the modern-day sheriff," says Freng, but minorities, numbers, poverty, and violence make this different from the old West. Cocaine, more powerful and seductive than other drugs, is, says Freng, a "rage drug."

Alan Sutherland, executive director of Travelers Aid International and earlier the staff director of the homelessness study carried out by the National Academy of Sciences' Institute of Medicine, believes that crack may lead to the end of the rebirth of our cities.[39] Sutherland is not the only responsible official thinking apocalyptically on this issue. Steve Freng, for instance, says: "Human beings have always liked to get high. Some can handle it and some can't. Now it is a world business. I fear sometimes that our workforce will disappear, because the 'eligible grunts' will all be drugged out."

One of the great tragedies of the crack epidemic is the babies born addicted. Pearl Pritchard of Oakland's Salvation Army shelter says that for an infant, withdrawal from crack takes three months. She says that more and more mothers are abandoning their children because of crack. She adds, "Some of these people will never straighten themselves out."[40] Freng says, "You will never see a fifty-year-old crack user twenty years from now. He'll be dead or in jail."

Reports come from all over about hundreds of newly homeless crack addicts. Alan Sutherland, however, is not so sure that there might not be more homeless without crack. It has become a financial mainstay of the ghetto, he believes. Whole families are being supported by teenage kids. Kathy Stout says that at Portland's Hooper Detoxification Center more than 50 percent of the clients are now there because of drugs. It takes three staff to subdue one crack abuser and get him into a holding cell. Because Oregon's crops were late in 1989, reports Stout, the low-income Hispanic population of Portland has increased substantially, and many of them are drug users.

Marcia Carlisle of Seattle's detox center states that there are now so many in Seattle on crack that "if we let in all the coke addicts, there would be no room for the drunks." Now, there are "maybe three to four times the number of addicts" in Seattle as there were a few years ago, she observes. "If they use both heroin and crack, we send them to methadone treatment, because it exists," Carlisle says. She cites a bill before the state legislature that addresses the problem of pregnant mothers on crack, because of the "appropriate hysterical fear of all these developmentally disabled babies who will be born."

"Druggies hit bottom sooner," says Portland's Jean DeMaster, so some of them can bounce back. Her staff go up to the jail twice each day to take out drug abusers awaiting trial, whose sentences would probably be thirty days. A "behavior contract" is entered into with each of them—a case management plan—usually a plan for how they will stay drug free so the charges can be dismissed. Sometimes, for those who have hit bottom quickly enough, this approach works.

No one really knows what to do about crack. Mostly, we try the same sorts of things that we do for any other addiction. We have the greatest amount of experience with alcohol, but after all these years of trying to end addiction to it, there still has not been any breakthrough. Crack is still new—only about five years old. Reportedly, the crack "high" is so pleasurable that many who have experienced it can no longer take a serious interest in anything else. Most who work in the field believe that crack is more addictive than alcohol, that addiction takes place quickly—perhaps after only a few instances of use—while alcohol may take years. With our success so limited in treating alcoholism, how can we expect to achieve great strides quickly in treating crack addiction?

Portland's housing director, Don Clark, sums it up: "Crack has stunned everyone."[41]

PROBLEMS AND CRISES come and go in America. Some of them are made up, some exaggerated, and some are real and proportionately understood. But we tire of them. We want to solve our problems and get them out of the way. Because of our rich human and natural resources, we have survived many crises, and often—in any fair sense of the word—we have triumphed. Sometimes we have not done so well when the enemy is ourselves, when it is human nature. Alcoholism, drugs, and the other addictions are matters of human nature, and while we may go to the moon and orbit the planets, neither we nor anyone else knows very much more now than we did a thousand years ago about human nature.

"How" is our family name in the American language, as in "know-how." It is inconceivable to many of us that we may not know how to do some of these things and may not have the foggiest idea how to find out. Alcoholism and drug abuse concern individuals and their decisions. For some the decision ought to be fairly easy: they have a good life yet destroy it for the feeling a drug gives them. For others, that good feeling is just about the only good feeling they get: maybe because they ruined their earlier life and cannot get it back or maybe they were dealt a bad hand from the start. We do not know why people do things. Perhaps we know the least about the most important things.

Social policy tries to come to terms with such questions. In Washington State, ADATSA has made high-quality alcoholism and drug treatment available to a great many more individuals, and it costs the taxpayers significantly less than they were paying before to support general assistance that kept drunks drunk and drug-gies drugged. That is good: ADATSA may help persons make better decisions about their own lives. Although the long-range impact may be reduced rates of alcoholism and drug abuse, it is evident that what we call "treatment" does not "cure" all or even most alcoholics. Many are soon back to their old ways, many others are improved and live better lives, and some recover permanently.

The public is entitled to be told these things as clearly as possible so that it can make informed decisions on the policies it will support. Even more important, though, the public needs to be told everything, because intuitively many know that much is not told—for a number of reasons, reasons perhaps of kindness but also reasons of professional or political self-protection. And this intuition contributes to a growing general distrust of our leaders and our institutions.

These problems exist not because we refuse to spend enough, but because the problems are genuinely difficult and efforts at change always run up against a complex web of conflicting interests. There are, as Nathan Glazer says, limits to what can be accomplished through social policy. Each policy, he says, takes the place of some prior arrangement, perhaps a tradition that served us imperfectly, but on balance may have worked better than the new policy.[42] We need to be modest in adopting policies and programs and to be aware, as General Eisenhower might caution were he among us, of the "welfare-industrial complex," or what Robert Woodson calls "the Poverty Pentagon."[43] This is not an argument for not trying things, but, in fact, an argument for greatly increased research and evaluation. If modest programs and modest accomplishments are all that we can attain, they count. On occasion, we find something big to do that is helpful. Most likely, however, it is not a program or a policy, but a new way of looking at things.

At one time, looking at alcohol and drug abuse as illnesses was just such a new way. We have, as we often do, gone too far with it. Now, some informed observers and treatment professionals are rethinking this point of view. A recent issue of the *New Republic* carried an unsigned article entitled "The Barry Bust," discussing the arrest of Mayor Marion Barry of the District of Columbia for the use of cocaine:

> The conventional explanation is that Barry had a debilitating disease: he was in the clutches of drugs, his volition smothered by liquor and cocaine. Barry's remaining apologists have explicitly pushed the disease alibi, and it was implicit in his maudlin plea for pity on the Sunday after his arrest: he was sick, so he would "begin to heal my body, mind, and soul"— after which he would presumably be all better (i.e., electable, or at least pensionable). This cycle is the medical equivalent of sin, penance, and redemption, with one difference: to admit sin is to accept blame: to claim illness is to duck it.
>
> The disease paradigm for substance abuse is open to question on scientific and logical grounds, but its practical upshot is what makes it finally unacceptable.
>
> At a certain point it may in some sense be beyond your power to step back from the brink. Still, when catastrophe strikes, it's all your fault, for two reasons: (1) you knew, or should have known, the odds when you went into the game; and (2) society can't afford to hand out blanket exemptions from moral responsibility.[44]

The current philosophy of ADAMHA is that "addiction is a chronic relapsing disorder."[45] Inasmuch as no inherent physical basis for these addictions has been proved,[46] and nearly everyone agrees that a person's decision to take a drink or use other drugs is a major factor, the word *disease* carries misleading overtones. The idea of disease was developed not from solid medical evidence but for strategic and tactical reasons—for instance, so that alcoholics would not be treated as criminals, and problem drinkers would not believe that they could take "just one drink." While these are reasonable, perhaps administratively sensible, and humane desires, in the absense of scientific evidence, they do not turn an addiction into a disease. Perhaps it is time to rethink this notion and look for a more helpful characterization.

Thinking about addiction and public policy, Mike Tretton sees the main issue as whether to confront the problem or just to continue to provide and increase resources that sidestep it. A large part of the problem is that human beings sometimes make bad decisions about their lives and that the communities that have helped them make good decisions are weakening. Somehow, when we don't know what to do about it, spending a lot of money makes us feel better—as if we are really trying. But it is an expensive delusion. Usually in trying to find shortcuts to social change, we make things worse: it is so much easier to destroy something than it is to improve things. Human life is an ecosystem about which we know astonishingly little.

In Alcoholics Anonymous and the other twelve-step programs, individuals get together and build themselves a small community where they try to help one another make and keep the decision to stay "clean and sober." Often this works, or at least it helps. No one in Alcoholics Anonymous is paid a dime in connection with the movement; it is entirely voluntary. What participants do is tell each other that everyone matters and that it is his decision and only his to stop drinking and stay sober. Right now, this is the best we know how to do.

The late homeless advocate Mitch Snyder (right) is joined by activist Carol Fennelly and New York attorney Robert M. Hayes in a protest outside the offices of the U.S. Department of Health and Human Services, August 19, 1987.

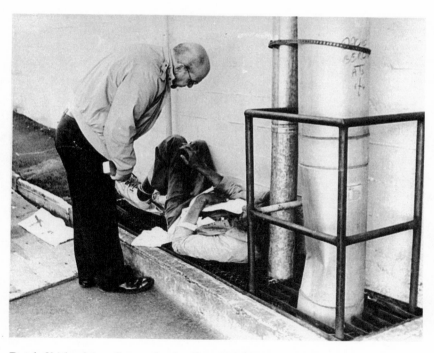

Dutch Shisler drives the van for the City of Seattle's program that picks up inebriates from city streets. Here he is seen offering a man a ride to Seattle's Hooper Detoxification Center.

Mike Neely leads the Homeless Outreach Program on Los Angeles' skid row. The shirt and matching baseball cap make HOP workers easy to spot as they walk the streets building support networks among the homeless.

Boona Cheema, director of Berkeley-Oakland Support Services (BOSS), has been helping East Bay homeless for twenty years.

4

Falling Through the Bottom of the Underclass

"SOMETHING HAPPENED in the mid-1970's—the population of skid row grew, constituencies broadened, geographical limits broke. Skid row as a way of life, not as a distinct place, is thriving in a way not seen for 50 years. . . . It is an option of desperation."[1] Kim Hopper, who works with the homeless mentally ill in New York City and writes movingly about them, so testified in December 1982 at the first of many congressional hearings on homelessness. Homelessness among the city's black poor is what he knows best, but the "something" that "happened in the mid-1970's" in his city appears to have happened at about the same time in many of America's urban black ghettos. Increasingly, men, women, and families were falling into an urban underclass.

In October 1989, I visited the Homeless Outreach Program in Los Angeles's skid row to interview its director, Mike Neely.[2] I had learned of him through a series of telephone calls I made after watching an extraordinarily thoughtful and candid documentary on public television, a piece by a young film maker named Tom Seidman about Los Angeles's short-lived tent city for the homeless in the winter of 1988–1989. Under pressure to do something for the city's homeless, many of whom were camping out at city hall, the office of the mayor had set up a tent city to shelter the homeless from the cold. Trailers were also set up to bring in all the social services in an effort to connect the homeless with jobs, training, welfare assistance, housing, medical care, or whatever they might need to overcome their homelessness.

Seidman's cameras followed the tent city throughout its brief history. At the end of three months, the city was dismantled, a failure. The mayor's office had tried and failed to find permanent sites that it could acquire to house these homeless individuals and families. Anything available was simply too expensive, according to interviews shown on the film.

Seidman, the young producer, had concluded anyway that what the homeless needed was more than housing, more than jobs. The city found them jobs, got them clothed for interviews, and helped them get there. Characteristically, however, in a matter of days the homeless were back on the street. Jobs and housing alone would not work: what each of them needed was a support system. The main problem was that they had lost their connection to a caring human network of friends and relatives. Without such a network, they would not stick to a job and would soon lose whatever housing they had gained.

Neely's office was a desk among several in one end of a large storefront in the 800 block of East Sixth Street. Neely, a light-skinned black man of about thirty, wore a bright lemon-yellow tee shirt and baseball hat, both with the initials of the Homeless Outreach Program prominently displayed. I had come to see Neely because others I had called to talk with about the tent city experience believed Neely understood it best. He had been homeless, and all his staff were former homeless persons. They were a support system for each other, all of them recovering addicts of alcohol, drugs, or both, met regularly in group sessions, and worked closely as a unit. Neely could explain Seidman's conclusion that the critical factor in homelessness was the absense of a support system.

I asked Mike Neely when Los Angeles's skid row homelessness had grown dramatically and whether he had any theories to explain it. He replied, to my surprise, "Feminism." At this laconic answer, I asked for more, and he gave it to me. Before the 1960s, Neely said, black men in the ghetto often had factory jobs that paid better than the domestic work their wives did. When they came home from work, typically they hung out with their friends; they commonly drank and caroused and not uncommonly beat their wives. The male derived his power in the family through the fact that he earned more than the female and was physically stronger.

Then, as Neely sees it, came feminism, and while black ghetto women did not burn their bras and march on city hall, they did decide that they had the right to more respect than they were getting. At the same time, factory jobs were moving out of the cities. Affirmative action was a requirement for employers, and black women were, Neely says, a "twofer." At the same time that factory jobs were declining, factory employers were being encouraged by the government to hire women. The service sector, in contrast, was growing. Jobs there, however, paid less than the usually unionized factory jobs. Young men entering the job market, with mostly only low-paying service jobs available to them, no longer had an economic position superior to that of their women.

As wife battering came into the open, women increasingly decided they would not tolerate it. The problem may have gotten worse, as men grew angrier and drank more as their economic power declined. Aid to Families with Dependent Children (AFDC), in those days, was available to mothers of young children only if no man resided in the household. All these factors combined to weaken the husband's position both at home and in the labor market, strengthen the wife's, make him angrier, lower her dependence on him, lower her tolerance for his behavior, and lead to his leaving or being thrown out. Because it often takes two incomes to avoid welfare, sooner or later the female-headed family would settle into an AFDC-dependent mode of living. Some of the males, rejected by their families and bereft of dignity, sought comfort in alcohol, or perhaps drugs, alone or in the company of others, and some of these found themselves homeless on East Sixth Street, deeply into an addiction.

"Housing is not the issue," insists Neely. "Jobs isn't the issue. If you got one of these dudes a house, he wouldn't last in it any longer than four months." What causes homelessness among these skid row dwellers? Addiction and the lack of a support system. "There is always at least one vacancy," according to Neely. "As long as there are vacancies, the problem can't be housing." And as long as there are job openings, the problem cannot be jobs. Overcoming homelessness requires the will to stop abusing alcohol or drugs and to stick to a difficult and often boring routine. And for that, one needs a support system—friends or family who care. What happened in the inner city, what happened to the underclass, was the destruction of the male's role and the disintegration of his place in the social setting. If Neely is right, the only way to prevent homelessness among black urban males is to build or rebuild a social structure where they have a valued place.

Clancy Imislund runs the Midnight Mission in Neely's part of Los Angeles. The mission serves 1,600 meals each day, mostly to homeless alcoholics. He says that when he first worked in the area about fifteen years ago, the proportion of whites to blacks was much different—about 85 percent were elderly white males. Now the area is about 90 percent black, he says. Many of the whites who would have been on downtown's skid row have drifted out into other neighborhoods. Skid row is still not mainly an economic phenomenon, he says, agreeing with Neely. The only way its people can get better is to "work their way better," he says, and "most don't want to."[3] Seventy of those who do work at Clancy's Midnight Mission.

I began this chapter with Kim Hopper's testimony that the homeless population of skid row America grew dramatically in the mid-1970s. "Something happened," he said to members of Congress. What happened may have been in part a delayed negative side-effect of 1960s progress in civil rights. William Julius Wilson, a sociologist at the University of Chicago, describes how improved opportunities for blacks provided by a growing economy, civil rights laws, and government programs enabled many of them to move out of the old neighborhood. This mobility drained neighborhoods of positive leadership and connections to better jobs. After a decade of such progress, the neighborhood was badly cut off from the economic mainstream. The struggle of the good citizens who remained to uphold traditional values such as respect for the law, hard work, self-discipline, education, skill development, sacrifice for the family, and church participation had fallen on hard times. Charles Murray writes:

> A community that subsists on illegal sources of income and that is victimized by widespread violent crime is socially disorganized in crucial ways. To put it roughly, good folks

> no longer set the standards. . . . The role models for the youth
> are not blue-collar working men who raise families but hustlers.[4]

Many of the new skid row homeless observed by Hopper were the products of the social disintegration of the inner city.

Based on the documented experience of 5,000 American families over the past twenty years, Murray has concluded "that it is extremely rare for a person to get into the labor market, stick with it, and remain poor."[5] Persons who fall to the bottom of the underclass are likely to be among the worst educated of those remaining after the exodus of the talented and the energetic. Alan Sutherland of Travelers Aid International tells me that 35 out of 100 homeless individuals in a study he knows tested at the level of mental retardation. The key to rising out of the underclass appears to be schooling or whatever it takes to complete school. John Kasarda, of the University of North Carolina, reports that "in New York City during the 1970s the number of jobs typically filled by people who had not finished high school declined by 40 percent, while the number of jobs typically filled by people who had attended college increased by 61 percent."[6] Murray finds poverty to be so closely associated with a failure to complete high school that among the 5,000 families there were too few adults who were poor and had graduated from high school to study how this happens: "Of working age black men . . . who had a high school education, only 5 percent were poor."[7]

Where the inner city has been isolated from the mainstream, Wilson writes, youths are no longer able to see how education contributes to economic improvement, and they do not know people to help them find a good job.[8] Negative opportunities abound in such an environment: inducements just to hang out, to drink and carouse, or, more seriously, to participate in the underground economy of drugs, theft, and prostitution. Isabel Sawhill of the Urban Institute writes, "Once crime, dropping out of school, teenage childbearing, and joblessness become commonplace, they are likely to become more acceptable. Such a shift in social norms leads in turn to more bad behavior."[9]

Barbara Sanders, who worked for several years in Oakland's public housing projects, told me that "many now believe that these are the final days." There is nothing to be gained by being good. So enjoy yourself along the way." Pimps are a joke now, she says. "A Cadillac? So what? You see fifteen-year-olds, no driver's license, [with] a Mercedes and a car phone. The only success models are drug dealers."[10]

Although some batten on this life, at least for a time, most who succumb to its blandishments soon find themselves in trouble, many of them cut off from family and friends. Murder is their leading cause of death, and prison a common experience. For many of those who lose control of their drinking or their use of drugs, there is skid row.

Social workers and program administrators in communities I have visited to gather material for this book have supported the observations of William Julius Wilson and others about the decline of well-paying industrial jobs accessible to inner-city residents. Gisela Bushey, director of a homeless program in Hayward, California, is one of several officials who supported this assessment.[11] No one, though, could mention a homeless individual who had been laid off from such a job. Instead, the problem was said to manifest itself in fewer new industrial hires, a disappearance of opportunities for young men to earn a good wage legally, and an increase in the relative economic attractiveness of the welfare system.

The nature of hiring seems to have changed. Bushey reports that it has become more common in the bay area to hire people for half-time work, because employers are not required to provide the same fringe benefits for such workers. Employers, Bushey says, are leaving jobs open rather than hiring someone they think will prove inadequate. Some reduced hiring in Alameda County has resulted from the shift from unionized low-skill heavy industry to nonunionized and education-heavy high-tech. What Bushey calls the "burp" of the recession in the early 1980s dislodged some people from their jobs and further hastened the shutdown of industrial plants. Growth in the labor market is mainly among smaller employers, who are not required to meet governmental affirmative action requirements. These days, she says, they prefer to hire someone who is white rather than black. This may be racial bias, but it can also be based on differential job qualifications, such as educational level, grooming and dress, and manner of speaking. Such differences may result from the deterioration of family and schools in the inner city or be unintended consequences of factors such as those discussed by Mike Neely, factors having little direct relationship to racism.

Men fall out of the bottom of the underclass and into homelessness when their drinking or drug habit costs them their job, family, and friends. Often, they land on skid row. The women and children of these men have the resources of AFDC to keep them off the streets, and they fall into homelessness more rarely. When they do, shelters, welfare hotels, motel vouchers, or other programs are generally available to them. Homeless families do not often end up on skid row, although about one individual in five who live there is a woman unaccompanied by children.

Female-headed families that become homeless are typically headed by teenaged mothers, or women who first became mothers in their teens and have never had an independent household. They and their children have always lived in the household of their own mother, grandmother, aunt, or some other friend or relative. According to Wilson, the disappearance of industrial jobs in the 1960s and 1970s made it increasingly difficult for young women in the inner city to find men whose employment income made them suitable for marriage. Having children without marriage, then, gained acceptability.[12] Murray attributes non-marriage more to the influence of welfare programs that gave the young mother an income without working or taking a husband.[13]

New research by Robert D. Plotnick reinforces Murray's view. Commenting on the fact that earlier studies had failed to demonstrate a link between welfare and illegitimacy, Plotnick says that such studies relied on "data from the mid-1970s and earlier." Plotnick explains that "by the 1980s [Plotnick's data are from 1979 to 1984] the stigma of bearing a child out of wedlock and the broad social controls that inhibited out-of-wedlock child-bearing had declined relative to their strength in prior years." So the economic incentive of a larger welfare payment was no longer offset by the social stigma.[14] Mike Neely's historical analysis recognizes not only welfare and male joblessness, but other factors as well in the increase in single-parent families, illegitimacy, and homelessness.

Murray points out that schools aggravated the situation by responding to demands for reform and changing their policies to allow unmarried mothers to continue as regular enrollees. "Schools," he writes, "formerly served as the validator of social morality." New policies "crippled an important deterrent function that schools formerly served and instead facilitated the fashion- ability of teenage pregnancy." He calls teenage pregnancy "a legacy of the social reforms of the 1960s."[15] Alan Sutherland of Travelers Aid says that for a teenage girl having a baby has become a rite of adulthood: "Now she is independent of her mother—she thinks."[16] But in a high-cost city like New York, Washington, or San Francisco, she abruptly finds out she cannot afford her own place on what she makes at McDonald's or on AFDC.

The Salvation Army's shelter for homeless families in Oakland has been in business for seventeen years. Its director, Pearl Pritchard, tells me that the shelter has always been full but that "more people are turned away these days."[17] Its doors opened in 1971, when large numbers of pregnant teenagers began publicly admitting their pregnancy and keeping their babies. Gretchen Kaufory, an elected commissioner of Multnomah County, Oregon, observes a recent "sudden increase" of this practice in her area.[18] Previously the pattern was to go away somewhere to have the baby, put it up for adoption, and return as though nothing had happened. Many Oakland and other East Bay girls used to do this at the Salvation Army's Booth Memorial Home in a secluded Oakland neighborhood. Formerly a home for unwed mothers and their children, Booth is no longer needed as a live-in institution, because today unwed mothers are allowed to stay in school, as Murray notes, and to use day-care programs. AFDC, rent sup- plements, food stamps, Medi-Cal, and other public programs enable them to maintain a separate family unit. Pritchard sees these young mothers when they are evicted, usually for nonpay- ment of rent, sometimes for association with drug dealers, for prostitution, or for other bad behavior.

Boona Cheema, who runs a large homeless program with branches in Berkeley and Oakland, informs me that at least 80 percent of area welfare mothers supplement their grant in some way—through working and not reporting the income or through prostitution or dealing drugs. For many, the grant is not suffi- cient to pay the area's extraordinarily high rent and still pay other necessary expenses. These young women can be evicted for nonpayment of rent or for activities undertaken to help pay the rent. Or they can leave a drug-violent neighborhood in fear for their safety and that of their children.[19] These are ways they fall to the bottom of the underclass, and this is when Pritchard or Cheema come to know them.

Judge Stella Schindler of the family court for the borough of Queens, New York, was Mayor Ed Koch's homeless coordinator. She tells me that "a huge number" of homeless women in New York head families without ever having lived on their own. After months or years of doubling up with others, they have used up their welcome, perhaps because of crowding or perhaps because of their behavior. Not only do such young women need housing, says Schindler, in the shelter market of New York City, decimated by rent control, "they also need skills in how to live."[20] Schindler, her successor in the mayor's office, Alberta Fuentes, and Phyllis Wolfe of Washington, D.C.'s program, Health Care for the Homeless, all agree that much of family homelessness originates in the practice of "babies having babies."[21] Schindler says she sees great grandmothers in their forties in her Queens courtroom. Hayward's Bushey says that one-third of the homeless mothers in her area are teenagers. Most of the remainder probably first became mothers at that age.

James Leiby of the University of California, Berkeley, School of Social Welfare, says that by the early 1980s in many parts of the United States increasing numbers of women, persuaded that they and their children should no longer tolerate physical or sexual abuse by a husband or someone else in the household, were hiding in shelters set up to protect them.[22] Steven Freng says that by 1981 Seattle's domestic violence had reached a "critical mass" such that social workers knew what to look for and were placing women and children in shelters newly set up for that purpose. Women who saw the shelters on television knew they had an alternative to remaining in a violent and destructive situation. Their addition to the ranks of the homeless was, sadly for them, an improvement.[23]

"JUST AS HEROIN in the 1960s contributed to the rise of the single-parent family," writes Senator Daniel Patrick Moynihan, "so will crack soon give us the no-parent child as a social problem."[24] Jean DeMaster of Portland's Burnside Project elaborates. "We are in the second generation of chemical dependency," she says, "addicts who are the children of addicts—often crack-using children who are the offspring of alcoholic parents. In an earlier time, all the clients here were alcoholics. Now many are crack users."[25]

DeMaster goes on to say that the phenomenon of the "me generation" aggravates the harm to families caused by crack addiction. These days it is not unusual for a parent who gets sober to decide she will take care of herself and leave the older children, sometimes even younger ones, to watch over themselves. The extended family has already dispersed, and no longer is a grandmother around to keep things together. We are seeing increasing numbers of "unsocialized people"—not malicious sociopaths, but asocial people, inexperienced at relating to other humans. In Hayward, Gisela Bushey remarks that people used to be able to fall back on an extended family. "Now we are a more transient society," she says. "And there is more divorce." Boona Cheema reports that in her agency's Oakland shelter, 85 percent of the homeless individuals there have used crack recently and that "there are almost no family ties." She adds that alcohol abuse has increased. Barbara Sanders says that women "weren't into heroin" but welfare mothers are into crack. Pearl Pritchard adds that the newest version of a family is men alone with children. When the male in a couple has a lesser drug problem, he may assume care of the children. Pritchard reports seeing cases where a young father has done "a complete turnaround" to take care of a new, crack-addicted, baby when the mother cannot because of her own addiction.

Elouise Greene, a professional social worker, refers to a new program for homeless men in Richmond, California, in which three-quarters of them are addicted to crack.[26] Mike Neely of Los Angeles reports that crack has just passed alcohol, 41 percent to 40, as the leading form of addiction there. Los Angeles's homeless projects coordinator, Robert Vilmur, concedes that there are hundreds of newly homeless men in south-central Los Angeles, the result of crack addiction.[27] Officials in Seattle, Washington, D.C., New York City, and other places report similar experiences. Crack cocaine is the principal producer of new homeless individuals and the great wrecker of mostly poor, mostly black families in the short time since its U.S. advent in 1985.

The family has been under attack in the United States for years but seldom from so many directions. Crack is just the latest, and currently the most virulent, of these attacks. Cheema believes that "the needy are more desperate now" than when she began working with the poor and the homeless in the early 1970s. Part of the problem, she believes, is that money support from welfare programs has not kept up with inflation. More women than ever are turning to unreported outside sources for income—legitimate activity such as babysitting or domestic work, done for cash; illegal activity such as prostitution and drug dealing. Sanders observes that most women who seek housing support from her office in Contra Costa County have some kind of job, even though most men she sees there do not.

Roger Starr, long a student of urban affairs for the *New York Times*, has witnessed a decline in support for family life from traditional institutions, particularly some of the religious denominations, he says. Starr complains that instead of providing moral leadership and practical help, religious institutions spend increasing time and moral capital on politics—local, national, and even international. They have been distracted from their traditional role in the community just when it is needed most. More and more people cannot cope with the problems of modern living, he says—teenaged mothers who cannot exercise the role of motherhood, fathers who cannot carry out their role.[28]

Jean DeMaster also points to the breakdown of the family as an important factor in the increase of homelessness, citing older people abandoned by their grown children and younger children who run away from their parents. She tells of parents splitting up and the children joining the one who first remarries: maybe the father of a teenaged son takes a young wife, and conflict ensues as he appears to have chosen the young woman over his son; the son gets in trouble, perhaps disappears. Moynihan writes of the importance of family breakup to position in American society: "Family structure," he says, "may now be the principal determinant of class structure."[29]

Mitch Snyder and Mary Ellen Hombs, in a chapter on the causes of homelessness that they wrote in 1982, concluded with these paragraphs:

The breakdown of social structures, relationships and responsibilities has meant drastic changes and deviations from time-honored ways of addressing all of the other problems. We no longer offer charity to the "village idiot," take our mother or our uncle into our home with much frequency, or maintain relationships that are not "working." While this is the one category with the immediate potential to keep a person off the streets, it just doesn't happen very often.

The conditions and problems discussed so far are all symptoms and expressions of a deeper malaise, which, in reality, reflects deep-seated changes that are a product of profound contradictions and systemic inadequacies in our culture. We have built our nation on an economic value system that is rooted in the false assumption that through competition and isolation, rather than through cooperation, compassion, and community, we can build a sane and livable world. We are figuratively moving away from one another and our own inner center. Is it any wonder that we are increasingly isolated, insulated, and separated?[30]

Starr, DeMaster, and others whose approach to homelessness and to changing the system may be very different from Snyder's can agree with much in this passage. Statistics from San Francisco, where a very large portion of the low-income population is made up of Asians and Hispanics, underline the importance of family deterioration in homelessness. A mayor's office shelter survey reveals that "a majority of the homeless population was white (55 percent), but both blacks (29 percent) and American Indians (2.5 percent) were overrepresented while Asians (2 percent) and Latinos (8 percent) were underrepresented.[31] The lower homelessness rates among Asians and Latinos can be ascribed to their traditionally stronger emphasis on commitment to the family.

Oakland A's pitcher Dave Stewart, on the way to his third straight season of twenty or more victories, has regularly taken time to work with kids at the Oakland Boys Club, where he was a member at age ten. Stewart's sister Carolyn Bolton now helps run the West Oakland branch. She says he

knows the kids of Oakland don't really get a chance to do a lot of things. When he was coming up our parents were there, but there wasn't a whole lot for him to do. Today, kids are having kids. There aren't the grandparents around to be supportive. The home life is not there anymore. So who do kids turn to? These kids are deprived of certain things, and it's gratifying to him to help them.[32]

It takes more than the devotion of an ace pitcher to replace or to rebuild our primary support system, the family—but it helps.

INCREASED HOMELESSNESS has resulted from the natural evolution of our economic and social institutions toward "modernity," from policy interventions in the operation of these institutions, and from individual problems and decisions. All these aspects of homelessness could be mapped to show cause-and-effect pathways from each to all the others. In Daniel Patrick Moynihan's phrase, "Everything is related." All components of homelessness have been proposed by some social critics to be primary and dismissed by others as secondary or even unimportant.

We may never know what is primary; maybe in some sense nothing is. It is, however, beyond argument that social dynamics are complex and related and that often their interactions are counterintuitive.[33] Although we can affect society through governmental intervention, the result is often quite different from the intent.

When mainstream social structures and safety nets such as unemployment insurance fail, welfare programs provide a backward counter system: "don't work, don't save, don't succeed, or you will lose your benefits," is the message. It is a counter economy, and it generates a counter morality. Once in, it is difficult to find a way out.

The disincentives of the welfare system in a market economy encourage a counter society. Once in the underclass, a person cannot see his way out. Both liberals and conservatives insist that there are pathways, but those are largely invisible to one who needs them.

Many conservatives believe the reverse incentives of the welfare system destroy low-income families. They also see the destruction of the family as the main factor in the pathology of the urban underclass. Charles Murray shows in *Losing Ground* poverty's steady decline in the United States from the end of World War II to roughly the declaration of the War on Poverty. Then a steep and prolonged increase in the number of single-parent families on Aid to Families with Dependent Children (AFDC) began. Instead of poverty continuing to decline, it shifted from an independent condition to pauperism—that is, to dependence upon others, in this case upon means-tested government programs—and a parallel increase in crime, high school dropouts, and so forth. Pauperism may be worse than the poverty it replaced according to Moynihan. "To be poor is an objective condition," he wrote in 1973, "to be dependent, a subjective one. . . . [Dependency] is an incomplete state in life; normal in the child, abnormal in the adult."[34] The best way to solve this problem, suggests Murray, is to end welfare for all but the elderly and the disabled, perhaps by gradually decreasing welfare grants (that is, in fact, happening through the failure of welfare to keep up with the cost of living) so that people have no choice other than work.

Challenged by Murray's analysis, Mary Jo Bane and David T. Ellwood, Harvard professors, developed quantitative evidence contradicting the theory that welfare programs are the main cause of low-income family breakup and illegitimacy. Drawing from recent work by William Julius Wilson, Bane and Ellwood found the declining position of urban black males in the labor market more likely to cause deterioration of a black family than the availability of welfare. There are fewer marriageable black males, Wilson argued because of the job situation. Consequently the number of unmarried black women is rising.

The percentage of babies born out of wedlock is also rising. The absolute number of such babies born each year, however, is in a moderate decline. An even greater decline in the number of babies born to married mothers during the same years explains this anomaly. Black women now marry less often; those who do now have fewer babies. A temporary bulge in the age structure, with more teenagers since 1975, also means that more babies will be born out of wedlock simply because there are more teenagers. Overall, Wilson showed, the proportion of babies in single-parent families is increasing only because marriage is decreasing and those who do marry are having fewer babies.[35]

To Wilson's argument, Bane and Ellwood added an analysis of the relationship of the size of welfare grants to the proportion of single-parent families. AFDC grants vary from state to state, they observed, and no positive correlation exists between the size of welfare grants state-by-state and the proportion of single parents in those states.[36] Rather, they found single mothers more likely to live separately from their own parental household in higher-payment states (thereby aggravating the shortage of low-income housing), while continuing to live with a parent in lower-payment states.[37] Women in the lowest-payment states often have the most children, contradicting Murray's model.[38]

Bane and Ellwood also demonstrate that while the purchasing power of welfare payments has declined across the country since the mid-1970s, the proportion of single-parent, low-income families has risen. Like Wilson, they trace problems of family breakup and decline in formation of new families primarily to the replacement of good-paying factory jobs in central city areas by low-paying retail jobs.

Wilson insists that social isolation, not a "culture of poverty," explains high rates of crime, drug use, and other pathologies of the inner city. Successful role models have moved out of the inner-city ghettos, leaving behind an environment of failure. He writes, "The combination of unattractive jobs and lack of community norms to reinforce work increases the likelihood that individuals will turn to either underground illegal activity or idleness or both."[39] We internalize norms in a culture. The problems of the inner city result not from long and deeply held customs and traditions but from the contemporary economic structure and its attendant life experiences. Policy emphasis, says Wilson, should, therefore, be placed not on changing sub-cultural traits but on changing "the structure of constraints and opportunities."[40]

Murray too insists that the structure of constraints and opportunities is important, but believes that welfare has played the critical role in this structure, rather than declining job opportunities. He responded to Ellwood's arguments in a 1986 article, "No, Welfare Isn't Really the Problem." By pointing out that although AFDC itself varies greatly from state to state, differences among total welfare packages—AFDC plus other benefits—are

modest in relation to cost of living for different states, he answered
the statistical argument against his position on the relationship
of welfare to family structure. Murray gave the example that in
1978 the welfare package supplied 66 percent of median household income for New Orleans and 65 percent for San Francisco.[41]
Then he elaborated a set of hypotheses that "exceed the capacity
of quantitative policy analysis." These hypotheses make up a
model intended to reflect "the way a real, live young woman who
is pregnant and poor might look at the welfare option."[42] While
welfare packages grew to enable a single woman to support a
child, men in poor communities became "less reliable." Men
began using women's welfare benefits, says Murray,

> as a way of getting along—sometimes living wholly off the
> woman, probably more often using the woman's apartment and
> other benefits as a supplement to his own income. . . . This
> makes it easier for him to leave a job, behave in ways that get
> one fired, or to delay acquiring a new job, all of which con-
> tribute to his long-term unemployability. At a community level,
> the hypothesis is that the existence of a large number of women
> on welfare leads to changes in peer values among young men.
> Getting a woman to support you confers status. Conversely,
> the status formerly associated with "being a good provider"
> disappears—even when the man is employed, he is not the
> pillar of support for the family; the welfare system is. . . .
> When welfare recipients are concentrated, as they are in the
> inner city, these dynamics create problems that extend far
> beyond the recipients of welfare. . . .
> But welfare all by itself is truly not the problem. . . . The
> changes in welfare *and* changes in the risks attached to crime
> *and* changes in the educational environment reinforced each
> other. . . . Together, they changed the incentive structure.[43]

Schools are important awarders of status. At one time pregnancy was stigmatized so the girl was often expelled in disgrace.
This attitude changed in the 1960s throughout the country, and
instead of punishment, many inner-city schools began to offer
special services for pregnant girls and young mothers. Gradually,
prestige became attached to premature motherhood.

At the same time, hustling superseded regular work for many
young men in the inner cities. Murray argues that these young

men, likely to end up in jail, are not the choice of husband of a young mother with judgment:

> At a more general level, a community that subsists on illegal sources of income and that is victimized by widespread violent crime is socially disorganized in crucial ways. To put it roughly, good folks no longer set the standards. In some cases, they are physically intimidated from setting standards (witness the situation in many housing projects); in others, the role models for the youths are not blue-collar working men who raise families but hustlers.[44]

In spite of their own conclusion that welfare per se has not been a major cause of family breakdown, Bane and Ellwood, with Wilson, share Murray's concern that an urban underclass has become trapped in a condition of dependence. The answer principally lies, they claim, in strengthening the job sector—moving the poor back up through the social strata. They set forth ideas about policies and programs necessary to bring about this change. Where Bane and Ellwood, and Wilson, make their political appeal, however, and how they structure the argument, are quite different from Murray.

Wilson makes his appeal overtly to "minority [group] leaders and liberal policymakers," asking them to recognize "the need to expand the War on Poverty and race relations visions to confront the growing problems in inner-city social dislocations."[45] He asks them to build a political alliance around a combination of universal (rather than means-tested) policies such as growth-oriented macroeconomic policies (partly in place), a national labor-market strategy, child support assurance, family allowances, and child care. Wilson also offers a set of "means-tested and race specific" strategies somehow to be supported in less visible ways because such strategies are unpopular.[46] The "hidden agenda for liberal policymakers," Wilson says, "is to enhance the chances in life for the ghetto underclass by emphasizing programs to which the more advantaged groups of all class and racial backgrounds can positively relate.[47]

Instead of appealing to liberal policy makers, Ellwood anchors himself in the American mainstream. He outlines his program in two recent books, *Poor Support* and *Welfare Policy for the 1990s*.

The primary message of *Poor Support* is that "the welfare system does not reflect and reinforce our commonly held values and expectations." He continues, "The history of [U.S.] social policy can be seen as a series of attempts to help people without interfering too seriously with the basic values of autonomy, work, family, and community."[48] Ellwood describes three conundrums for policy makers attempting to help the needy without undermining those four basic values. The first and oldest is the *security-work conundrum*: "When you give people money, food, or housing, you reduce the pressure on them to work and care for themselves." The second is the *assistance-family conundrum*: What is the impact of welfare on marriage, divorce, and childbearing—the subject of greatest argument between Wilson and Murray? The third, least commented upon yet most important, is the *targeting-isolation conundrum*: "The more effectively you target, the more you tend to isolate the people who receive the services from the economic and political mainstream."[49] Ellwood writes:

> Until recently, social policy succeeded in avoiding the dilemmas to a remarkable degree. But it did so by eschewing pure welfare forms that would offer generous benefits to all needy applicants, choosing instead to rely chiefly on nonwelfare forms of support linked to specific problems. . . . We must look more to other nonwelfare supports that reflect the diverse causes and effects of poverty.[50]

On the theme of mainstream values, Ellwood comments that our present combination of policies hurts the working poor worst: "They get so little aid they are actually the poorest group after transfers. Over a third have no medical protection."[51] Expressing skepticism that any "welfare-based solution," including workfare, "will ever take us far," Ellwood cites the inherent flaws in such approaches: they inevitably reduce the incentive to work, support mostly single parents, and isolate and stigmatize. He disagrees with conservatives, he says, that welfare "has been a large part of the problem," but agrees with them that it has never been a long-term solution for the healthy who are able to work. "Conservatives are right," he explains, "when they assert that welfare does not reflect and enforce our basic values."[52] We must adopt, he argues, policies and programs that encourage and reward work and responsibility.

In a major four-year study of the economic status of inner-city black youth, the National Bureau of Economic Research (NBER) found that youths from welfare homes "do far worse in the job market" than youths with the same family income and other attributes from nonwelfare homes. Whether it was a female-headed family or a family with adults of both sexes did not seem to make much difference in youth job performance. The relationship of the family to means-tested government programs, however, did matter. The authors of the NBER study conclude that the explanation for the difference would be factors such as "information and 'connections' or attitudes and 'work ethic,' " since young blacks are more likely to hold jobs if other members of the family are employed.[53]

Much has been made of the disappearance of the better-paying unskilled jobs from the inner city,[54] but according to the 1980 Census young blacks in the inner city did not do much worse in finding and holding a job than did similar youths outside the ghettos—38 percent versus 32 percent.[55] Looking to see how New York City's growing number of downtown office jobs has affected the employment of dropouts from city schools, Bernard J. Frieden found that commuters from outside the city hold a slightly higher percentage of the remaining manufacturing jobs than of the office jobs.[56] "Failure of strong downtown economies to do more for city residents," he concludes, has at least three explanations: city residents lack information networks and company representatives do not recruit in the inner city, many lack the education needed for either office or manufacturing jobs, and many are not in the job market. Frieden believes that it would help if downtown employers worked more closely with the schools.[57]

Lawrence Mead sheds some light on what happens to job attitudes when a family becomes involved in the welfare system. He observes that some feel they cannot work "unless someone else handles the logistics—finding them a job and arranging child care, training, and transportation," and many are choosy about what they will do. Citing Nathan Glazer, who complains of reluctance to "work steadily at menial jobs that in previous generations supported families," Mead wants to know why the "architects of government jobs" think that "disadvantaged job seekers deserve relatively comfortable, well-paying positions in public agencies, on the assumption that they are otherwise unemployable, when aliens who are no better prepared are washing dishes in American restaurants." We are, Mead says, back to the issue of rights versus responsibilities, "of apportioning responsibility for coping between the individual and society."[58] "The real issue," he continues, "is whether the worker should be held reponsible for meeting the needs of the economy or vice versa." His answer has placed him in the political center:

> Americans today clearly do not want jobless people to have to wander endlessly in search of work or to be paid the pittance that farm workers earned in the 1930s. Conservatives must be willing to join a debate about what working expectations should be and must cease trying to avoid it by appealing to impersonal economic laws. . . .
>
> Liberals, with their demanding view of what a job should be and their reluctance to expect serious work effort from the poor, are distinctly out of step. . . . [Success] must be earned by performance that commands the respect of others. The liberal view ignores the demand for reciprocity, for effort in return for support, that emerges so strongly from polls about welfare policy.[59]

Ellwood has proposed to refocus the major assistance of social policy on working families.[60] According to his proposal, children would no longer live in a neighborhood or grow up in a family in which government assistance is the principal source of income, and low-income adults would have the opportunity to work and no longer have not working as an economic option. The following is a summary of Ellwood's recommendations:

- *Ensure that everyone has medical protection.* There now are about 37 million Americans who have no health insurance except what they can pay for themselves. In a crisis they may present themselves at a private, or more likely a public, medical facility and receive treatment of varying quality. The cost is borne by local taxpayers and is reflected in charges to other patients or, more often these days, in higher premiums for those who are covered by insurance. Ellwood thinks we need a plan for collecting health premiums from persons otherwise uninsured through payroll taxes that vary by income level.

- *Make work pay enough that working families are not poor.* He recommends increasing the take-home pay of working families to bring all of them above the poverty level, through a mixture of plans. He would, for example, increase the Earned Income Tax Credit (EITC) and make the credit a refund for those not earning enough to benefit from it as a deduction; begin government wage supplements of half the difference between a worker's hourly wage and, say $6 per hour; and make the child care tax credit refundable.

- *Adopt a uniform child support assurance system.* Ellwood proposes identifying all absent parents and requiring them to pay a percentage of their income as child support, withholding it from their paychecks like an income tax. Such an experiment is under way in Wisconsin.[61] The federal government should make up the difference between the amount collected and some minimum.

- *Convert welfare into a transitional system designed to provide serious but short-term financial, educational, and social support for people who are trying to cope with temporary setbacks.* At present, about three-fourths of the persons who receive AFDC stay in the program only a short time. The remaining one-fourth stay on it more or less permanently. Ellwood's proposal establishes a maximum length of perhaps three years on transitional support.

- *Provide minimum-wage jobs to persons who have exhausted their transitional support.* At the end of the maximum period, some people will not yet have jobs. Some may prove incapable of holding a job. Everyone would have as a last resort a federally funded job at the minimum wage. While Ellwood does not say so, I would presume that not all the wage supplements would be available to such workers.

Ellwood has guessed that "to do everything right" it would cost the taxpaying public about $20–30 billion more than we spend now.[62] Welfare programs—SSI, SSDI, and related payment programs—would be confined to persons who are unable to work because of disability. AFDC and food stamps would be among the programs to end. The major component of the $20–30 billion in added costs would be in new benefits to poor families not now on welfare—added income to bring them above the poverty level—and health coverage, as nonwelfare families, except for the elderly, are not now covered by government health insurance. The increase in governmental costs for those who now receive AFDC and food stamps would be nearly offset by terminating old payments as new ones begin.

Ellwood has not discussed the effect on able-bodied adults who despite these incentives do not work, do not work enough, or are too unreliable or unpleasant to hold a back-up, minimum-wage job. The last comprehensive look at most such persons was when they were in school, and, as Moynihan observes in *Family and Nation*,

> They lack the basic skills and, more dismayingly, the basic attitudes that would make them attractive even as entry level employees. They don't know how to seek the help they need, and worse, they positively frighten those who feel the urge to offer help.[63]

Until we test Ellwood's policies, we cannot know how many persons cannot hold a last-resort job, but the number may be considerable.

While maintaining their disagreement with conservatives such as Murray about the relative importance of changes in the labor market or the advent of welfare and antipoverty programs in bringing about the pathologies of the inner city, Ellwood and his coworkers have proposed policies that suit both explanations—policies that replace welfare with work. A growing number of academic social scientists have followed their lead and have rejected important assumptions of welfare liberalism that previously enabled this school to share a common agenda with Socialists. This group has adopted in place of those ideas the new assumptions and policy ideas compatible with an activist, socially concerned conservatism. Their ideas are attractive; their direction worth serious consideration. They would establish a single economic system for all who are able to work. Although there is no one "answer to homelessness," a policy that strengthens working families and brings as many welfare families as possible into our economic mainstream should do much to alter the home and the neighborhood environment, as well as the economic situation, that contribute to falling through the bottom of the underclass.

Bane and Ellwood are at the heart of the American social policy community, so their powerful analysis and fresh thought will generate waves throughout academia and government. Some waves are already evident in the report of a major welfare policy conference held in Wisconsin in June 1990. Billed as the Midwest American Assembly on the Future of Social Welfare in America, it was a major finding of the conference that our welfare system fosters dependency: "The principles of individual responsibility and individual accountability for one's own well-being should guide any changes in the system that are proposed."[64]

Included among the conference's short list of recommendations designed to completely overhaul the existing social welfare system were payroll deductions of child support from absent parents, increases in the Earned Income Tax Credit to raise the income of the working poor to a "socially accepted minimum level," and "encouragement of community support and 'watching out for one's neighbors.' "

The Progressive Policy Institute (PPI), a new think tank in Washington, D.C., that provides research support to the Democratic Leadership Council (the *New Republic* describes the DLC as the Democratic party's center-right caucus, "a coalition of neo-liberal intellectuals"), draws heavily upon the work of Ellwood and Bane.[65] "We're trying to fashion approaches that work as economics and correspond as politics to the basic values of the public," says PPI chief economist Rob Schapiro, formerly on the staff of Senator Moynihan.[66] There seems to be little doubt at the new research institute that a nonwelfare approach will be less politically divisive than the current policy if only because it will help the many low-income families who go to work, not just those currently supported by public assistance.

Robert D. Reischauer, director of the Congressional Budget Office (CBO), has pointed to projections indicating that labor

market conditions for entry-level and low-skilled workers are likely
to improve in the 1990s. He has argued that this trend makes
the 1990s a particularly good time to emphasize job-related
policies.[67] Ending AFDC itself will, according to Reischauer, create
a great many jobs for which previous experience in caring for
a family is useful. Working welfare mothers will automatically
create opportunities for child care workers. As many as one in
six welfare mothers would find such employment. We will also
need more managers and workers for community-living situations for the seriously mentally ill. The aging population also
needs more human-care-services workers.

A recent news report from Royal Oak, Michigan, tells of
fourteen welfare mothers hired under a state program at $21,000
per year as foster mothers to disabled children. "These women
are capable of doing something, but for the most part they are
happy being moms," says state legislator Shirley Johnson, credited
with helping to get the program funded. "I was scared at the
beginning," she admits. "How would you match the right mom
with the right child? But it has worked beautifully."[68] Experience
in taking care of one's family will be valuable in many of the jobs
emerging in the next few years.

Housing secretary Jack Kemp and others have promoted a
concept called enterprise zones, in which private corporations
receive dramatic benefits such as forgiveness of capital gains taxes
for investing and locating operations in depressed areas of the
inner city.[69] The tax incentives are a 5 percent tax credit for the
first $10,500 of wages paid in the zone to each lower-income
worker, a tax deduction of up to $50,000 in newly issued stock
of small corporations, and elimination of the capital gains tax on
tangible investments in the zone. The idea, of course, is that good
jobs will result from the investment and that ghetto residents can
take these jobs. This policy should be approached carefully, for
it could also make things worse. It encounters the same phenomenon that generally results in higher rates of homelessness where
jobs are plentiful: escalating land values. David Osborne has
analyzed the problem in a recent *New Republic* article, "The Kemp
Cure-All: Why Enterprise Zones Don't Work":

> The problem is simple. Deep tax incentives may shift invest-
> ment geographically, but they cannot change the way the

market works. [N]o amount of tax incentives entice firms to hire people who can't reach the required levels of proficiency quickly. . . . Meanwhile, zone residents who don't get the new jobs nonetheless have to pay higher rents when real estate demand drives up rates. Poor residents—and sometimes struggling businesses—can even be forced out of the neighborhood when landlords begin rehabilitating properties, just as in any other gentrification process.[70]

Osborne cites statistics from ten experimental enterprise zones in Indiana, where zone residents got only 6.3 percent of the new manufacturing jobs. He argues instead for an approach that ties creation of such zones to a program of comprehensive economic development and social services for the area. He quotes Stuart Butler, domestic policy director at the Heritage Foundation: "Working with community-based organizations to address a lot of social problems within the zone—crime and that kind of thing—seems to be very important." I fear that the economic realities indicated by Osborne may be too powerful. When a local program is carried out superbly well, it will work. But implementation on a national scale may fail.

Secretary Kemp's proposal would create fifty zones nationally in four years. Cities and counties will compete for selection; communities must convince Secretary Kemp, who has taken ownership of this idea and staked his reputation on it, of their capacity to carry it out successfully. Neighborhood-based enterprises, such as those promoted by Robert Woodson, a prominent black community organizer, are a factor in selection, and their participation in the enterprise zone would be encouraged.

The evidence that enterprise zones will work, HUD officials admit, is largely anecdotal. Each zone is unique to its city's combination of participants from neighborhoods, city government, and business. HUD must develop selection criteria that takes into account many variables; yet the best of criteria and review methods make selection an art, not a science. Discretion by officials at both the federal and the local level is necessary for the program to work. That, however, creates the potential for political favoritism and corruption. Without strong leadership from HUD, the program could become a disaster.

HUD faces the additional challenge of coordinating its participation with the policies and programs of other federal agencies such as the Department of Labor, the Internal Revenue Service, the Department of Health and Human Services, and those agencies' state and local counterparts. HUD might take the clear lead for this program with all agencies cooperating to draft the selection criteria and review the proposals under HUD's chairmanship. All involved should be included with objective outsiders in a continuing evaluation of the results of the enterprise zone program.

Enterprise zones and other elements of the Homeownership and Opportunity for People Everywhere (HOPE) program proposed by the Bush administration, as well as the Ellwood proposal for replacing welfare with tax credits and other supports for working families, fit with mainstream American values of work, family, and private enterprise. At the same time that inner-city families would be given opportunities to earn more than welfare through tax credits by working, private job creation would be under way. The Government could present the program as a comprehensive, bipartisan program to rebuild inner cities, strengthen working families, and end public dependency. Without such a coherent value-based policy, public dependency will continue to increase: our natural institutions of family, neighborhood, school, and church will lose the ability to support us and hold us together. Homelessness, even in a prospering economy, will continue to grow.

This combination of policies presents an opportunity for productive political realignment. Most individuals will not change parties, but the evolution of a bipartisan, working majority in Congress provides common ground with Republican administrations on important issues. This political center could coalesce around the principle of strengthening working families in a context of democratic capitalism. Instead of fighting battles over the ideas of the Right and the Left, this new political center can generate ideas for which testing and adoption are not partisan.[71] Congress will still debate important issues such as how to pay for new programs, how fast to go, and what should be done by each level of government or the private sector. Because of heavy interest-group lobbying, battles will rage over ending ineffective programs or approaches.

A working majority for a new domestic agenda will develop. Activists of moderate temperament from both the Democratic and the Republican party will come together, perhaps only for a time, around a limited set of policies and programs. This active center, already beginning to take shape around preliminary experiments in welfare reform, would agree on the need for a government policy that empowers families and individuals to govern their own lives and life in their communities and places a clear expectation on them to do so.

5

Housing, Housing, Housing

"IT IS NO EXAGGERATION to say that there is a three-word solution to homelessness: housing, housing, housing."[1] This proclamation by Robert M. Hayes, the New York attorney whose 1979 lawsuit established a right to shelter in that state, is exactly what he says it is not—an exaggeration. From our examination so far of the homeless themselves and of the history and dynamics of deinstitutionalization of the mentally ill, the nature of alcoholism, and the formation of an urban underclass, it should be clear both that housing is not the *principal* problem of the homeless and that decision makers have good reason to be hesitant about adopting new policies or appropriating large sums of money for sweeping solutions to homelessness. Having disposed of the idea that homelessness is mainly a housing problem, I must acknowledge that lack of appropriate housing nevertheless is an important contributory factor. Housing that is acceptable to economically marginal families and individuals and those with special problems has been disappearing, even while the supply for many of us has been increasing and improving.

In the 1989 book *New Homeless and Old*, Charles Hoch and Robert A. Slayton trace a long-term decline in the supply of places to live for low-income single individuals—single-room occupancy (SRO) housing. They report that "members of the single working poor [have been] victimized by urban policies that encourage the destruction of SROs and other types of low-income housing" and argue persuasively that "the loss of SRO hotels was more the result of public initiative and subsidy than of the economic pressure of the urban land market."[2]

Until about 1920, according to Hoch and Slayton, a vigorous and generally unimpeded private market had supplied housing in the central cities for low-income and seasonal workers. This housing had become less profitable to operate over the years as demand declined: the railroads that joined the regions of the country were largely completed by then, labor demand in the mining industry had become less erratic, and agriculture was increasingly mechanized. New regulations aimed at safety for residents were making it less profitable to build or to rehabilitate shelter for the poor. While quality and safety were probably improved in the units that were built, the trade-off was an inevitable reduction in the total available.[3]

Then Big Science appeared. At the University of Chicago, a theory of "human ecology" took hold, and its advocates in the academy aggressively worked to define an agenda of social reform. This was the beginning of the end for a natural low-income housing market. Robert E. Park, a professor of sociology, wrote that there were "natural areas," each of which had a "natural function." There was a natural process, with urban growth, of "differentiation and segregation."[4] His colleague Ernest Watson Burgess wrote, "As a city grows its structure becomes more complex, its areas more specialized." There was a "natural" division into social classes, so where the classes were mixed things were "disorganized."[5] The hotel-dweller lived downtown, not in a residential area, so he contributed to such disorganization, which impeded the natural and healthy development of the city.

A few years earlier, New York City had imported from Germany the concept of "zoning codes," in the first place "to keep residential sections separate from potentially harmful industrial activities."[6] In the hands of the human ecologists, such codes in time became a comprehensive instrument to shape the growth patterns of cities in line with their theories about human nature— theories, of course, borrowed by real estate interests to serve their purposes. According to Hoch and Slayton, "The most important of these was to rationalize land investment and thereby help maintain central area real estate values."[7] In the 1920s and early 1930s, decisions on where to build, what to save, and what to destroy were worked out between local governments and private interests, and they were mostly about private money. Generally this arrangement kept the destruction on a moderate scale, say, one building at a time.

"The Great Depression of the 1930s," write Hoch and Slayton, "consummated the shift of dominance in housing policy from the private sector to the public sector." This change came about as part of an emerging consensus "that government was now responsible for the welfare of the citizenry."[8] During the depression, federal money became available for the destruction of buildings that local governments determined to be undesirable. Localities, wanting to get all the federal money they could, used the available tool of code enforcement to tip the economic balance so that owners of older buildings would agree to their removal.

Federal funding and policies provided an incentive for the destruction of downtown SROs during the 1930s, but it was not until after World War II, with the passage of the Housing Act of 1949, that federal funds were made available for the wholesale destruction of neighborhoods and areas of cities. This process was called by the inspirational name "urban renewal." The goal of the act was "to make decent housing available to every American citizen," by coupling the construction of public housing to the "clearance of slums."[9] "Redevelopment agencies" were established in cities under the terms of the act and worked with local progrowth coalitions of developers and leading citizens to tear down and rebuild huge sections of town, usually adjacent to or part of the urban core, and inevitably containing large numbers of SROs and other low-income housing units. The idea was that the cities could be made more beautiful and more livable for everyone through the elimination of blight. As these programs were undertaken, a housing shortage for the poor in some of the neighborhoods involved might not have been foreseeable, as vacancy rates were often quite high in the most rundown areas. In a study of forty-one cities, four out of ten households displaced by urban renewal simply relocated in other "slum" areas, which soon resulted in overcrowding even where it had not been the case before.[10] According to Martin Anderson, writing in 1964, the urban renewal program "eliminated 126,000 low-income homes . . . and replaced them with about 28,000 homes, most of them in a much higher rent bracket."[11] By early 1963, Anderson estimated from Urban Renewal Administration data that over

609,000 persons had been moved.[12] Urban renewal came in some quarters to be derided as the "Negro removal" program. Little new housing either for poor families or single individuals was built relative to the amount of housing lost.

The demolition of old housing in the inner cities had always upset the lives of low-income workers and alcoholics who depended on it for affordable housing. Its large-scale destruction in the 1960s and 1970s coincided with the release of increasing numbers of patients from mental hospitals. The earliest patients discharged from mental hospitals usually had been relatively good candidates for living in the community. Two-thirds of them went to live with their families or independently in their own apartments. As time went on, though, patients who lacked family ties began coming out in larger numbers. There were few halfway houses for them. While some of these patients were placed in nursing homes and boarding houses, others joined the low-income workers and alcoholics living in the shrinking supply of SROs. By the mid-1970s it was reported that almost a quarter of the 100,000 persons living in New York City's SROs were "severely mentally dysfunctional."[13] As older structures continued to make way for office buildings, convention centers, condominiums, highways, and other more profitable uses and as the discharge of mental patients continued, derelict alcoholics and mental patients were increasingly living outside.[14]

Apparently we have no authoritative national figures for the loss of SRO housing over recent decades. To judge from local reports, though, the frequent observation that nearly 50 percent of the remaining supply disappeared in the 1970s does not seem unreasonable. In Chicago, for example, SRO units declined 80 percent between 1960 and 1980. Most of these units were lost before 1973, when about 36,000 remained in the city as a whole. By 1984, half the remaining units had been "converted, abandoned, or destroyed."[15]

The urban renewal program still exists today, but the name has been changed several times, first to "Model Cities," then to "Planned Variations," and now to "Community Development Block Grants." "Enterprise Zones" may be next. In the block grant program, the federal government has largely withdrawn from the planning process, leaving it to states and localities. With each name change, the requirements for planning have been strengthened, particularly the provisions regarding participation of neighborhood leaders, and the process has been slowed down.

Throughout the country the last fraction of these SROs are under threat—either through urban renewal programs or, increasingly, gentrification, perhaps stimulated by urban renewal improvements. According to Roger Starr, land values have surged in the central cities, as older structures have been replaced by office buildings, shops, condominiums, tourist centers, parks, freeway intersections, and other hallmarks of prosperity. In many cities, particularly in the Sunbelt and on the West Coast, where corporations are more frequently locating their administrative headquarters and their technical operations, downtown land values have risen because of sustained economic prosperity. Although urban renewal may have played little or no role in many cases, it is difficult to isolate such urban dynamics. The result is the same: the poor are squeezed out.

In such instances, it is clearly the general prosperity rather than an economic downturn that aggravates homelessness. The ratio of high-paid jobs to available housing has contributed to what might be called a "trickle-up" process: instead of the traditional pattern where the poor benefit as housing is passed down by the better-off, the better-off and their developers are buying the housing lived in by the poor and either tearing it down or fixing it up. In Washington, D.C., for example, $395 apartments have gone to $850 in five years.[16] In the past twenty years, there has been a net loss of 22,000 low-rent units in downtown Seattle.[17] The downtown shelter director in that city tells me that an increase in the number of homeless singles there in the past five years has corresponded directly to the loss of these SROs.[18] While Filer and Honig find no definitive research supporting claims that a million SRO units were lost during the 1970s alone, nearly 50 percent of the national supply,[19] data from many communities suggest that major losses occurred during that period and continue. Hoch and Slayton have compiled figures on several cities from a variety of sources.

Although research efforts got under way in the late 1970s, it was the homeless crisis of the early 1980s that sparked widespread concern about the loss of SRO hotels. Studies conducted across the United States documented and deplored the loss. New York City lost 30,385 units in 160 buildings between 1975 and 1981, for a decrease of 60 percent overall. In San Francisco 5,723 (17.7 percent of 32,214 units disappeared between 1975 and 1979. Denver, which had 45 SRO hotels in 1976, had fewer than seventeen left in 1981. In Seattle the number of SRO units dropped by 15,000 between 1960 and 1981. San Diego lost 1,247 units in thirty hotels between 1976 and 1984 and has only about 3,500 units left. [New York City's policies have resulted in the creation of 2,000 more such units since these figures were compiled. San Diego's innovative and effective program will be discussed later.] Smaller cities lost hotels as well. Portland eliminated 1,700 units in the 1970s. Cincinnati lost 42 percent of its SRO units during the 1970s and has only fifteen hotels remaining with 875 units.[20]

SROs still face a strong economic threat in San Francisco, where hotel owners would like to rent many of those remaining to tourists: in a recent telephone survey I made of sixteen south of Market SRO hotels, I was able to find only one monthly vacancy; there were numerous vacancies at the higher daily or weekly rates tourists would expect to pay.

An example provided by Hoch and Slayton shows how resources are combined from federal, state, and local government to subsidize the conversion of low-income SRO housing to housing for better-off renters. "Presidential Towers," they write, is "the product of Chicago's urban growth coalition."[21] The first phase of Presidential Towers provides 3,000 units for middle-income singles and couples with rents starting at $745 per month. The project is built on urban renewal land cleared more than ten years ago and left vacant in the interim. The apartment towers are forty-nine stories tall. First, the city sold the land to developers in 1980 for the 1968 market price, capturing none of the subsequent increase in land value. Real estate transfer taxes of $20,000 (a pittance) were waived. The city paid for the removal of an SRO remaining on part of the site and for sidewalks and street lighting. At a time when the prime rate was pushing toward 20 percent, the city sold $180 million in municipal bonds at 9 percent interest to make a short-term construction loan to the developers and also made a long-term loan of $5.8 million at 2 percent financed by the interest earned from the 9 percent bond money between the time it was borrowed by the city and the time it was drawn down to pay construction costs. The federal government insured a $158 million mortgage, keeping the interest rate at 9.5 percent. The developers, with the help of their congressman, got three federal exemptions: $3 million in mortgage penalties was waived; developers were permitted to use accelerated depreciation in calculating their tax losses, saving them $7 million; and they were allowed to ignore an earlier commitment to rent 20 percent of the units to low- and moderate-income households. Altogether, the cost to the public and the benefit to the developers from special breaks of one sort or another was about $100 million.[22]

Thoughout all the years of "human ecology," "slum clearance," and "urban renewal," very little recognition and less care have been given to the human ecosystems disrupted and displaced to serve the theories of sociologists and the visions of developers and growth coalitions. Hoch and Slayton cite census data showing that 68 percent of the SRO dwellers in the Chicago of the 1950s had lived in the same apartment for two years or more.[23] In a current survey, about nine out of ten Chicago SRO residents report they are satisfied with their living arrangements. Almost as many know the managers or desk clerks personally, and more than half know the owner. Staff take phone messages, distribute mail, screen visitors, and carry out "other small but important services."[24] Local retail establishments in SRO districts provide services valued by the residents. Employment bureaus are the most valued, and next are those providing food and drink: a disappearing custom is the provision of a free meal with the purchase of alcoholic beverages. Seen as blight by reformers, saloons are social centers, and second-hand stores and pawn-shops are important economic supports.[25]

Not everyone chooses to live a life where they are daily responsible to others for providing income, minding a demanding set of manners they have never been convinced are important and that they find awkward, keeping to a clock based on some predetermined starting and ending points, and avoiding comestibles, potables, or inhalables that seem to make life an adventure instead of a trial. "Let me tell you about Skid Row," says Clancy Imislund. "The people on it can't cope with the conflict of a structured life."[26] SRO life has increasingly become the sidewalk or the alley life as the SROs have disappeared. We did not mind it so much when these people were in the SROs.

The value and the fragility of social and economic relation-ships in a low-income section of Richmond, Virginia, undone by urban renewal are described in *The World of Patience Gromes: Making and Unmaking a Black Community* (1988) by Scott C. Davis. The story, writes the author, is of "a black community: its birth in the country at the end of the Civil War, its move from country to city, its disintegration during the war on poverty."[27] It is about "the community that came to Fulton [Virginia], stayed for sixty years, then was lost. . . . men and women such as Patience Gromes who possessed an idea of grace throughout history, an idea for want of which a culture is broken, scattered, and unable to find its way."[28] The culture of Fulton remained "largely intact" in spite of all the changes going on in America and the world, "until urban renewal arrived in March 1968." The most powerful ingredient holding Fulton together was the faith of its best citizens that through right living—hard work, thrift, mutual support, and the observance of strict morals—they could progress both spiritually and tangibly. "Good character," writes Davis, was seen as "the prime weapon against all that opposed" the people of Fulton.[29] Evidence of such character was their houses, gardens, and families.[30] They were devoutly religious, and Davis's phrase "an idea of grace" beautifully captures the mystery and the fragility of life in a poor neighborhood where cultural values are sustained.

There were always plenty of Fulton residents who did not adhere to such high standards, and they lived next to and across the street from the righteous, in a kind of uneasy truce. Family members strayed from the path. After World War II, much of the industrial base left the area, and welfare and retirement benefits more and more became major sources of income in the community.[31] But the values of work, family, and faith continued to hold their own until urban renewal and the war on poverty.

The parents of Fulton's elderly citizens had worked hard and saved to purchase farmland "as a way of anchoring their lives," and houses "provided an equivalent opportunity" for such rootedness in the city.[32] Houses proved that hard work brings success in this world. But when Fulton was declared an urban renewal area, even though demolition and rebuilding would take years, government officials advised local homeowners not to keep their houses in repair. It would be "money down a hole," said one planner.[33] Thus toppled one important cultural bulwark.

Renewal promised "benefits far beyond the ability of an individual family to obtain through their own work." Increasingly, the ability to "manipulate government" replaced hard work and saving, let alone truthfulness, as values that were seen to pay off.[34] Urban renewal was "a perplexing variation on an old theme of evil"—something for nothing.[35] The professional planners were admired for their apparent sophistication but seemed to be getting paid without having to work—"a lot like bootlegging."[36] In fact, former bootleggers and artful dodgers were recruited to be community organizers, sending a signal that the old values were no longer in force.

Fulton was already nearly destroyed culturally by the years of urban renewal planning before it was destroyed physically. The actual destruction was begun by an unplanned event, a flood, and completed by the urban renewal program. Not only did a community die, reports Davis, but a large number of its leading citizens died within weeks or months of relocation. Patience Gromes died a week after moving, in the act of registering to vote.[37]

NEW YORK CITY enacted rent control in 1943. Today, high estimates of the homeless in that city run around 60,000. The city currently has access to about 250,000 abandoned housing units, most heavily concentrated in a close-in area of the South Bronx, and has taken title to many of them in rem, that is, for nonpayment of property taxes. In 1989, the city government decided to rehabilitate all these units over the next ten years at a cost of $5.1 billion and make them available to the homeless and others of limited income.

These houses and apartments had been abandoned in most cases because the owners, under a rent freeze, could not meet operating expenses and pay taxes out of the rent. Each month they took in less than they paid out. They could not sell the property as there was no market for land and buildings that would only lose money.

For New York City, at least, we have a partial price tag on the cost of rent control: $5.1 billion in lost housing. We are also able to see that there are at least four times as many abandoned housing units as there are homeless people. The families that were housed until recently in welfare hotels such as the notorious

Martinique described in Jonathan Kozol's book, *Rachel and Her Children*, were victims of rent control.[38]

In no other place in the nation have stringent rent controls such as those in New York City been in effect for nearly so long. Housing abandonment is not typical in other places with rent control, as rents have generally been allowed to rise in some relationship to operating costs. In addition, in many communities rents are unfrozen when a tenant vacates and then controlled again with occupation by a new tenant. The effect of rent control then is to reduce profitability, and where the reduction is large enough to make other investments comparatively attractive, it discourages the production of new rental housing. Over time, the housing supply in such places is further reduced through conversion to condominiums or other forms of owned housing.

Rent control unquestionably increases the number of homeless to the extent that it discourages the production of rental housing and leads to the withdrawal of such housing from the market. There has been much heated argument in the past several years about how frequently this actually happens. Most of the argument centers around research presented by William Tucker in the *American Spectator*, the *National Review*, Heritage Foundation reports, his recent book *The Excluded Americans*, and elsewhere. Tucker has insisted that rent control is a major cause of homelessness, basing his contention largely on the statistical analysis of data from a sample of cities. The way the sample was selected has not held up under questioning by the Economic Policy Institute (EPI),[39] and his regression analysis has also come under attack. John M. Quigley writes that Tucker's "widely publicized claim that homelessness in America arises from local rent control is *just plain silly*."[40] Tucker tries to support his conclusion with a statistical analysis of data from cities with and without rent control, and Quigley points out that Tucker has not included price (rent level) as a variable. When price is introduced, says Quigley after reanalyzing Tucker's data, the effect of rent control disappears. Homelessness correlates with a combination of rent levels and vacancies. The problem is not rent control, but the unavailability of housing at a price within the means of potential low-income renters. Rent control does not cause homelessness, he says. High prices and low incomes do.

Quigley's analysis, in turn, has the weakness that regression analysis does not establish the time sequence of the variables being analyzed. Rent control disappears as a factor in Quigley's analysis not necessarily because it is irrelevant but perhaps because it affects homelessness indirectly, not directly, by discouraging production of new units and leading to withdrawal of existing units from the market or, in the extreme case, abandonment of units. That is, rent control does not cause homelessness, but rent control causes or contributes to higher rents and lower vacancy rates, which in turn cause or contribute to homelessness. Even if this equation were correct, it would still be difficult, unless one could determine which events came first in time sequence, to prove whether high rents led to rent control, rent control led to high rents and vacancies, or they fed on each other, with rent control an aggravating factor—perhaps, in some cases at least, a very serious one.

As will be seen, however, the EPI study appears to demonstrate that rent control correlates with homelessness only where extreme versions of the policy are in place now or have been historically—in places such as New York City; Cambridge, Massachusetts; and the California cities of Santa Monica, Berkeley, and Cotati. EPI reports that about 200 cities and counties have "some form of rent control" but that most of them "permit rent increases sufficient for the landlord to maintain an adequate return on investment," exempt all new construction from controls, and allow rents to rise to market levels whenever units are vacated. EPI calls such policies "moderate rent controls" and "insists there is no evidence that such moderate policies discourage investment in rental housing or contribute to homelessness."[41] EPI presents a tabulation of such studies, with the results of each.[42]

Bradley Inman, a syndicated real estate columnist who in the early years of rent control sometimes offered advice to investors and the public as an official of the Bay Area Council (San Francisco), reports that at first he and his associates advised against investing in rental housing. After a time they concluded that, in such moderate rent control situations as described in the EPI report, rental housing could still be a good investment and began to advise their public accordingly.[43] Inman notes that rental housing production in many cities with rent control is quite brisk.[44] Rent control appears to have no continuing adverse effect on the construction of new rental housing or on the numbers of units continuing in operation as rentals. While moderate rent control must take some of the profit out of rental housing, the effect does not seem to be strong enough to make such investment less attractive than the alternatives, which for real estate investors would usually be such ventures as single family housing, office buildings, and shopping centers.[45]

In the few cities with more extreme forms, the story is very different. In 1980, when rent control was new, Berkeley and Santa Monica had vacancy rates of about 6 percent. Lately they have been around 2 percent. Rental unit construction has virtually come to a halt in those cities, while every year many rental units are taken off the market.

In spite of Berkeley's being one of the most desirable places in the San Francisco Bay region to live, rents are half the bay area average. The story in Santa Monica is similar. Rents had risen sharply in recent years when, in 1977, Proposition 13, a tax-limitation ballot initiative, was passed, saving many landlords considerable money. Renters had been led to believe this tax break for landlords would lead to rent reductions, and it did not happen. Economists were not surprised, as prices, they believe, are set by supply and demand, and Proposition 13 had little short-term effect on either. Its longer-term effect would presumably have been an increase in rental housing supply: as rental housing became more profitable, it would compete more successfully for investors' money. But before that effect had time to take place, local rent control measures were passed, and construction of new rental units in many cities came to a standstill. In cities where stringent rent controls take most of the profit out of rental housing and subject landlords to severe regulation, prices are low, and homelessness is high. Rental units, understandably, are often sublet at higher rents and do not reach the open market for newcomers.

My conclusion is that rent control has been an important factor in the origin and persistence of homelessness in New York City especially and in others with extreme policies. In cities with moderate policies, rental housing construction was discouraged in the early years, while investors took stock of the situation, watched implementation, and assessed alternative investments. After a while most of them moved into the market again, although some rental housing was lost in the interim. The continuing effect of moderate rent control in reducing the supply of rental housing, thereby aggravating homelessness, appears to be negligible in economically vigorous cities with moderate policies.[46]

IN EARLIER TIMES, homelessness was usually associated with economic downturn. Today in most parts of the country, this is not the case. Counterintuitively, most of the cities with large numbers of homeless are, if anything, booming. The prosperity itself is a key factor in homelessness.

The principal economic variables contributing to the size of a city's homeless population are housing and jobs: not enough housing, too many jobs, or a combination of the two. The existence of jobs is the principal demand factor in the housing market. Jobs, of course, do not just happen. Historically jobs have been created by trade route intersections, natural seaports, agriculture, or mineral resources. Today climate, natural beauty, cultural amenities, and the presence of one or more major research universities are more likely to be factors. Local governments' land use policies are also important. Writes Leo Saunders, president of the California Association of Realtors,

> The lack of affordable housing in the Bay Area and throughout coastal California is one of the prices we've paid for the tremendous economic growth the state has enjoyed in recent years. Strong job formation and in-migration of workers to fill those jobs have created a huge demand for ownership housing, as has the attractiveness of living in California and the Bay Area.
>
> By contrast, housing demand declines when the economy is less healthy.[47]

Where employment is booming and housing cannot keep pace, there will be no room for the poor. "Trickle up" happens to everything. Rising rents in low-income neighborhoods and the gentrification of old downtown housing stock that used to house the poor are generally consequences of an excessive ratio of jobs to housing. Palo Alto, home to Stanford University and site of the fabled garage where in 1938 Hewlett and Packard played their role in starting what became Silicon Valley, is an example of a town suffering from prosperity.[48] "Palo Alto sees down side of upscale living," blares a page-one headline in the local section of a recent edition of the *San Francisco Examiner:* "Businesses leave and families can't afford to live there." Traditional stores are closing because the rent is too high, sales tax revenue is falling behind inflation, the city is laying off workers and cutting back on service, and school enrollment is declining, so school programs are being scaled back: "The city's problems stem from its very desirability. The first city to capitalize on the Silicon Valley explosion, it boasts three jobs for every resident."[49] Palo Alto's mayor points out that a new hiring company moves in soon to replace each one that moves out because of the shortage of affordable housing for its workers, and a new retail business moves in that can pay the higher rent. Young families with children cannot afford to move in; the families that do are mostly older and wealthier.

Another variation on the jobs-housing theme is reported from Fairfax County, Virginia, a western suburb of Washington, D.C. Construction workers building houses to cost over $400,000 are pitching tents in a campground for $8.50 a night because there is no better accommodation in the area they can afford to rent. They can find affordable housing in the towns they are from— places like New Martinsville, West Virginia, and Newtown, Pennsylvania—but there are no jobs for them there. They are, in a sense, today's hoboes. "These are our migrant workers," says a professor at nearby George Mason University who has studied the situation. They are the "virtual homeless," because they cannot find work where they live, and cannot find housing where they work.[50]

The Association of Bay Area Governments (ABAG) finds that housing is the San Francisco area's "most serious constraint to economic growth." The association reports that "many communities are seeking job growth without commensurately encouraging increased housing production." One might expect that next ABAG would advise against promotion of job growth. But instead, ABAG offers a different caution: "Without policy changes, there is a real possibility that job growth . . . will not reach the forecast level." More housing and transportation, not fewer jobs, is the agency's first prescription. "Policy debate," says ABAG, "should focus on three actions": expanded housing production in places where job demand already far outstrips growth in the labor supply, more freeways and public transit, and finally in areas where labor shortages are expected to emerge in the future, a reevaluation of "policies encouraging further commercial and industrial development at the expense of housing production."[51]

IN THE PAST, says Stuart Butler of the Heritage Foundation, cities have been able to change dramatically without homelessness. Cities can absorb the in-migration of high-paid workers if the housing market is flexible. Then the poor migrate to other neighborhoods where they can afford to live. But where anti-growth policies hold sway, then there is a problem. The organized resistance of people in the suburbs to growth is different now, greatly worsening homelessness.[52]

William Tucker joins Butler in this view. He attributes the lack of housing for low- and moderate-income families and individuals not to an excess of jobs but to interference with the housing market through the imposition of rent control and through exclusionary zoning and growth controls. The "biggest impediment" to housing, says Tucker, "has been the growing determination of municipalities to make it as difficult and expensive as possible to put up new housing within their borders."[53] Once people move into an area, they want to maintain or improve the quality of life that attracted them there. They can do this through restricting further development, and—since present residents and not future ones control city government—there is nothing stopping them. Through zoning and building control, one cost after another is added, and the approval process is lengthened: more land per housing unit; more square feet inside; higher-quality construction; payment for roads, sewers, sidewalks, and underground utility wires by the developer; and contribution of land and money for parks, schools, and even day-care centers. Where in the past a project might have taken two years from conception to completion, now it takes five—if it is built at all. Existing owners see their own property values surge as a result of curtailed supply: not only do they protect and improve their neighborhood this way but also they enhance their own wealth—at no cost at all to themselves.

Where this strategy might actually cost existing homeowners something is in higher property taxes, but ways are found around that problem. One is the "welcome stranger assessment," an insiders' ironic name for charging higher property taxes to later arrivals. Typically, the local appraiser simply sets the value of new houses higher than older ones, so new arrivals pay higher taxes. It takes them a while to figure this out, and by then they are old residents who will benefit from the process in the future themselves, so they do not complain about it. In California such "welcome strangers" have been built into the state constitution through Proposition 13. The base tax rate for each house in the state begins from the price at which it was most recently sold. A house bought fifteen years ago for $100,000 often sells today for $600,000. The person who bought it in 1975 pays $1,000 plus a 1 percent increase per year plus his share of any local voter-approved bond issues—say $1,200 total. A person who buys this house in 1990 will start paying taxes at $6,000. Welcome, stranger![54]

The latest trend is morally lofty talk about stopping all new construction until clean air standards are met. It is, writes Tucker, "only a matter of time before the majority convinces itself it is doing the Lord's work."[55] A recent segment on "60 Minutes" illustrates this: movie actor Martin Sheen was shown taking Holy Communion, then appearing before neighbors in Malibu to advocate growth controls in that now unincorporated beachside district of Los Angeles County, and then walking East Sixth Street in downtown Los Angeles, hugging and greeting homeless people. Tucker could not have asked for a better juxtaposition of activities to prove his point.

Tucker makes his case powerfully about the adverse effects of self-interested local government policies presented as community minded. I am sure that growth control and exclusionary zoning policies play an important role in the cost and availability of housing. I believe they are the principal inflationary factor in cities undergoing normal job-growth rates but showing a rapid rise in housing prices and higher-than-normal proportions of homeless families and individuals. But where jobs are growing rapidly in cities that are already very large, prices will be on the rise no matter what, except on the distant periphery of the metropolitan area and in rundown neighborhoods. They will be very high indeed in safe neighborhoods close to the principal amenities of the area. Prices will stay down only in places where people do not want to live—where the housing is in bad condition, the neighborhood is unattractive or dangerous, or the schools are poor. Even there, prices will be higher than in similar neighborhoods of less prosperous cities. In Los Angeles and Orange counties, prices are very high even though many parts of the area have only minimal growth controls. Housing is going up all around the edges and out for miles and miles, houses and small apartment buildings in built-up areas are being knocked down and larger ones are being constructed in their place, mountains and canyons are being turned into new Bel Airs and Brentwoods.

Economically, there is a single housing market; there are not separate markets for different income groups. Housing is subject to the rules of arithmetic: each house built in any price range ultimately means that a house becomes available for a low-income family, through a process known in the trade as "filtering" or disapprovingly as "trickle-down." Each family moves up into a house vacated by another family when it in turn moves up. One house built for a rich family results in one house for a poor family. Poor families move into apartments vacated by the middle class, generally better places in better neighborhoods than what is usually built for the poor. This has long been the way most Americans have improved their housing, including most low-income Americans.

Unfortunately, this process no longer works as well as it did. Tucker documents convincingly how local no-growth and exclusionary zoning policies and practices have interfered with the operation of the market in many communities, restricting the development of housing and increasing its price for everyone. The issue that Tucker does not address is that the housing market is becoming national, even international in some cases. Therefore, in a community with too many jobs, jobs that were probably attracted to the community by the climate, natural beauty, presence of world-class universities, or other features not readily subject to the market, someone from outside the area is likely to come in and buy the house vacated by someone moving up, thereby exporting the vacancy. The poor family that benefits will be someone in the city the in-migrant family came from—a city where there may already be an excess of houses. Filtering does not result in housing for those on the low end of the chain in an area that is growing more rapidly than housing construction can keep up. Thus the numbers of homeless swell.

Prosperity causes homelessness through the two factors of rapidly increasing jobs and artificial restrictions on the housing supply. The jobs increase because employers find the area desirable and want to locate there. Housing is being restricted not just because the people already there are trying to protect and enhance their advantages, as Tucker demonstrates, but also because the area is really deteriorating—the air is polluted, traffic is heavy, and open country is disappearing. Is it unreasonable for the people who live there to want to halt the area's decline before it reaches equilibrium—an equilibrium that will not logically be reached until the area declines to the national or, ultimately, the world average for livability? That is what would happen in a completely free market. In fact, why shouldn't the locals try to make their town pleasant and keep it that way? Providing, perhaps, that their definition of nice includes a reasonable mixture of people. And they do not leave people who seek safe shelter out in the cold.

Very little has been written about the important subject of how the age distribution in our population is affecting the demand for housing and the incidence of homelessness. Certainly this is an important omission. "Demographics is destiny," as they say, and no less so for the homeless. James Wright has commented that just as the baby boom resulted in crowded classrooms in the 1960s, and will lead to a peak in the demand for gravesites in the middle of the twenty-first century, it is currently placing an extraordinary demand on housing.[56]

FRENCH ECONOMIST Jean Baptiste Say coined a phrase that underlies what has come to be called "supply-side economics." It is that "supply creates its own demand."[57] Direct evidence now shows that the provision of services at least contributes to an increase in the homeless count and to homelessness itself if one accepts the way the term is used by the government and most researchers, namely, that persons in homeless shelters are homeless. "Families arriving at shelters are overwhelmingly drawn from housing, not from the street," writes Robert C. Ellickson. He cites official city figures: "Seventy-one percent of these families had been doubled up with family or friends during the previous night. Another 18 percent had been living in their own places."[58] They come to New York's shelters from the homes of friends or family, either because their hosts—the "primary tenants"—can no longer accommodate them or no longer want to or because they choose to move out. In Fremont, a city of about 170,000 people twenty miles south of Oakland, California, the police counted homeless persons and found thirty-two. Only three of these thirty-two were willing to go into the shelter when it opened. The shelter, though, was full from the first night. Sixty percent were from Fremont and two neighboring cities and the other 40 percent from the northern part of the county, mostly Oakland and Berkeley. Most of those from Fremont the police had not counted on the street were coming from violent home situations or from the homes of relatives and friends.[59] Either the family or its hosts are likely to have considered the availability of free city accommodations in deciding what to do. In New York City, the right to shelter has been established in court (*Callaghan* v. *Carey*), and in that city the per capita incidence of family homelessness is about five times the average for other large cities. "The most obvious explanation," says Ellickson, "is that during the 1980s New York City had become one of the few cities to offer free shelter, with no questions asked, to all families that showed up at emergency intake sites.[60]

Advocates make an argument for broadening the definition of homelessness to include everyone not living in a place of his own. According to them, someone living with relatives is homeless. So are the thousands in Los Angeles and other cities living with permission in poorly furnished garages and storerooms, perhaps even paying rent to stay there. It is argued that for a time, with the provision of increasing numbers of spaces in well-run and reasonably comfortable shelters, people will continue to come out of these undesirable situations into the public eye. After a time perhaps the need for such spaces will be met, and the numbers counted as homeless will stabilize. Then we will know how many homeless we actually have: maybe it *will* be the advocates' 2–3 million.

Undeniably, millions of Americans may be living in undesirable situations. And, in a sense, they are homeless. Surely, homeless is a relative term (that is, living poorly) as well as an absolute one (that is, living outside). But it is simply not the same problem to make it possible for every adult individual or family to have a place of their own (now imaginable but surely unprecedented in human history) and to make sure that everyone can be indoors at night.

In the Manhattan Institute report, Filer and Honig point out that waves of immigrants to New York City throughout its history have shared housing, but not until now was there a legal right to shelter. They think back ninety years and wonder, "How many 'homeless' families would have existed at the turn of the century if the government had announced it was legally obligated to provide a hotel room to any family without an apartment who requested one?"[61] Alan Sutherland answers that immigrants doubled up in anticipation of getting their own place and that many of today's homeless do not see how that is going to happen.[62] He is probably right that immigrants had more hope of getting a job and acquiring their own home than many of today's doubled-up families, but I do not believe that these newcomers—and their hopes—would have prospered so well if the government had taken care of their problems "better."

Not only does the availability of free and unlimited shelter space generally attract families and individuals into the homeless category, but their numbers vary directly with the quality of shelter offered. It became known in New York City that if a family applied for shelter during normal business hours, it would likely be sent to a minimal barracks-type shelter with little privacy. The shelter might have private bedrooms, but kitchens and social and recreation areas, if it had them, were likely to be shared with other families. After hours, the assignment was more likely to be to a room in a commercial hotel. For no other reason anyone is aware of but the better accommodations, almost three times as many families reported came to sign up as homeless after hours. According to various studies reported by Filer and Honig, as many as three out of four families turn down city offers of shelter and continue to make other arrangements until they are offered a hotel room. Many clients make it clear to intake officials from the beginning that they will accept only a private apartment or a hotel room. "This suggests," write Filer and Honig, "that these families may have been attempting to improve their assignment rather than being newly homeless."[63] Perhaps if the system were working better—say, if there had not been those decades of rent control in New York City—these families might have a decent place of their own to live, instead of with friends or relatives. But this situation is not the same as homelessness, and certainly not the same task for a city or nation to undertake as making sure that no one has to sleep on the streets.

Pearl Pritchard believes that people would rather stay almost anywhere than in a homeless shelter. "There are so many rules," she says: curfews at 10 P.M., rigid meal times, no alcohol, no drugs, and no smoking in the rooms. The demand for space is held down by the management needs of the shelter.[64] Indeed, when Los Angeles decided to replace free hotel vouchers with space in a National Guard armory, demand declined by 72 percent.[65]

Two professors at New York University, James Knickman and Beth Weitzman, performed the original analysis of the New York City data cited by the several authors earlier for the city Human Resources Administration. Their assignment was to determine why some welfare families become homeless and others do not, so that an early warning system could be developed for the prevention of homelessness. One of their discoveries was that among women on welfare the percentage of pregnant women and women with new babies who seek shelter is many times higher than that of other welfare mothers. Obviously, a new baby can place a strain on a doubled-up household, but there is little reason to think that simply being pregnant should have such an effect. The authors explain that it was city policy at the time of their study to place all pregnant women and new mothers in private rooms; other clients were promised less privacy. Pregnant women and new mothers were eligible for city help in finding permanent housing earlier than other homeless women. These policies would have increased the relative attractiveness of the city's offer over other options, such as continuing to share housing.[66]

Their experiences suggest that a count of the homeless might be more meaningful if it excluded those staying in shelters. I am told that this method of counting is the concept adhered to in Europe.[67] Because nearly all homeless families with children are in shelters of one sort or another, such a practice would greatly reduce the count of homeless families in America and could even wipe out the statistical support for claiming that families and children are the fastest-growing group among the homeless.

Homelessness, as most define it today, does not simply include people living outside because they have nowhere to go, although that is part of it. The number varies greatly according to the amenities offered: Supply creates its own demand.

"INTELLECTUALS DO NOT have better moral judgment than people with little or no education, they do not live more wisely, they are certainly not more compassionate, they have not fewer but *different* superstitions, and they are capable of the most mindless fanaticisms," writes the sociologist Peter L. Berger.[68] It is patently unfair for Wright and others in the welfare establishment to contend that the reluctance of responsible officials to adopt new policies and programs stems solely from "our current political and economic climate." We have little reason to believe that solutions are "within our reach," certainly even less for us to believe that we should hie ourselves to the experts with open checkbooks and plead that they take our money and make things better.

Neither, however, is there evidence that the somewhat mythical "private market"—mythical given the present extent of government intervention on behalf of all manner of special interests and even sometimes the general interest—would, if left alone, produce an adequate supply of affordable housing or bring an acceptable portion of the able-bodied lower-income population into the economic mainstream.

6

Blueprints

ALTHOUGH EXAGGERATING the part housing problems play in homelessness is as unhelpful as unwarranted major new federal programs and fund allocations, we should give thoughtful attention to carefully planned governmental action. We have good reasons to believe that the right kind of housing, in combination with other policies, could help many of the homeless. Solutions to homelessness must give prominent attention to many kinds of housing.

The variety of existing and proposed policies and programs aimed at increasing the availability of housing to low-income families is truly bewildering. Over the years federal housing assistance has assumed three forms: direct dollar assistance through grants or loans either to suppliers of housing or to those wishing to rent or purchase it; interventions in financial markets such as mortgage insurance and related programs; and tax incentives, especially the mortgage interest deduction. Until recently federal housing policy has been spectacularly successful for most Americans. They have been able to buy and live in their own homes. In the 1970s and 1980s, however, housing prices rose dramatically in many areas and skyrocketed in booming cities, pricing middle-class families, particularly would-be first time home buyers, out of the market. In response, increasing numbers of middle- and upper-income families have begun purchasing houses in low-income neighborhoods. This "gentrification," discussed in Chapter 5, reverses the filtering-down process that historically provided housing on the private market for low-income families. At the bottom of the scale, some families and individuals, usually otherwise troubled, lose their housing and cannot find another place to live.

Three conflicting and sometimes contradictory schools of thought about low-income housing strategy have led to the present quandary. "Industrial liberalism"—the mainstream school —is the most prevalent. The two others, smaller but still influential, are recognizable under the headings "socialist" and "libertarian." Believing that all three schools operate from flawed assumptions, I call for a fourth approach whose distinguishing feature is an emphasis on building responsible self-governance. Specific recommendations are offered at the end of the book.

In drawing conclusions about the efficacy of approaches to low-income housing, I have asked how well each accomplishes these three objectives, which are implicit in other policy judgments throughout this book:

- Make the product or service available: How much appropriate housing will result for low-income families and individuals, and what will it cost?
- Build self-governance: What is the effect on the exercise of responsibility by individuals and primary groups over the quality of life in their homes and communities?
- Foster economic growth and distributive equity: How is the growth of the total economy affected, and how are the benefits distributed?

After applying these three criteria to the major approaches to low-income housing and offering my own for consideration, I conclude by offering some policies and programs with promising features.

RECOGNIZING THAT THE MAINSTREAM American housing system has serious problems, leaders in the housing industry—public and private—formed the National Housing Task Force (NHTF), with James M. Rouse, arguably America's most renowned housing developer, as chairman. It set forth findings and recommendations in "A Decent Place to Live," the final task force report.

NHTF has proposed "a new federal delivery system" that it calls the Housing Opportunities Program, along with $3 billion for grants to states and local governments in the first year. A new bureaucracy would be set up, the Housing Corporation of America. The report also calls for federal leadership in creating new sources of capital for low- and moderate-income housing, increased emphasis on preserving and improving the existing stock of low- and moderate-income housing, "a complete modernization" of existing public housing, tax policies that stimulate development of new low- and moderate-income housing, rental assistance tied to federal housing quality standards, improved access to federal mortgage insurance (easier down payments, for example), continued support for the current housing finance system, renewed and extended efforts to combat discrimination in housing, and special emphasis on rural housing.

The mainstream theory is that housing for low-income families and individuals will never be profitable in an unregulated free market but that such housing can be produced successfully both publicly and privately with the proper mixture of subsidies and other palliatives. Open discussion centers around which programs work best and cost least. The unstated agenda is to ensure something for all the important players in the housing industry to guarantee their political support in the passage of new laws and the adoption of new or revised policies.

The NHTF comprises a broad spectrum of leaders from the U.S. housing industry. They know how to produce housing. But the task force has given short shrift to the most critical element in the problem—local government practices. Despite any programs it may add to those already in effect, then, little progress will be made. Madeline Landau has called the continuous addition and revision of programs to solve a problem "hyperinnovation." She traces the history of the War on Poverty in a monograph, *Race, Poverty and the Cities* (1988), and attributes many of the failures of these efforts to a constant resort to changing and adding programs, making the whole so complicated and diffuse that no one understood how it was expected to work. The system survived as long as it did (most parts are still alive, some quite healthy) because so many people had a stake in each of its parts, not because they added up to some conceptual whole.

The task force report's recommendations are another example of hyperinnovation.[1] These recommendations might also be called "comprehensive tinkering."

Many broad-based study groups do the same thing: it is in the nature of the beast. Because everyone participating has a different agenda, it is impossible to focus on any one thing as primary. When the task force leaders try to, they are likely to offend members whose ox is gored. Such task forces have difficulty saying that any existing program is unnecessary: each such determination will offend someone whose support is needed. It is expedient, then, to include something in the recommendations for every participant.

Like many other proposals, those of the NHTF include recommendations for direct government construction subsidies. These, however, do not work as a policy for producing low- and moderate-income housing, although sometimes they appear to. Such subsidies may produce several hundred housing units here and there, but hundreds of thousands are needed each year—and only the private market has the potential to produce such volume. Chester Hartman, a leading socialist whose views are discussed at length below, inadvertently makes this point:

> In the forty-five years since we began subsidizing housing for poor people . . . all of those programs together, rural and urban, have provided roughly 4.5 million subsidized housing units. That is what the private building industry provided in two good years, back-to-back.[2]

Nonprofit housing corporations should be encouraged for their good work. Whether federal cash subsidies should support the nonprofit corporations is a separate question; William Tucker believes not, and I agree with him. What such entities can accomplish is minuscule compared with the need, and they distract the public's attention from solutions that might work.

The fundamental problem with the NHTF proposal, however, is that it has glossed over the main problem. Rouse and his colleagues are as close to the political center in their housing views as Ellwood and his on welfare and jobs (see Chapter 4). The difference is that Ellwood's position is grounded in an analysis of the fundamental dynamics currently operating in the welfare-jobs situation, while the NHTF has simply stapled together many ideas, all of them perhaps true to a degree. Ellwood has reconceptualized the issues based on analysis and then told us what to eliminate, not just what to add.

MITCH SNYDER and the National Coalition for the Homeless have a different point of view. This socialist position, based on the class-struggle theories of Karl Marx, has been developed over many years by Chester Hartman and others associated with the Institute for Policy Studies (IPS) in Washington, D.C. Those of this persuasion want to take housing "for all consumers, renters, and owners" out of the profit sector and put it into nonprofit ownership with government aid. The current IPS position is set forth in *Safety Network* (October 1989), the newsletter of the National Coalition for the Homeless:

1. The creation of a large social sector for new, rehabilitated, and existing housing, to which all government subsidies would be directed; this housing would never be sold for profit;
2. Elimination of the principal housing cost for all consumers, renters, and owners—the repayment of money borrowed to build or purchase units—by substituting one-time up-front capital grants and permanently retiring the existing debt on already built units;
3. Adequate government funding—$49 billion a year under the Dellums bill, H.R. 1142, $89 billion under the maximum option outlined in the program.[3]

Safety Network calls the IPS booklet "a key resource for all interested in the creation of decent, safe, affordable housing." It says the "booklet places critical information . . . into the hands of . . . grassroots advocates" and "bring[s] vital concepts into the hands of local shelter providers, housing activists, and non-profit developers, while providing factual accounts of American families in crisis."[4]

When Hartman was living in the San Francisco Bay area in 1976, he helped IPS with a housing blueprint specifically for Berkeley, California. The local socialists and Communists had not yet achieved a majority on the city council, as they did shortly thereafter, so Berkeley's extreme form of rent control had not yet been implemented. IPS stated its position without reservation:

> Community ownership of housing and real estate is the ultimate goal . . . approached through tenant unions, rent control, a neighborhood preservation ordinance, rehabilitation and code enforcement programs, and cooperative ownership conversion. Each of the these reforms is intended as an interim step towards cooperative and community-owned housing by limiting property speculation and thus deflating or partially expropriating income property values.[5]

If the profits are completely removed from building housing, a step at a time, ultimately the government will have to build it: this is the IPS goal.

Hartman's IPS colleague Jill Hamberg wrote a laudatory article on Cuba's housing policy that was published in 1986. She set forth Cuba's program as a model "in sharp contrast to the rest of Latin America." "Cuban families," she wrote, "enjoy security of tenure and low housing costs that would be the envy of many U.S. and Western European households." Since the purpose of rent control is to expropriate property, there is no need for it in socialist Cuba. According to Hamberg, Fidel Castro decided against setting maximum rents because they would be "an administrative nightmare to enforce." He anticipated complaints "about exorbitant rent levels" but believed that "the only way to overcome this situation . . . [was] to build more housing."[6]

Rent control favors existing tenants by holding down their rents, but it tends to reduce the availability of housing to all prospective new tenants and raises the rent of uncontrolled housing. Although it helps low-income renters who stay in the same apartment for many years, its principal long-term effect is to reduce the profitability of rental housing and thereby to encourage its provision by government. With socialism, rent control is unnecessary. It is, in Castro's words, simply "an administrative nightmare."

Not only is rent control unfair to prospective tenants and inhibiting to production of rental housing, but also it is often,

perhaps typically, a socioeconomically regressive form of expro-
priation. Tucker shows that landlords in New York City are usually
from the working class. Most own only a few units. The biggest
landlord in the city owns only a tiny proportion of the units. In
an Arthur D. Little survey of 700 landlords, only 49 percent had
completed high school. The skills required for landlords have
typically been janitorial, so landlords are typically carpenters
and plumbers, not real estate moguls.[7] Buying the place next door
and fixing it up has often in the past been a step in accumulat-
ing capital taken by working families. It has been a way of
acquiring economic security without a college education, the other
principal method being to save, borrow to start a small business,
and make that business a success through relying on the work
of everyone in the family. Most landlords are not members of
the new upper–middle class, a certificated elite which has
achieved both its social and its economic status through higher
education. Instead, landlords mostly come from the infamous
"school of hard knocks" that achieves its status directly through
working and acquiring capital.

The conflict between landlords and tenants in New York City,
Berkeley, Santa Monica, and other cities is essentially a class
conflict, but a type opposite of what most people think. Tenants
working for rent control in those cities tend to be members
of the educated middle class, whereas landlords are of the
working class. Looking back on his experience as a member of
the Berkeley City Council, William Segesta observed, "During
the public hearings over rent control, it became obvious that
if Berkeley did have a working class, it was the landlords
themselves."[8] Gregory McConnell resigned as rent control chief
in Berkeley. "The only blacks I ever saw in my office," he said,
"were landlords"—and the only Asians. At tenant meetings, he
said, "All I'd see were affluent yuppies, college students, and what
I would call the 'perennial hippies.' "[9] James Baker, head of a
landlord group in Santa Monica, explained why rent control has
been turned down by Long Beach voters even though 66 percent of city residents are renters. "You have to have a very large
tenant majority, but you also have to have an educated elite,"
he said, to pass rent control legislation. Long Beach, he added,
is a working class town. Not so in such rent-control towns as

Beverly Hills, West Hollywood, Santa Monica, and Berkeley.[10] Tucker labels the certificated elite "the paperworking class." This class devises a set of rules, procedures, and legal formalities with which it is quite at home but which are foreign to landlords. When landlords have trouble with the system, tenant representatives complain that these landlords "can't handle the paperwork" and should do something else.[11] The skills of being a landlord have evolved from janitorial to bureaucratic as the paperwork class has succeeded in redefining the rules. Thus do the educated expropriate the wealth of the uneducated.

Recent studies and accumulated experience, as discussed in Chapter 5, have brought into question Tucker's contention that rent control throughout the United States is a major contributor to homelessness. In its moderate forms, rent control does not seem to have discouraged the construction of new rental housing except for the first few years after implementation. The evidence is inconclusive. Rent control, like so many social and economic policies, may affect adversely smaller firms and individual landlords. Larger developers may have an increased competitive advantage in a market changed by moderate forms of rent control. Such rent control policies, often designed specifically to take the profit out of speculation, may have eliminated a once outstanding opportunity for poor families to lift themselves into the middle class through real-estate pyramiding and sweat equity. The left-wing policies are completely unsuitable: they discourage work, throttle wealth-producing economic growth, and set up a separate class of dependent families outside the economic and social mainstream. They are based on an economic theory and a social philosophy that has failed everywhere it has been tried. They impale the poor on the horns of all three of David Ellwood's dilemmas (see Chapter 4).

WILLIAM TUCKER has analyzed the mushrooming of housing costs over the last two decades and demonstrated that the problem lies primarily in local government actions that hinder production— a libertarian approach to the homelessness problem. Because all housing in the United States is produced locally, local government permission is needed to build. Michael Carliner, a respected housing expert, adds credence to Tucker's view of the role of local government:

The local role in regulating land use, construction, and the operation of private housing markets has probably, on balance, been inimical rather than conducive to the production and retention of low-income housing. Exclusionary zoning (such as requirements that lots be larger than necessary) and other controls tend to raise the cost of housing and direct new construction toward the high end of the market. Overly strict building codes have inhibited the construction and rehabilitation of low-cost housing. Housing codes have encouraged abandonment. While these codes ostensibly protect poor people, they effectively rank homelessness as preferable to substandard housing.[12]

Tucker goes further, demonstrating that local government has been not merely "on balance, inimical" to low-income housing, but profoundly so to those of low income and to newcomers in general. Exclusionary zoning and growth controls present the major problems. As a result, housing is not built because there is nowhere to build it. Tucker believes that local government policies on land use, along with rent control, may explain half of contemporary homelessness.

Tucker has explained the way local governments respond to pressure from constituents who stand to gain much and lose nothing by resisting further development of housing. He attributes housing scarcity to free-lunch "rent-seeking" by present property-owners:

> Residents of any community can improve the value of their homes and turn their community into an exclusive enclave by practicing exclusionary zoning. . . . It is this use of the political system to gain unearned advantages that is at the heart of the housing problem.[13]

If Tucker is correct in this analysis, and I believe he is, there is surprisingly little understanding of the problem either among housing specialists around the country or among advocates for the poor. The NHTF report mentions exclusionary zoning and growth controls only in the details of its discussion and never mentions rent control. Much of the housing literature vastly underrates or ignores completely the role of local government in the housing problem. Perhaps Rouse and the NHTF deserve some credit in the matter, since the casual mention they make gives the local government problem more ink than it usually gets.

While assigning great importance to local government practices for the scarcity of low-income housing, Bradley Inman believes the industry itself is behaving badly. Inman has compared the U.S. housing industry of the 1980s to the U.S. auto industry of the 1970s. According to him, the industry is running out of markets for expensive houses; during the 1990s developers may have difficulty finding buyers. Yet developers have done nothing to prepare themselves to produce smaller, less expensive houses. Even as family size was declining in the 1980s, houses continued to get larger. Inman recalled that in 1949 the average house size was 800 square feet for a family of 4.2 members. Today's houses cover nearly 2,000 square feet; yet the average family has only 2.3 members. As the auto makers did, the housing industry points elsewhere to explain why it cannot build a smaller, less expensive product. It was too easy to make a profit in the 1980s: the industry "got carried away with the last decade's excesses," said Inman. He believes the industry can, should, and possibly will recognize the need for change and then address unmet needs as market opportunities. Foreign competition may get our housing industry to change, just as it did Detroit. Recently, he pointed out, the first Japanese company announced plans to team up with a U.S. firm to finance a building project. Maybe more of this joint activity is what it will take.[14]

Advocates at the national level assume the solution requires major federal action. They give little or no attention to how policies and practices of either state and local government or the construction industry affect the problem and might be changed without recourse to massive federal intervention. They seem to be unaware that housing construction is one of the most localized industries in America, totally unlike the centralization of automaking. These advocates have come to set the terms of discussion for their counterparts across the country, just as civil rights first and then antipoverty politics have been focused since the early 1960s on getting the federal government to pass laws and create programs.

A recent experience I had in San Francisco illustrates how little attention national advocates pay to local government actions or to practices that local housing developers can easily change. The Center on Budget and Policy Priorities (CBPP) was touring the United States to promote a series of reports that publicized the shortage of affordable housing "in all regions" of the United States and called for "major action on the part of the federal, state, and local governments, as well as the private sector."[15] It held a press conference in San Francisco in April 1990, after which I joined local agency representatives for a briefing on the study findings.

The CBPP study gave no attention whatsoever to differences in the structure of the problem among regions of the country, no look at how local economies work, and no glance at how the problem results from interference with the private market. The only entries about local government in the report were a few words of praise for local promotion of low-income housing. Neither did Edward Lazere, author of the report, mention local government in his oral presentation. CBPP appears to see the state and local government role as that of adding dollars or other support to programs initiated by the federal government. It does not refer to local government prevention of housing development or to ways state and local governments might play primary roles in encouraging housing.

Until I did, no one in the audience had raised any of these issues. The local attendees readily accepted CBPP's national mind-set about public policy, but I felt like an alien. When I asked if there was some reason why the report makes no mention of the effect of local government policies and practices on the housing supply, Lazere's answer was that CBPP is not equipped to deal with local issues because it has a national perspective. No one raised a protest. Lazere's response suggests the need for federations of local institutions that believe in private markets to come into the open, attend these conferences, develop a public position, and focus attention on what is needed to let markets operate.

TUCKER HAS REJECTED most of the past and present federal grant programs that subsidize construction or rehabilitation of low-income housing as being too expensive. With all the added costs under government regulation, a unit of low-income housing costs as much or more to build than a private-market unit of middle-class housing, but its quality is not as good. Administrative capacity and funding limit the potential to build housing this way. Consequently, such programs serve only a small minority of those who need housing. Moreover, it is means tested and therefore stigmatizes. Housing produced by federal grant programs is a form of welfare that adversely affects the people living there (for example, they cannot move without losing the subsidy). Such housing provides too many opportunities for corruption.

Tucker has said nothing about the mainstream superstructure of federal housing subsidies. The tax breaks for home ownership and the mortgage insurance programs that have enabled most middle- and upper-income families in America to buy homes and that have also provided mortgage money at below-market interest rates for the construction of rental units must continue for Tucker's recommendations to work. Tucker suggests that steps be taken to empower the poor to participate in the mainstream housing market—to become responsibly self-governing. Under his program, special housing for the poor would be eliminated; public housing sold to the residents, where feasible; subsidies eliminated for construction or rehabilitation; and housing vouchers issued so the poor can afford the minimum rents in the area (where vacancy rates are high enough). Interference by local government with the housing market should be curtailed, Tucker argues: rent control prohibited and exclusionary zoning and growth controls either outlawed or, more likely, local government jurisdictions made to pay the costs of their policies so that restricting new housing production is no longer a "free good."

Tucker says that if he were secretary of housing and urban development, he would propose to Congress an antihomelessness act that would do these three things:

- double the number of housing vouchers issued by the federal government each year (at a cost of about $5 billion)
- require municipalities that exclude apartments or multifamily homes (usually through down-zoning developed land or refusal to rezone undeveloped land) to compensate property owners and support the construction of multifamily housing in other communities
- abolish rent control except for national wartime emergencies[16]

Cities like New York could set up a fund to help tenants now under rent control adjust to a normal housing market. New York already plans to spend $5.1 billion on rehabilitating 250,000 abandoned units. The money could, Tucker says, be used for his program instead.[17]

Tucker also believes that a change of attitude is important. According to him, we need to develop a positive view toward developers and landlords: without them there is no housing. And we should stop revering as civic heroes no-growth advocates and pseudo-environmentalists. "If we are going to make room for each other in a more crowded America," Tucker observes, "we are all going to have to be a little more tolerant of each other's presence." Taken together, he says, the above actions "should be sufficient to create enough room in the country for all Americans," certainly enough for those "pushed to the fringes of our society and beyond—America's homeless."[18]

Under the "takings" provisions of the Fifth Amendment of the Bill of Rights, "nor shall private property be taken for public use without just compensation," it is foreseeable that an increasingly conservative Supreme Court may make the second two of Tucker's proposed legislative provisions law by court decision. "Sooner or later," he writes,

> some court is going to have to take a look past the fiction that zoning is aimed only at protecting the "health and safety" of the community and admit that the privacy, solitude, and property values of people within the community are also at stake. In addition, someone is going to have to acknowledge that a community's responsibility to future and potential residents is just as important as its responsiveness to the contemporary majority.[19]

Tucker's approach falls short in its failure to recognize that low-income housing is not profitable without government subsidy. All housing in this country is subsidized in one way or another, if only through a tax deduction for mortgage interest. Most middle-class homeowners also benefit from government-subsidized mortgage insurance. Although draconian attempts to increase efficiency might result in the elimination of many federal housing programs and activities, many would either be continued or housing, and not just low-income housing, would find itself in much bigger trouble than it is. Mortgage insurance and tax deductions in support of home ownership and of rental housing construction are relatively simple, administratively inexpensive, and effective. These federal programs do not discourage personal responsibility. Perhaps such programs should be extended to those further down the economic scale.

Most people I talk with do not believe that Tucker's recommendations, even if joined to a healthy package of government subsidies, would enable the private market to solve the housing problem in booming cities such as Los Angeles and the San Francisco Bay area. Rapid job and population growth exerts too much pressure on the availability and price of land. In an area where jobs are growing more rapidly than housing, the market if left to function freely will result in great and geographically distant income segregation attended by heavy, dense traffic. Under a laissez-faire policy, most of the vacancies created as high-income families take the new, upper-end houses will be exported to the communities from which the in-migrants come rather than filtering down to low-income families in the congested metropolis.

In booming cities, the question of how much growth is too much is constantly debated. These cities have no way to sidestep the issue and no objective way to settle the argument over controlling, slowing, or stopping the growth of a city or a metropolitan area. The logic of Tucker's argument is "never." Never is plainly not acceptable; that leaves these choices: control job growth (demand), administer the housing (supply), or let the natural (market) price of housing rise until the inflow and outflow of jobs reach equilibrium. An increase in housing prices pushes the ratio of higher-skilled jobs to lower-skilled jobs continuously upward. The smaller number of low-paid workers have to travel ever-greater distances through more and more traffic. In fact, the market is heading toward equilibrium. Silicon Valley companies, for example, are moving their low-paid jobs to other places as fast as they can. Companies are leaving, but others with higher ratios of managers and professionals are taking their place. Growth control and exclusionary zoning expedite the process, but it would happen anyway. Left alone, the housing market will ultimately achieve an equilibrium between supply and demand. The community, because of high prices and overcrowding, will arrive at the point where it no longer attracts more jobs than it exports. Ultimately, housing prices will stabilize at very high levels, rise further only with inflation or actual improvement of the area, and then decline slowly as the quality of the area deteriorates, or rapidly if the area economy dives. People then leave as rapidly as new people arrive since it is no longer as desirable a place to live. As this process proceeds, the number of homeless will stabilize.

Filtering down usually works in local housing markets but fails where large numbers of in-migrants are attracted to new housing units supposedly created to meet rising local demand. Executives and professionals are largely in a national rather than a local labor market. Manual workers and low-wage workers in general tend to circulate in local or regional labor markets. Houses built for a working-class market, therefore, may not recruit outsiders and may actually result in a filtering down that extends to the poor.[20]

WHICH OF THESE APPROACHES should we use? Federal assistance, in the form of mortgage insurance and loan guarantee programs, generates millions of housing units, either by helping buyers in financing a home or the industry in constructing one. The main problem now is that these programs do not extend down the economic scale far enough to reach low-income families, because housing prices are too high and because the incomes of many families, even with two full-time workers, are too low.

To the extent that any program uses tax money inefficiently— that is, produces the desired result at high unit costs—it retards national growth by taking capital away from more productive uses. Direct construction of federal housing surely has this effect, as does most directly subsidized private construction. Mortgage insurance and other loan guarantees can be carried out efficiently and be used to leverage multiples of the amount directly allocated. Because these policies produce amounts of goods and services comparable to those one might expect if the funds were left in the free market rather than collected as taxes and disbursed as mortgage insurance and loan guarantees, the effect of these programs on national growth should be neutral. The redistributive effect can be positive if these programs are directed to low- and moderate-income families.

Because mortgage insurance and loan guarantees give responsible choices to individuals and families about where to live, such programs need not create ghettos of stigmatized families. Direct housing subsidies and public housing do create such ghettos, weakening a culture of responsible self-governance.

Mainstream programs will continue to fail to provide adequate amounts of low-income housing in growing cities until the local government practices Tucker has described are changed. Building new housing in communities where exclusionary zoning and growth control are predominant has become so difficult and expensive, cautions Stuart Butler, that any increases in federal housing appropriations (such as those recommended by the NHTF) will likely force up prices of existing units instead of creating new ones.[21]

Libertarianism is based on the idea that government should let families and individuals manage their own lives, make their own decisions, and earn their own way in a free market. It is the pure opposite of socialism. The probable result under such a regime would be greatly increased total wealth, huge distributive inequities, and—except for the likelihood of congested living conditions—a good living for anyone quick enough to catch the economic train and strong enough to hang onto its straps. Without some of the mainstream programs that help ordinary people along and without steps to deal with problems that accompany rapid economic growth—such as high land costs—the market may produce enough housing and adequate quality of community life for only those in the train's probably very large first-class section. Those riding in the chair cars will not do so well, but those who fall off this fast-moving train will always be a problem. In view of the severe distributive inequities, libertarianism is not responsible self-governance. The concept of self-governance implies not only that each person or family can take care of itself but also a mutual obligation for the quality of our lives. If it were not for the scarcity of land in a growing economy and the scarcity of related resources such as water and energy, Tucker's program would work well. Most of the time, the market works, and the voluntary transactions that take place form the basis for a healthy social order. Land and water, however, are finite, and not everyone will be able to compete effectively for these resources.

The housing market will perhaps absorb the low-income families and individuals in the rapidly growing cities, or perhaps not. Tucker's policies leave us with the questions: Do we want to live in a world in which economics clearly segregate our lives? Are we willing to allow cities to grow until pleasure and pain come into balance?

The socialist approach fails utterly to meet any of my criteria. One need only look at anywhere it has been tried to see that it slows national growth. Products and services of all kinds are shoddier and scarcer. Senator Moynihan was among the earliest of a series of critics who have demonstrated that in spite of its fundamental claim to improve fairness, socialism does not smooth out disparities of wealth, income, or political power but instead makes them even worse.[22] Socialists typically look like liberals, and many of them like to think of themselves as liberals. Usually they simply join with liberals in advocating more and bigger housing programs. On occasion they push adoption of more extreme policies, and sometimes they succeed, as in the case of Berkeley's rent control.

Many socialists have prominent roles in movements advocating low-income housing policies and other matters concerning the problem of homelessness. The best example may be Chester Hartman. Recently I received a bulletin advertising the most important conference yet to occur on housing for the homeless. Three agencies of the federal government were to sponsor it. At the invitation of federal officials, who were aware only of Hartman as a prominent housing expert, he was invited to serve as conference chairman. When the significance of this appointment was noted at a higher level, a cochairman was selected as well. Hartman was to write the final report of the conference, but this plan too was changed. Still, he played a strong role, as he has done over time in the American housing policy arena. Socialists, however, seriously harm public policy in two ways. First, their insistence, often through research carried out specifically for its propaganda value, that more federal funds and programs are needed diverts attention from the potential for improvement through strengthening state and local self-governance. In this approach, the socialists are natural allies of most government program officials. This alliance surely has some effect on increasing the number of federal programs and the amount of money spent on them. (From this perspective, Hartman fits nicely into the chairmanship of a government-sponsored conference on housing.) Second, their relentless pressure for the expansion of personal rights, such as a right to housing, carries no promise of commensurate responsibilities. Berkeley's rent control is one of their more visible successes in this campaign. Discredited almost everywhere it has been adopted, socialism remarkably holds its own here.

A workable approach must incorporate mainstream loan-guaranty programs such as those administered by the Federal Housing Administration (FHA), the Farmers Home Administration (FmHA), and the Veterans Administration ("GI loans"). Such an approach, like Tucker's, will emphasize that a change in local government policies and practices is essential. Several particularly worthy existing and proposed policies and programs already contain some of the elements of a workable housing strategy.

SAN DIEGO DECIDED to employ municipal land-use policy as the principal means to get low-income housing built downtown by the for-profit housing industry. The city kept subsidies either to developers or renters to the minimum possible. The free market, rather than a means test, determined who would rent the units. If the policy worked as intended, predominantly low-income individuals and couples chose to rent these units.

To achieve its objective, the city zoned the downtown redevelopment area for apartments designed to appeal only to a market of low-income singles and couples. It then sold the land to private developers at full market value.[23] To hold construction costs down and to limit market appeal to low-income renters, the city modified several building code provisions as part of its zoning decision: units had only partial kitchen and bathroom facilities, and they could be as small as 120 square feet, although most are larger (the maximum is 220 square feet). Since the development area is within walking distance of most downtown facilities and near public transit, units were not required to have parking spaces at a full one-to-one ratio. Costs were further reduced by allowing sprinklers as a substitute for various fire-resistance requirements and for some of the fire extinguishers and hoses.

These and related provisions kept the land and construction costs of the units low enough—in one project about $16,200 per unit—that low-income singles and couples with 50–80 percent of the area's median income could afford to pay the full rent. The rents, ranging between about $270 and $400 per month, provided an adequate profit to the owners. Minimum-wage workers, SSI recipients, students, and retired persons have rented them, improving the living conditions of these individuals and freeing other SRO housing to filter down to renters with even less money. A low-interest loan for the purpose has enabled the landlord to set aside 20 percent of the units for very-low-income renters—those with less than 50 percent of the median income in the area—at $258 or less per month.

Since San Diego started this program in 1987, 1,000 units of new housing have been completed, and 1,000 more are scheduled for completion in 1990. HUD secretary Jack Kemp visited this project recently and has since modified federal mortgage regulations to include single-resident-occupancy hotels. In the past, the National Housing Act was interpreted to prohibit using FHA insurance for SRO hotels, which were defined as transient lodging. By requiring SROs to set up leases for a minimum of a month, even though residents may be expected to pay the rent weekly, HUD now covers this housing with FHA insurance. HUD is also waiving the usual rules prohibiting discrimination against families with children.

With the San Diego experience in mind, the Bush administration has initiated a nationwide program of mortgage finance assistance for SRO housing. According to Kenneth R. Harney, editor of the *Washington Real Estate Newsletter,* SROs financed in the national program, like those in San Diego, will carry no direct federal subsidy.[24] They will depend for their profitability on the market itself, supplemented only by any state and local code waivers, tax abatements, grants, or loans.

It remains for a city to do the same type of thing for family housing—surely more of a challenge. Possibly what can be done without subsidy for singles and couples, who require only one room with few amenities, cannot be done for families with children. Around the country, funds are increasingly being appropriated to improve the affordability of housing. In California, for example, taxpayers voted historically unprecedented billions of dollars for low-income housing in the two most recent elections. The federal government spends $250 million per year on low-cost rental housing in California alone, and a low-income-housing tax credit approved by Congress in 1986 has, according to columnist Inman, just now become "an attractive tax-avoidance technique for corporations and investors and a plentiful source of funds for low-cost housing."[25] In addition, Inman cites several other new sources of funding. The problem increasingly will be where to put the housing: not in my back yard.

In the 1990s many military bases will close, with much of the land becoming subject to local government allocation. Huge chunks of this land are in housing-short cities; thousands of acres in several choice parts of the San Francisco Bay area, for example, will be available. Competitive bidding by private developers could be opened on this land with conditions spelled out: a certain percentage of it to go for residential housing with a certain percentage of this housing set aside for high-density, low-rise, multibedroom rental units. Owners need place no upper income limitations on rentals, but a surplus of rental units would be produced, land and construction costs would be kept down by the way the bidding process was carried out, and the relatively spartan characteristics of the units would, as the San Diego SRO program has demonstrated, be unattractive to high-income clients.

IN ST. LOUIS, housing and social service programs for homeless families have been set up that embody community-building leadership principles I have also found in Portland, Oregon. Ecumenical Housing Production Corporation (EHPC) is a public-private partnership that brings together business, nonprofit, and religious leaders to tackle housing problems. Eight years after the first such meeting, many of the original participants still serve on EHPC's board of directors. A big difference between Portland and St. Louis, according to Lynn Broeder, director of EHPC, is that in St. Louis officials of the county and the housing authority have been "very little help." She said their main role has been watching critically. "It never lets up," said Broeder. "No matter how good a job we have done, if we screw up tomorrow they will be on us."[26]

EHPC specializes in families with children in need of three or four bedroom homes. This task can be difficult since houses suitable for large families are particularly uncommon in many of today's low-income neighborhoods. The company seeks houses and lots in stable neighborhoods with public transportation and good schools, purchasing and rehabilitating run-down houses and sometimes building new ones.[27]

Tenants are selected carefully—thirty hours are spent on each tenant application. Many are multiproblem families, and EHPC finds a high incidence of various sorts of abuse, typical in almost any large group of homeless families or individuals. But EHPC ensures that the families selected are headed by adults who, according to its own statement, "have goals for the future for both themselves and their families." About 60 percent of the adults have full- or part-time jobs, 20 percent are looking for work, and 15 percent are involved in job training or education programs.

The residents are not viewed or treated as victims but as reponsible members of the community. EHPC seeks to give the homeless, in the old phrase, "a hand up, not a handout," and to this end, EHPC makes sure families accept their responsibilities. Paying the rent on time is a must, for example. According to Broeder, about 20 percent are behind in their rent at any given time. EHPC counselors encourage residents to see that paying their rent on time and keeping up the house and yard are ways they maintain a position in the community. The house, in EHPC's culture, is the physical embodiment of the residents' relationship to the community and to each other. As both a symbol of this culture and a practical device, EHPC makes certain that every one of its houses has a working lawnmower. In the words of one commentator on the EHPC program, "Tough-love is sometimes needed, but because it is love and relationships are personal, centered on the well-being and advancement of each family, the program works."[28]

As of early 1990, EHPC had 111 houses and apartments with a total of over 500 persons, 300 or so of them children. These families have an average income of less than $7,000 per year, about one-fifth the median income in the St. Louis metropolitan area. They must pay 30 percent of their income in rent; HUD vouchers pay the rest. Single parents head 85 percent of these families. The group has a 98 percent on-time rent payment record, and twenty-one families have achieved "independence": that is, they have moved off the rent subsidy.

According to EHPC's figures, client rentals, including HUD vouchers, account for 54 percent of the corporation's income. Donations make up the balance—19 percent from industry, 17 percent from churches and synagogues, 3 percent from foundations, 3 percent from individuals, and 4 percent miscellaneous. Federal mortgage insurance and tax policies favoring nonprofit housing developers significantly reduce expenses.[29]

One of several important aspects that distinguish this program is its reliance on the social fabric of the community. It emphasizes using, and thereby strengthening, the role of traditional institutions such as the churches and the business leadership structure, and it relies extensively on volunteers instead of creating or augmenting governmental or nonprofit bureaucracies of professionals in downtown offices. The staff of EHPC includes a few experts that deal with complex financing arrangements, but much of the technical work is done by volunteers from local business firms, churches, and the public. Although the job would be vastly more difficult without federal programs, these programs are not allowed to define the EHPC's effort. EHPC builds and helps to sustain the self-governing ability of the community at the same time that it deals with the immediate and long-term problems of homeless families.

HOUSING VOUCHERS are useful in communities with surplus housing; actually, according to Irving Welfeld of HUD, the great majority of American cities have a surplus of housing. The 1987 vacancy rate of 8.1 percent nationally and 8.9 percent in central cities was "the highest level in over two decades."[30] Even California's vacancy rates reached a twenty-year high in 1987, despite low vacancies in some cities.[31] Welfeld points out, however,

> an adequate housing supply can coexist with a housing crisis for families and individuals who cannot afford to pay the rent for the available housing. Housing does filter down, but if the rent roll does not equal the operating expenses the housing will filter right out of the market.[32]

Housing vouchers can bring the amount a renter can afford to pay up to the level of the apartment's operating expenses in such a market and provide for a profit margin.

Portland, Oregon, is one example of a community with a housing surplus, partly because of a slow economy and partly because of policies local government has followed over the past twenty years. Tim Gallagher, executive aide to Mayor Bud Clark, believes that Portland's biggest asset is its readily available stock of low- and moderate-income housing.[33] Its availability, he says, is a product of recent recessions in the lumber industry and, to a lesser extent, of a city policy requiring approval to demolish a dwelling. In Portland, property taxes have actually declined in recent years, after an exodus of about 5,000 people in the early 1980s left many housing units abandoned. In the late 1980s some houses were still selling for $5,000 to $10,000 in this city, even though since 1987 Portland has bounced back from the recession. Families on AFDC or earning the minimum wage can still find a place to live, and with a voucher they can do better.

Housing vouchers are particularly appropriate for working families, less so for those on welfare, according to Robert B. Hawkins, Jr., of the Institute for Contemporary Studies (ICS).[34] Private landlords often prefer not to rent to families on welfare. Homeless families, as a rule, are likely to be even less desirable. "Landlords of low-rent buildings," says Irving Welfeld, "have to be selective about their tenants—given the precarious nature of their operation," and the "housing homeless" usually become homeless "because of non-payment of rent or less than standard behavior."[35] Despite vouchers, even in a market favorable to renters, many of the homeless still have difficulty finding a place to rent.

Vouchers do not work well in booming markets where the production of housing cannot keep up with demand. They help the lucky recipient who finds a place he can afford with the aid of the voucher, but they exert an upward pressure on all rents through the increase in demand they create. From the standpoint of the local housing economy, the problems just get worse.

PUBLIC-PRIVATE PARTNERSHIPS, such as the Bridge Housing Corporation in the San Francisco Bay area, could potentially enlist large amounts of private capital and serve as an instrument to direct resources into housing development for low-income families. Companies invest capital in Bridge partly because the lack of affordable housing for workers imperils their own growth. Bridge's board of directors is made up of top San Francisco Bay area corporate leaders (finance, construction, and real estate), politicians, and academics. The company's capital base comes primarily in the form of donations from corporations and foundations. Bridge plows its surpluses back into new projects.[36]

After 859 housing starts in 1988, Bridge went on to become the 125th largest housing developer in the United States and the first nonprofit to appear in the industry's top 200.[37] By then Bridge, in its sixth year, had over 1,700 units completed and occupied and about 1,000 more in various stages of planning. The units are located in about thirty different places, including some choice ones, around the San Francisco Bay. They are beautiful.[38]

Bridge is able to offer its houses at below-market prices because of donated capital including land, nonprofit tax advantages, tax-exempt bonds sold by local governments, surplus public land purchases—unused school property in particular—and local government land-use concessions, such as higher density allowances and waiver or deferral of development fees.[39]

Bridge's strategy is to take advantage of all the laws, regulations, needs, and sentiments that favor nonprofit developers and low-income home buyers and renters to develop high-quality units affordable to low-income families. There are three crucial differences between what Bridge and San Diego are doing. First, of course, Bridge builds for families instead of for individuals and couples. Second, Bridge builds units whose market value greatly exceeds what buyers or renters are asked to pay for them. When its most recently completed 114 units (appraised at up to $400,000) were placed on the market at between $99,000 and $149,000, 3,271 families applied.[40] Bridge chose the winners by lottery. Third, buyers and renters must pass a means test: because the units are sold below market value, in addition to a minimum income to qualify for their purchase, there is also a maximum. On the other hand, to qualify for a loan to purchase a unit, applicants must have been at a job for at least two years, have good credit, and be able to meet the monthly payments.[41]

Bridge has bought up projects of failed savings and loan institutions to convert them into low-income housing. It paid American Savings $800,000 for one in Pacifica, California, spent four years persuading city officials to double the number of units allowed, got the voters to agree to an exemption from Pacifica's growth-control plan, raised $1.8 million by selling low-income tax credits to Chevron, got the city to defer its development fees, and secured $5.5 million in tax-exempt bond financing. If American Savings had been able to do all this, maybe it would not have gotten in trouble. There are several reasons why American Savings could not do all of this, though: first, Bridge is brilliantly run and superbly connected; and second, the laws provide non-profits many breaks that the profit-making institutions do not get. Mike McKissick, a for-profit developer, expressed his own mixed feelings about nonprofits' taking over such failed projects: "If you were to give the so-called "failed" developers all of the special tax credits and exemptions from zoning rules and development fees, they could probably make this project pencil out too."[42]

What this developer was asking is close to what San Diego has done to enable private developers to make a profit building and renting SRO housing at free-market rents. Where there are such city policies and activities, it does not require the brilliance of a Bridge Housing Corporation to do the job: mere mortals can do it. Whether San Diego's way can succeed for working families remains to be seen.

Giving nonprofits privileges that mainstream institutions in the same business do not have is fundamentally harmful because it undermines the capacity of these institutions. This practice differs from giving special breaks to museums and symphonies whose purpose is not economic. Making houses available to the poor that middle-class families cannot afford weakens the main-stream system of incentives. The way to get housing built for everyone is to restore the filtering down process and, where that is not enough, to zone land so that profit-making developers can build housing that is less expensive, that only low-income families will want to buy or rent, and that tenants move out of as their economic conditions improve. Bridge, for all its talent and resources, produces fewer than 1,000 units of housing per year. Only the private market can attain the necessary production level to alleviate the housing shortage for low-income people.

PORTLAND'S CENTRAL CITY CONCERNED (CCC) is an agency that provides housing for clients enrolled in substance abuse programs sponsored by other agencies. CCC is a nonprofit corporation that runs SRO housing in Burnside, the downtown, skid-row area of Portland, Oregon. In business since 1978, the agency has managed SRO buildings and owns three of them with a total of 719 beds. Accommodations vary: some buildings have central kitchens and dining facilities, while others have pullman kitchens in the rooms; some units share bath and shower rooms, and others have private baths. The management does not divide males and females, but the ratio—this could be expected anywhere in the United States—runs abut six-to-one male, with no children in residence.

CCC only incidentally supports alcohol and drug treatment programs. One building has forty-five units on an alcohol- and drug-free floor where, Don Hendrix, CCC director, told me, monitoring is "heavy" and eviction is "instant." The limit for residence there is ninety days.[43] Other than that one floor, no special place is provided for recovering addicts. They live with the general SRO population, which includes many individuals actively drinking and taking drugs. One of the buildings, not owned by CCC, even has a liquor store on the ground floor. As a landlord, CCC evicts anyone the neighbors complain about enough or who appears to be endangering the premises. The place, then, is much like an apartment or a room one might rent in a "good neighborhood." The rooms are smaller, of course, and the rent is cheaper, as the tenants live on very low earnings, some form of welfare, or a small pension.

Kathy Stout of Hendrix's staff said that one of the SROs has a drug problem. Laws that make eviction procedurally complex make such problems in the SRO hard to solve. The federally funded legal services agency promoted these laws in the legislature to protect tenants against major landlords seen as unfair. CCC works cooperatively with the local bar association's legal aid society, which, Stout observed, "understands what CCC is trying to do"—trying to provide a safe and healthy environment for low-income tenants. Under these legal conditions it takes six months to "clean up" a building, she continued. Organizationally separate from CCC, Burnside Projects runs the city's largest homeless shelter on the problem building's first floor.[44]

More difficulties are occasioned by the fact that the outdoor social life of the SRO tenants takes place mainly on the local sidewalks, as it has going back to the period before CCC was founded. The numbers of people on the street attract drug dealers to the area. Stout was unsure whether the dealers use the crowds mainly as camouflage for dealings with outsiders who meet them there or as their primary market.

CCC usually hires the managers of these SROs from among the former tenants, Stout explained. The janitor, the desk clerk, the building assistant, and the manager are all likely to be former tenants doing the job at the minimum wage. In addition, the building assistant gets half his rent free and the building manager gets all his rent free plus some extra cash. A small pool of money even enables building managers to take a vacation.

These SROs run at about 90 percent occupancy. During past summers, in spite of affordable vacancies for the homeless at CCC, numbers of homeless have continued to sleep under Portland's bridges. In 1989 it was better; some who had previously slept under these bridges moved into the SROs. Stout has interpreted this as a sign of progress, a sign that trust is building between the homeless of Portland and the agencies trying to help them.

CCC's Everett Hotel set aside a cluster of twenty-eight rooms for clients in outpatient substance abuse treatment programs operated by the Burnside Project. These clients' rent is paid from their SSI, Veterans Administration, or general assistance check.[45]

Burnside pays client utility bills from federal Low Income Energy Assistance Program funds. There are no full-time staff. The part-time manager who oversees the facility and acts as landlord, "makes sure that everything is okay," in Burnside director Jean DeMaster's words. A council of tenants enforces house rules and forces people out if they are drinking.[46]

Burnside case managers handle responsibility for the clients in treatment. The state Department of Corrections supports four of these case managers. Burnside takes in 600 people a year from the jails, about 120 of them long-term prisoners. Burnside assigns twenty-three corrections clients to each of the four case managers. These clients are among those the agency places in CCC's hotel rooms.

Another CCC building, the Estate Hotel, has a resident manager and fifty-one rooms, all of them set aside for clients in treatment and follow-up. Physically, although these two hotels are SROs, they are organized as recovery hotels—set up and staffed to provide a needed measure of stability in support of client recovery. Burnside places clients in one of these recovery hotels immediately after five days in detoxification.

In addition to the outpatient treatment Burnside provides with CCC's hotels, DeMaster's agency also operates an inpatient program. She called it "a live-in treatment center" for "beginners"— abusers who still have a family support system. After detox, they move into the center, for intensive treatment. Either it works for them, or it does not. During treatment, the clients begin a twelve-step program that will continue after treatment is completed. After intensive treatment, they go home and either stick to their decision or not. Intensive treatment, she said, is like "taking a course." It is pointless to take it more than a few times.

THESE SEVERAL EXAMPLES of programs and policies are quite varied, but they have some important things in common: first, they are focused locally, recognizing that the housing industry in America is local; second, they treat the market as a tool rather than as a problem to be circumvented; third, they recognize the importance of the policies and practices of local government in housing. These three elements are necessary ingredients in any low-income housing policy for it to succeed in producing large numbers of suitable and affordable housing units where they are needed.

The largest underutilized potential for progress in housing currently resides in state government, and advocates would do well to campaign at the state capitols. The reason for this is that states set the rules under which local governments must operate, not that states have money to spend on housing. Most, as a matter of fact, do not have money to spend, but this should be no impediment to action. The principal need from the state level is for leadership in governing, not for programs and money.

Where there is money to deliver, as the voters through initiative ballots have recently instructed California to do, this money should be incorporated into a strategy to change local practices so that the market can function more effectively, not as a substitute for local leadership or the market. As we have seen, only the market has the potential to solve the low-income housing problem. And as we have also seen, intelligently designed and managed policies at all three levels of government are necessary to provide an environment in which the market can work.

II

Leadership

7

The Big Argument

FROM LONG EXPERIENCE working at the administrative level with antipoverty and United Way officials from social work backgrounds and from public statements and writings of both academic and professional welfare leaders, I had not gained much hope that social workers could help solve America's difficult problems. What I heard from their leaders was "give us more money" and "the poor are victims." Local social workers typically seem to see their work as "mobilizing resources" to support agency budgets or at best to assist clients in "meeting their needs." Such a picture has given me little confidence in the ability of the social work profession to address problems of poverty and homelessness. During the research on this book, however, I changed my mind. What the universities teach and what the public leaders and typical government bureaucrats in these professions assert are very different, both philosophically and practically, from what thousands of good social workers across the country do.[1]

The fundamental and dramatic difference is in the allocation of individual responsibility. High-profile leaders and academics overwhelmingly emphasize the victimization of the poor by "the system," placing little or no responsibility on persons for their own condition. In contrast, effective social workers insist that their clients accept a measure of personal responsibility for their condition, for improving it, and even for helping others.[2]

THE EXPERIENCE OF Elouise Greene, whose day job is counseling students in an Oakland, California, community college, illustrates the issues centering around the concept of responsibility. One day after responding to an advertisement in the *West County Times,* she found herself working evenings too, as the swing-shift counselor-manager of a rather unusual homeless shelter in downtown Richmond. Sponsored by the Volunteers of America (VOA), this shelter was intended as a three-month experiment while VOA prepared to use the facility for another purpose.

Greene was to start the program and run it. She was told that the doors would close at 9:30 P.M. and that clients could sleep in the chairs, for there were no beds in *this* shelter, only chairs and other furnishings, particularly a television set. Greene's shift was to be 6 P.M. to 2 A.M.—from after the soup kitchen that used the building in the daytime closed until the night replacement came on duty. The program was announced at meals in the soup kitchen, and word was put out in the community.

At first only a handful of men came, and sometimes one or two women. Within a few weeks about three dozen came regularly. About 75 percent were black males, generally between the ages of thirty and fifty. Sometimes a few teenagers showed up who had been booted out of their family home for the night. Participants would watch TV, fall asleep in the chairs, play cards or dominoes, or sometimes fight. Greene had to referee the fights. All knew it was a temporary program.

After three weeks of this, Greene concluded that they were wasting their time. So she arranged the men and the few women into a circle and asked them each to say something about why he or she was homeless. She challenged them: this place is closing in four weeks, she said. "What will you do in the time remaining to deal with your problem?" She used the chalkboard: "What is homelessness?" "Why can't you look for a job?" Each person wrote on the board what he or she needed to become productive.

Words appeared on the board: toiletries, a place to clean up, clothing, housing, jobs, job training, and so forth. To make them feel responsible for each others' needs, she organized them into committees, each with responsibility for one of the needed items. Every day, each person took on an assignment, reporting back to the committee on something he or she had done that day for the group. The groups developed housing lists, arranged buddy systems to live together in multibedroom houses or apartments, found hotels that would give them shampoo, wrote letters to Safeway asking for food contributions, requested surplus clothing or donations of suits to wear for job hunting.

When Greene noticed that on the first two days of the month very few men were present, she asked why. It was explained to her that most of the men were on crack and that all the men were on either general assistance or Supplementary Security Income (SSI); they took the check on the first of the month and visited crack houses. She learned that at least three-fourths of them had had a family and a place to live before—before they began using crack cocaine and lying and stealing to support their habit. In most cases, the drug use began about two or three years ago. The families, the extended families, and the friends of these individuals had given up on them and thrown them out.

An experienced hypnotist, Greene decided to try a voluntary hypnosis group. After each committee meeting, those who were interested adjourned to a corner of the room. In the beginning only four of them stayed; eventually she had twenty of them in mass hypnosis. Greene's first hypnotic suggestions were to improve self-esteem and create a positive self-image; she then moved on to encourage personal accountability. After each session, they talked about how they felt. Crack, she found, was definitely the major problem. Only a few in this group of men had a serious problem with alcohol.

Under hypnosis, she asked them to recall and experience their best high. She then told them they did not need the drug to get high, stressing that they were destroying their minds with it. In hypnotic regression, she had taken them back to good times. She observed that drug addicts fall into a hypnotic state easily because they "know the feeling."

Greene said the night shift expressed amazement at the morale of the clients as they left in the morning to undertake their day's responsibilities. She always left them with a posthypnotic suggestion that the next day would be a productive one. They knew, she said, that someone cared and had expectations for them.

About fifty clients were reached before the three-month life of the program expired, according to Greene. She believed these men needed another six months of aftercare to ensure that their new habits held permanently and to internalize the concepts of personal responsibility and accountability that are critical to the success achieved. Early on she said to the men, "No one out there expects you to be any better than you are—an addict, a liar, and a thief." Then she asked them, "Are you satisfied with that?" She cited behavioral transformation as the therapy she practices, referring to the writings of Jim Hoke, particularly *I Would If I Could and I Can.*

"They got themselves into this, and they can get themselves out, with time and a support system," Greene has said. "First they need a place to stay so they can work out the problem." Then she recommends weekly group sessions and a counselor as needed. This approach, she believes, could have achieved much with the men even without the hypnosis component. "If they could clean up their act and stay clean," she claims, "most of these men could return to their homes and families. In that sense, they are not homeless. One problem is that no one asks these people why they are homeless." Everyone has some theory about it. "The key is client responsibility," Greene emphasizes, "and it needs to be built into any program. Agencies make clients dependent on them, strip them of what makes them men." Greene holds that these men are inherently no more "losers" than anyone else.

The program is now over. After the several weeks with Greene, about ten of the men still appear frequently at the soup kitchen. Three have joined the California Conservation Corps. She does not know where the rest have gone. If VOA had decided to make the facility available permanently for the program, it could have been continued for about $125 per day, she says. A political effort was mounted in the community to continue the program, but it was not enough. Anyway, she says, they had a great party at the end of the program.

What Elouise Greene told me was so different from the public and academic face of social work that I decided I needed to go back to sources. I called a friend on the faculty of the University of California, Berkeley, School of Social Welfare, Bob Pruger, for advice. Pruger offered to give me the complementary copies of textbooks he had accumulated in recent years from publishers trying to persuade him to adopt them for his introductory course on the welfare profession. These textbooks, I thought, would give me a good idea what social work students are being taught in the universities. Pruger also suggested I talk to Professor James Leiby, the school's historian of the profession.

Leiby described what he calls the "big argument." The intellectual history of social welfare, he told me, can be seen as an argument between helping individuals adjust to society—that is, individual change—and trying to affect the social and economic environment—that is, institutional change. Those who look to institutional change for a solution insist the problem is capitalism, rugged individualism, and exploitation. This "social action" orientation includes a broad spectrum of views, ranging from the looser perspective that the diverse economic interest groups sometimes get together and sometimes do not to the notion that inequality and injustice are inherent in our system and can be tempered only through a radical change of political and economic structure. The social action range of perspectives has dominated many university schools of social work. Students entering graduate programs seldom object, as they have assimilated the common ideology of American undergraduate educational institutions that the poor and minorities are victims.

The School of Social Welfare at Berkeley, belying the university's public image, is one of the more conservative. More than four out of five of its students are enrolled in a "direct services" track, specializing in a particular group of clients—children, the aging, parents, and even the obese. The faculty, Leiby said, has not interested itself in teaching social action. "Our faculty traditionally," he observed, "has been interested in incremental improvement through legislation rather than radical polemics and 'empowerment.'" "The more academic schools are like this," editorialized Leiby. "We are not much interested in the Glide Memorial approach," he said, referring to an activist church in central San Francisco. Students often come to Berkeley expecting a radical approach, Leiby reported, and his school "tries to make them more realistic."

Leiby contrasted Berkeley's program with San Francisco State University's School of Social Work Education. "I don't know whether this is still true," he said, "but in the 1970s State sought out social activists." As part of its admissions process, he observed that a student committee interviewed the prospective students on their plans to change society with what they learned.

There is no "bill of responsibilities" in America, Leiby pointed out, and as a result arguments in welfare policy are typically couched in terms of rights, often stated as property rights versus human rights. In the welfare field, arguments that favor personal responsibility can be traced more to the religious thought of earlier times than the political—to the notion of a "Protestant ethic." The "success literature" of the nineteenth century was not political but "religio-economic." Husbands in such literature were expected to be good providers—it was their personal responsibility.

The present focus on rights dates to the Progressive Movement of the early 1900s. The emphasis began to shift from individual and community responsibility to social legislation: child protection, housing, health, and social insurance. The religiously based notion of personal responsibility proved awkward for social workers of that period to defend, Leiby explained, as they struggled to fit themselves into a world whose discourse was increasingly secular and "scientific." Most social work had been based on the notion of Christian charity. The residue of this older view can be seen today in the profession as a belief in solidarity, "caring-sharing," self-determination in the sense that people want to do their part, one for all, mutual help among groups. In earlier times, caring-sharing was not conceived of as a government responsibility. Then when people were in difficulty, social workers, or "charity workers," as they were often called, worked to reestablish natural support groups. Today, caring-sharing is seen by many as the responsibility of government.

Throughout, social workers have struggled to attain professional status for their activity. In the late 1900s they made up a very small part of the labor force in human services, holding positions mainly in child welfare and mental health. Their largest single employer today is the military—particularly the Veterans Administration. In the active service they often work with the families of soldiers.

The profession should "get it straight," according to Leiby, "that an MSW [Master of Social Work or Social Welfare] needs to see both A and B: (A) to be committed to helping people take responsibility for their own lives (B) in a society where opportunities are available for them to do so." Social work is concerned with the art of living together, in Leiby's view, and the notions of personal responsibility and social responsibility should be reflected clearly in the ethical code of social work and in the doctrine taught in schools.[3] Applicants for jobs in social work should be advised about that point of view. The functions of professional social work are different from medical therapy or legal advocacy, closer to the work of the clergy than to medicine, the law, or the military.

The principal organization speaking for the social work profession is the National Association of Social Workers (NASW). It is usually unrepresentative, said Leiby, because two important groups are too busy to support it—executives of large welfare agencies and faculty of social welfare schools (faculty assigned to assist students in obtaining field work assignments are an exception). The profession will not be strong until academic and administrative leaders participate more, though. While NASW does not pay much attention to social work in the military, noted Leiby, the association looks kindly on private employee assistance programs, much the same sort of activity. It is a handicap that the most visible leadership group in the welfare profession does not involve more of the intellectual and administrative leaders of the profession and practitioners in the military and corrections.

Another Berkeley professor, Paul Terrell, continued the analysis. He told me that throughout the history of social work a point of view has prevailed that the psychotherapeutic approach and the community organization approach are mutually exclusive—workers in these two activities are not really in the same business. But they are both called social workers and taught in social work schools; they coexist in the NASW. In part because these two forms of practice stem from different and conflicting theories, no principle in the social work profession declares that one is to assist the client to take or to share responsibility for his own situation. To make an issue of this point would be institutionally divisive. In part for this reason, the field overwhelmingly ascribes most problems to social and economic institutions rather than to individual decision.

Pruger's stack of complimentary textbooks from publishers adds up to fourteen. Searching the appendixes, in one I found the NASW Code of Ethics mentioned by Leiby. Reading through the code, I could find no ethical requirement, explicit or implicit, that even suggests that social workers should help clients assume responsibility for their own lives. But the code insists that an ethical social worker "advocate changes in policy and legislation to improve social conditions and to promote social justice."

Searching the indexes of all fourteen books for the word *responsibility,* I could not find it. Where I find a mild implication of client responsibility is in brief discussions of "case management" that appear in a few of the books: the client is to agree with the case worker upon a case management plan and to do his part in carrying it out. This important notion is buried within hundreds of pages of text about social needs, service delivery issues, social change strategies, funding, women's issues, social justice, professional associations, organizational theory, social problems, racism, the coming-out process for lesbians, the nuclear threat, and what the Pentagon's budget means to the reader.[4] A few of the books mention helping clients to achieve independence and self-reliance,[5] but none mentions their being helped to assume responsibility for their condition. I believe that in instances the writer intends this view, but important words are left unsaid.

Social workers I talk with emphasize responsibility repeatedly. For the social workers I perceive as most effective in achieving positive client outcomes, helping individuals to assume effective responsibility for their own lives and for their role in social relationships is the central notion in social work. This principle divides much of the visible leadership of social work from grass-roots social workers and social work program directors. The fundamental issue separating them is whether the system is wrong and needs to be changed, or whether the answers lie within individuals and their relationships with one another. In the second view, the social worker represents the system in a partnership of mutual respect with the client, where each has the right to expect something from the other. In the first view, the client is seen as a victim; he or she is denied the respect and dignity of human strength and fallibility, good and evil, and seen as a mere victim of oppression, without will in regard to his or her problems or accomplishments, with rights to demand but without the blame or the credit that comes with responsibility.

Alberta Fuentes, homeless coordinator for the New York mayor's office, told me about a woman who was recently charged by the police with beating her child. The woman held the little girl up against a car, pounding her and berating her for inadequate panhandling. She, in her early forties, had three of her own children with her and was taking care of two of her grandchildren, one of whom was the child she abused. A daughter of hers with two other children was living in another shelter. Each of these women, Fuentes angrily stated, is "leaving a trail of babies." When I asked Fuentes what should be done about this kind of situation, she responded,

> We should start by telling them, "Enough is enough!" So much of this is a failure of our value system. We used to ostracize irresponsible behavior. Now we just leave it as a matter for the welfare system. Let's get selfish about this: they are living off the rest of us.[6]

Fuentes says nowadays we just get these women birth control devices instead of saying, "Don't!"

Anna Kondratas, HUD secretary Jack Kemp's assistant secretary for community development and a former public policy analyst, told me that she does not believe it is a good idea for the government and public institutions to tie a moral stigma to unwed motherhood: public officials, even teachers, should not tell unwed mothers that "sex between unmarried persons is evil or sinful," because other social institutions should transmit religious values. But this stricture does not absolve schools and other public institutions from transmitting social values. It should be made clear to young people that out-of-wedlock childbirth with no means of support is irresponsible behavior. Kondratas wants people to internalize and act upon the principle that "bad judgment and stupidity in life have consequences."[7]

Judge Stella Schindler of the Queens family court said that people must be held accountable for their behavior. She remembered that when she was a schoolteacher, teaching classes of troubled children, one of the most troubled called upon her years later for a character reference. She asked him, "Why me?" He replied, "You're the only who expects something from us." This student had assaulted one of the teachers, and for all Judge Schindler knew he is dead by now. His cry, though, was to be held accountable.[8]

SOCIAL WORKERS frequently tell how they have changed their own ideas about personal responsibility since they began working with clients. Bill Hobson, director of the Downtown Emergency

Shelter in Seattle, works with the homeless in that city. He is a former university professor and still describes himself as a left-wing political activist. He said to me, "The value is beginning to enter social work that people need to accept the consequences of their actions. That is therapy." Most people who come to the downtown shelter do so in part because of bad decisions. Gangs such as the Crips and the Bloods have made a poor decision stemming from their frustration and anger. Although there is a lot of injustice in America, Hobson observed, this country does "a pretty good job relative to other countries in maximizing opportunity. Still, there is a lot of inequality."[9] Marsha Moskowitz, Multnomah County, Oregon, director of community services, described herself as "one of the new type of liberal" who find the "exaggerators and the no responsibility people," those who "stress the importance of not blaming the victim," harmful to the profession.[10] Boona Cheema of Berkeley has noticed that working in homeless programs has made her "more conservative." If the client, for instance, is not doing something to help himself, after about a week in her program they throw him out. It was not that way when she started the program in the early 1970s.[11]

Some social workers do not consider the responsibility issue as political or even as philosophical—it is just a practical matter. Pearl Pritchard of Oakland's Salvation Army sees the problem sometimes as the client's fault and sometimes not: "Maybe they lost control of the situation and need help. But they need to take responsibility too."[12] Marcia Carlisle, administrator of the King County, Washington, detoxification center speaks matter-of-factly of "shared responsibility" between client and case worker for the effectiveness of therapy.[13]

The foreward of a book from the stack Bob Pruger gave me states that many, if not all, overviews of the field provide only one ideological frame of reference, usually liberal and occasionally radical.[14] The book later defines *liberal* in a way that leaves room for the notion of personal responsibility:

> Liberals assume the basic values of capitalism (individualism, acquisitiveness, and competitiveness) automatically serve the best interests of society [but they] wish to modify capitalism . . . to minimize the number of people not benefiting from the

system, but not to fundamentally change the economic system itself. . . . People must be motivated by want or need to be productive . . . [and] liberals see government as the proper instrument for correcting the deficiencies of the marketplace.[15]

What would a conservative view be to these authors? Barry Goldwater is quoted: Welfare changes a person from a "dignified, industrious, self-reliant, spiritual being into a dependent." Based on such a view, a conservative would, the authors say, "limit welfare to private voluntary charity." Conservatives stress unlimited free will and the idea that the individual can overcome anything: "The causes of social problems are located in the moral character of the individual; the economic system (capitalism) is blameless."[16] Clearly, both of these philosophies admit the notion of personal responsibility on the part of clients. A liberal view could insist upon it, allow it, or ignore it. A conservative view (the one never seen in social welfare textbooks) insists upon it.

What would a radical view be? A radical would dwell on the imperfections of modern capitalism (some would say social democracy) and how he purports to demonstrate that the liberal and the conservative welfare philosophies in practice function to mitigate these imperfections so that the system can survive. In the radical view, the client is not responsible, but a victim of oppression.[17] Any attempt to place responsibility on the client, or to share responsibility with the client, is blaming the victim.

By this set of definitions, all fourteen of the textbooks that I examined are indeed either liberal or radical. Most are liberal but sympathetic to a radical criticism of the system. None either defends capitalism or exercises the liberal's option to emphasize the client's share of responsibility for his condition. This view of liberalism, however, is so broad as to include all of the Left short of outright abolition of private capital and all of the Right much short of pure laissez-faire capitalism.

Using this broad description of *liberalism* is not unreasonable, but it is not very useful in differentiating the politics of Americans. Under this definition nearly all Americans are liberals—for instance, all but a small handful of the members of the U.S. House of Representatives and every member of the Senate. It necessitates further refinement to be useful in categorizing the fourteen texts I examined. If all the members of the U.S. Senate are liberals, then some are radical liberals, some moderate liberals, and some conservative liberals. On that basis, the books cluster heavily toward the radical end of the liberal continuum, and none is close to being conservative liberal, let alone conservative. In a passage that epitomizes the evident attitudes of several authors, one book states as though it were undisputed that capitalism requires a 7 percent unemployment rate for its success.

A more systematic analysis of social welfare textbooks than mine was published by two University of Maryland professors in 1982.[18] They attempted to get at the "prevailing ideological assumptions of social work education" and arrayed the positions taken by the books along a continuum from "Left" to "Right":

> The Left pole . . . encompasses the position that individuals' lives are circumscribed and heavily influenced, if not determined, by political, economic, and institutional patterns within society. The Right pole attributes to individuals and families a great deal of leeway to determine their individual and interpersonal experiences.[19]

The professors found a cluster of four on the Left, viewing social work as "fundamentally related to social change"; four in what they called "the center," asserting the "connections between social work clients and societal forces and events" but not "overtly" advocating the need for social changes; and three viewing "societal forces as part of the field within which individuals and families exist." No text was said to be on the Right, that is, to accord families "a great deal of leeway to determine their . . . experiences."[20]

The authors made no specific mention of the concept of assigning responsibility to clients for their actions or of the notion of shared or mutual responsibility, which might be a satisfactory definition of the center. The notion of mutual responsibility, although it is unstated, does appear to be compatible with the point of view of all but the four textbooks on the Left. The problem is that it is unstated.

The attempt by social workers I talked with to attach a label to their ideological position within the field may stem from an effort to understand and deal with the disquieting realization that their own professional views, once held so certainly, are changing. This is my own story. Such labels may not fairly represent and probably will not help to resolve the important and, perhaps, increasing divergence between the social work philosophy commonly communicated to social work students in our universities and what good social workers, whatever their political ideology, think and do. What might help would be to make all the professors and administrators who are so certain of the victim theory go to work with clients.[21]

In several of the books that I examined, a social work practice with no ideological overtones is briefly mentioned whose implementation logically and practically leads to the client's assuming a share of responsibility for results. My interviews indicate this practice is gaining popularity in social case work: it is case management. While there is nothing new about the idea, social workers increasingly see it as an effective vehicle for working with homeless clients.

Anna Kondratas believes that the McKinney Act, under which Congress funnels most special homeless funds to states and communities, places too much emphasis on emergency aid and not enough on root causes. One such cause, she thinks, is the failure of our welfare apparatus to function effectively as a system. She says that because the homeless are often the poor who do not have the wherewithal to negotiate this system, we need to fix it by making it easier for clients. One approach would be to assign a case manager to each client. To simplify the whole system of agencies, programs, and benefits would be a task of incredible and insurmountable difficulty. Instead, the case manager would help the client negotiate the system.

Kondratas and Stuart Butler, of the Heritage Foundation, wrote a book together, *Out of the Poverty Trap: A Conservative Strategy for Welfare Reform*. In our discussion Butler told me the practice of case management is growing. He believes its essence to be the notion of a contractual relationship between case worker and client. He likes the term *case manager* better than the more traditional term *case worker*, because the new expression implies a reciprocal relationship of responsibilities. Goals are set *with* the client. Butler sees the one-way notion of client "rights" and system "obligations" as part of the "poverty trap."[22]

"We give you the opportunity, and it is up to you to make it happen," Marilyn Miller, executive director of Portland Impact, tells homeless families in that city. She says that her agency's case management contracts with clients are designed to make clients "feel like they've done it, feel respected and empowered. We won't let them use system barriers as an excuse." If they run into a barrier, they are to try to negotiate it. If they can't, then they need to ask for help. She says,

> We have about 30 to 35 families to a case manager. The case managers get a mix of kinds of problems. The case manager is the administrator of the client's program—volunteers and other resources. There is a weekly meeting of the case manager with each client. The case manager is also the therapist. Treatment needs are often farmed out.[23]

Robert B. Huebner, the evaluation coordinator for the homeless initiative at the National Institute on Alcohol Abuse and Alcoholism (NIAAA), has pointed out that the concept of a services broker originated in the social work profession and goes with the term *case worker*. He believes in a broader case management concept that encompasses the broker function. Under case management, there is a "living negotiated arrangement," where the manager "represents a lot of fields, not just social work."[24] As Portland's Miller puts it, while the manager often farms out various treatment needs of the client, the manager is accountable, with the client, for the results. Boona Cheema says that too often social welfare schools appear to assume that clients come to an agency with one problem or maybe two. In fact, she says, there is almost always an array of problems. Her agency has shifted its focus to become "fully case-managed," in part based on this recognition. At Maxene Johnston's Weingart Center on Los Angeles's skid row, the case management system is used with hundreds of clients, and the mutual responsibility for keeping to it is emphasized.

Cheema puts a little different twist on the approach. She says the case manager should act like a surrogate parent, firmly but with affection, insisting the client keep his end of the bargain.

Case management is a key element in the organization of successful alcoholism or drug treatment, says Mike Tretton, director of Seattle's Central Area Community Alcohol and Substance Abuse Center. Case management is vital not only to establishing mutual responsibility but also to building a new support network for the client.

> We assign forty cases to a counselor. The counselor sets up four therapy groups of ten each, who provide each other moral

support, help each other, network, etc. When treatment is completed, these groups continue to meet weekly. They are tied
into a twelve-step program, and as friends for each other
constitute a replacement for their old drinking buddies.[25]

Everyone I talk to agrees that the importance of replacing an
alcoholic's group of "bottle buddies" with a new group of friends
who agree on sobriety cannot be overestimated.

The entire community of Portland's service agencies has
recently recognized the case management concept as a strategic
element in dealing with homelessness. According to the Reverend
Spencer Marsh, a recently drafted master agreement among
twenty-one organizations emphasizes a single case management
system, neighborhood multiservice centers, and more transitional
and permanent housing to replace mass emergency shelters. The
local chamber of commerce has committed itself to raising all the
several million dollars needed to pay for case managers.[26]

Gisela Bushey's family shelter in Oakland calls its approach
to clients case management, although there is "no specific contract
with the client." She says the essence of case management is a
"philosophy of empowerment": clients must be made to feel they
can succeed. Staff time is thus spent building skills and self-esteem.
All clients clearly understand that they must be working to
improve their own situation and are challenged to take responsibility. Although the staff helps them get to where they can get
assistance, they must then use the assistance. The shelter enforces
certain rules. It maintains an 8:30 P.M. curfew, for instance. In addition, anyone who comes in drunk or high has ten minutes to pack
up and get out. In fact, before they are admitted in the first place,
they must have kept themselves clean and sober for fourteen days.[27]

As client loads are established for case managers, the situation
must be structured so that case managers can give an appropriate
degree of attention to each client. There is no magic number of cases
a manager can handle. This number depends on factors such as
the difficulty of client problems, distances to travel, and—very
important—the other resources commanded by the manager. Fifteen
would be too many for some kinds of clients, while in other cases,
and where group processes are used, forty might work well. The
problem is not so different from any other management span-of-
work (sometimes called span-of-control) problem.

SELF-DESCRIBED AS A CONSERVATIVE, Stuart Butler of the Heritage Foundation likes to cite liberal Senator Edward Kennedy for holding "a truly paternalistic view of the poor." The senator is on record opposing voucher programs because he thinks the poor will choose badly. With the concept of responsibility must go empowerment— the opportunity and the wherewithal to make choices.

The process of building and rebuilding responsibility in clients is mentioned with increasing frequency these days. Judge Schindler of Queens says the homeless are often people who miss all their appointments and as a result, miss out on their welfare benefits. Many just do not follow through on their responsibilities, because of their disordered and chaotic lives. Berkeley-Oakland Support Services (BOSS) has learned from experience, says director Boona Cheema, to tell clients who do not want to take some responsibility for their own lives to "buzz off." She says that while her Berkeley program is hardly conservative in the usual sense of the word, its rules are. "Rules are necessary for people to live together," she says, and many of the homeless are homeless at least in part because of their inability or unwillingness to follow simple rules of living with others. They need help learning to comply with such expectations. The Reverend Marsh, however, cautions against giving them more responsibility at the beginning than they can handle.

Cheema says that while with experience she has come to think of herself as conservative, she distinguishes herself from many by a strong belief in empowerment for the homeless. Many conservatives, she believes, do not care about the poor, do not "give a damn." She registers the homeless to vote and helps them get to conferences on homelessness. She has been troubled by conferences on homelessness where the "experts" on the subject are all professionals—architects, planners, and the like. She believes in self-governance—empowerment and personal responsibility. When Heritage's Stuart Butler addresses groups of social workers, he likes to make one particular point. He tells them that social workers who assume the client is a victim of the system make the error of failing to condition aid on performance: this is self-defeating. It may or may not be true that the client is a victim, he allows, but to provide aid under this assumption does not work. Like Cheema, Butler employs the parental analogy: as we would with our own son or daughter, if we want someone to take increased responsibility, we need to make this a clear expectation. The Salvation Army's Pearl Pritchard says that regardless of fault, the homeless need to take responsibility. The client should be expected and empowered to make decisions, and while not all of them will be wise, it is the client's life. Boona Cheema places a limit: for an alcoholic mother who beats up her children, sometimes the only thing that can be done is to call the protective service to take the children away from her. Seattle's Tretton says that "we've gone way too far" in treating alcoholics solely as victims. They do have a choice, he insists, "even though alcoholism is a devastating illness that kills people and makes people insane."

Mike Tretton is himself a recovering alcoholic. As one, he does not believe in "enabling"—for instance, helping an alcoholic to get the cash he is "entitled to" under welfare programs, with the inevitable result that he will use the money to drink. He says that many social workers are such enablers, who "believe the alkies' sad stories." "They don't do real case management," he says. "They help the person to qualify for a payment and get it for them." "Most of these people have had a lot of help," he continues. "That has not solved the problem. The social worker says, 'They have a disease, so they are entitled to benefits.' " "It is a disease," Tretton complains. "But it is a disease with a difference." There is a solution rather than a cure, and social workers should use it. It is "tough-love"—like the love of a good parent for an errant child, kind but firm treatment. Enormous personal support is needed for recovering addicts. "When an alcoholic stops drinking, it is like his closest buddy died," Tretton says. Tretton knows: he is one.

Tretton finds some good in the terrible news of the crack problem. "The silver lining," he says, "is that crack is bringing the drug problem to a head." Human services workers, he believes, are beginning to address their role as enablers of drinking and drug abuse and are facing the fact that they have become institutional codependents of addicted clients. When they learn how to modify this behavior of their own, they will take a giant step toward solving the problems of chemical abuse.

From his tiny office in the shadow of Seattle's famous old Smith Tower, Bill Hobson, the downtown shelter director, talks about enabling: "Enabling means contributing to . . . illness."

Hobson declares that in spite of his radical politics, he has never supported the "drunk check," what they call a general assistance welfare payment in Seattle. He believes that it is killing people. In Tretton's program, under recently enacted state legislation, the welfare check is managed for the clients. "We are giving them a ninety-day opportunity to save money and to line up a place to live," Hobson says. "During that time we help them to 're-socialize' themselves." When they complete the program, a case manager will continue to control how they spend any general assistance they may receive. The State of Washington has declared itself against enabling and has determined to correct its own such behavior.

Such a limitation appears to conflict with the notion of empowerment, however. Hobson, who supports the limitation strongly, says that "personal empowerment is what it's all about . . . giving people more decisional control over their lives." But, he says, they need to be told, "even coerced," about deviation from their commitment to stay clean and sober. "Enabling," he says, "is not the same as 'empowerment.' "

Marilyn Miller observes that in the academies more and more social workers are being trained as detached professionals. Like a parent, though, the most effective social workers get involved and show emotion. Clients need to be reintegrated into a social support system, and this effort takes more than money and services. The social worker, according to Miller, should show personal commitment to clients as well as independent judgment, because they lack emotional support. The worker, with the client, is central in building a new support system.

Boona Cheema adds the office setup to this discussion of professional distancing. It is important, she insists, "not to keep a certain kind of distance" that is characteristic of government offices. In her program, no counters with receptionists behind them separate the professionals from the clients. The counselors are directly accessible to anyone who walks in the door. Doubtless, of course, this arrangement leads to an occasional harrowing experience, and counselors often take a considerable amount of verbal abuse from some angry clients. One social welfare intern from a local university complained to the dean that it was unsafe to work at BOSS. BOSS then decided not to use such interns any more because these professionals are convinced that the bureaucratic style impedes the development of a client support system: physical barriers become emotional barriers.

Miller says a social worker, like a parent, should be a role model. Clients tend to live up to their perceptions of a case manager's expectations. It is less often recognized that successful clients are also role models. Miller's agency focuses attention on its successful clients, bringing them back to help in the program as board members, volunteer workers, and sometimes as paid staff. At BOSS, Cheema says that not all, but many, of the clients do turn their lives around, and some of those are hired by BOSS as counselors and other staff. The former homeless make the best counselors, according to Cheema. She says that social welfare students have come to her agency with many preconceived expectations that do not work out. Even after an internship, many still maintain romantic ideas about clients. Former clients often have more realistic ideas about themselves and about the homeless. Two of her center directors, for example, are former mental patients. Tom Neely, director of Los Angeles's HOP, and all his staff are former homeless persons.

Pearl Pritchard has identified three styles among professionally trained social workers. First is the effective worker, who helps people help themselves. "Then there is the worker who just counsels and counsels," she says. The third kind simply "likes to think of herself as a social worker, use all the words. She accomplishes nothing." Mike Tretton believes that many social workers were "the hero" in their home and that is why they went into social work. They enjoyed that power. Pruger stresses that social workers are not free actors; they all work for someone else who sets the rules. Social workers, he says, "value values." But in the end they behave very much as anyone would among clients with serious problems: "They agonize a lot." Many program directors believe they overcome some of these problems by including former clients on the program staff. They find that former clients do not have the same set of problems and are more able to accept, and to work within, the limitations of clients and the job situation.

CASE MANAGEMENT is a most useful idea for helping all kinds of homeless families and individuals. It is a simple idea, and merely performing it represents an accomplishment. Our national policy should provide every homeless person with somebody, a case manager or someone else, to stay in touch with, to know how to find him. No one in America should be lost and forgotten. Nor should anyone become so alienated as to lose and forget the rest of us.

Beyond staying in touch, a case manager's goal should be to reintegrate his homeless clients into a social structure that will empower them to reestablish themselves with shelter, work, family, and friends.

While all the rhetoric flies in the press, on the floor of Congress, at the meetings of professional associations, and in university lecture halls, practicing social workers quietly tell us that the proper basis both for national welfare policy and for a case manager's relationship with his clients is the principle of mutual responsibility.

Under a plastic sheet a homeless man faces the first snow of the season, in Lafayette Square across the street from the White House, November 11, 1987.

A homeless man in New York's Grand Central Station, three days before Christmas, 1986.

Thanksgiving dinner was served to Washington, D.C., homeless across from the White House in 1983.

"Street of Dreams," November 26, 1943.

8

Homelessness and the American Dream

HOMELESSNESS SHOCKS many of us because it suggests the American Dream is failing. "Send these, the homeless," says the inscription on the Statue of Liberty, seen by millions of immigrants arriving on our shores:

> Give me your tired, your poor,
> Your huddled masses yearning to breathe free,
> The wretched refuse of your teeming shore,
> Send these, the homeless, tempest-tossed to me:
> I lift my lamp beside the golden door.

"Home Sweet Home," reads the stitchwork sampler, probably the most printed American motto. Home symbolizes everything enduring that we work and fight for: it signifies country, family, neighborhood, community, friends, warmth, security, and comfort. No word better expresses the American Dream. In an important sense, *freedom* and *liberty* are really about home. The "pursuit of happiness" is bound up in owning and maintaining a home. Nearly all of us go to work to achieve that goal. It is why we pay taxes and why we vote. Homelessness is nothing less than a metaphor for the failure of our civilization.

Homelessness disturbs everyone: each new poll shows most Americans willing to pay substantially more taxes to help the homeless. Homelessness is not only a problem, or more correctly a complex set of problems, but also a haunting specter. In a symbolic sense, a count of the homeless is a count of those who have lost the American Dream.

In the late summer of 1988, at the Souper Center in Richmond, California, I met Mitch Snyder for the first, and sadly, the only time.[1] Snyder had just driven a succession of old cars across the country, from Washington, D.C., to Richmond, California, stopping along the way to talk to groups in thirty cities and towns to recruit people for demonstrations and a hunger strike in Washington. He was a week late, as one after another of his cars died along the way. One caught fire somewhere in the Midwest; another lost a transmission in the mountain states.

Snyder, a middle-aged man with shaggy brown hair and tired eyes, wore an army colonel's fatigue jacket, jeans, and a navy blue sweatshirt. Several of those attending were from a west Contra Costa County "peace committee." Most were local program or administrative officials, some private, some governmental. Two reporters from a large suburban newspaper attended.

Snyder began by telling us that the problem of the homeless was caused by Reagan's housing cuts. "People who are committed to justice of any kind," he declared, "need to address the question." Civil rights and peace are cited as examples of such campaigns for justice. He assured us that George Bush could not get elected because he was a "blue-blood with no charisma." Michael Dukakis would be the "captain of the *Titanic*"—after him, the right wing would rule America for twenty to forty years. "Progressive people," he said, "must get behind the housing issue to test whether "Reagan maniacs" would control our future. Snyder wanted these progressive people to force the government of the United States to appropriate at least $15 billion per year for the next ten years in support of low-income housing. He told the group that the money should come from "getting some of it back from the rich." An effective shortcut to getting homeless shelters built in the meantime was to "find a building . . . not being used and tear the doors off." Snyder himself paid no taxes, he said. He was receiving about $100,000 per year in speaking fees, which he put "all into the program." He said he "wouldn't give the government a plugged nickel." Once again I found myself wondering what it was that constituted charisma, because that bedraggled man exuded it. In spite of myself, I wanted to agree with him, with everything he said, and follow him. "We don't have a Gandhi in America," he said, "but we do have a community of conscience, people who keep after the issues year after year, people who are real."

Attending the Snyder meeting was Jean Siri, the mayor of El Cerrito, California, and a paid-up member of Snyder's "community of conscience." Siri told me that Contra Costa County has the highest median family income in the state and the greatest disparity of income between rich and poor. One day, after noticing that the water in her fishpond had taken on a skin of ice, she became concerned about the homeless. Although county officials had denied any problem, the staff of shelters and soup kitchens reported otherwise. Siri then decided to organize a clothing, blanket, and sleeping bag drive. Since then she has helped organize and carry out several drives on behalf of the county's homeless and has worked to publicize the situation. The previous winter the county Board of Supervisors for the first time voted funds for homeless programs. Siri said they decided as a fund-raiser to have a house tour of the rich and to match any funds raised privately fifty-fifty. Another project was "Hands across the Lafayette Reservoir." The dollars raised were used to set up a shelter program.

In addition to local advocacy and resource mobilization for the homeless, Siri and her associates actively supported Mitch Snyder's national effort to obtain a huge increase in the federal housing budget. Earlier their issues were civil rights and the war in Vietnam. Siri was a strong and active proponent of mandatory busing to achieve racial integration in the Richmond Unified School District. After reading sociologist Lillian Rubin's critical book *Busing vs. Backlash,* she now believes the way busing was carried out was mistaken. She is now as convinced about the need to push for housing programs as she was earlier about busing. She is one of the people who, in Snyder's words, "keep after the issues year after year."[2]

A few months after our interview, I read in the newspaper of a plan to develop housing on open private land in Siri's neighborhood. She spoke out vehemently against the planned development. If she were aware of any irony in her position on the proposed development and the lack of affordable housing, it was not reported.

Robert Hayes is a prominent figure in Snyder's community of conscience for the homeless. From 1978 to 1989, day after day, operating out of a cramped suite of offices a little off the path from midtown Manhattan to city hall and Wall Street, Hayes proclaimed injustice and demanded remedy. Earlier, as a Wall Street lawyer, he had often noticed people on his way to work sleeping in rags on heated subway gratings and in doorways. He felt he had to do something. Perceiving injustice, he sued and won an order from the court for the city to provide shelter to all who need it. He started the National Coalition for the Homeless, running it as general counsel at low pay and long hours. We can be sure that he is a "good person" because he gave up a job leading to great wealth in one of Wall Street's most prestigious law firms in order to do good. He stayed at this work full time until late 1989 when he assumed the volunteer position of board chairman and went back to the private practice of law.

Hayes dreams of justice for the poor and cannot understand resistance by officials to his and other homeless advocates' demands except in terms of venality. He says that it is the "callousness" of such officials "which has permitted our government—President Reagan, states and cities too—to preside over the spectacle of two million Americans homeless and to do virtually nothing." (As shown in Chapter 1, the number of homeless in America is dramatically less than two million.) The problem will be solved, he says, when Americans "of good will" come to "recognize that homelessness is unacceptable" and "demand that it be ended."[3] He makes it clear that this is a moral crusade, with the community of conscience on one side and everybody else on the other. The community of conscience dreams of a right to shelter and of the people rising up to insist that the government guarantee such a right, cut other parts of the budget or collect new taxes, and pay whatever it costs. This community assumes the resistance of others to its demands derives from ignorance, obliviousness, cruelty, or misplaced priorities. It believes that if we only muster the public will, we can solve the problem.

Alberta Fuentes, as homeless coordinator for Mayor Edward Koch, found homelessness not to be a problem of political will but of human complexity. She does not know how to solve it. She says that the people living in shelters are damaged "perhaps even before birth" and that just providing them a place to live is not a solution. She insists that the young boy who sits and stares at the wall in a shelter or welfare hotel probably sat and stared at the wall where he lived before. Women go on having baby after baby, with no husband and no source of income except welfare. Men take no responsibility for their children. It seems almost as though the more we try to do the worse it gets.[4]

Alberta Fuentes and Robert Hayes share a dream of an America where the streets are safe and clean and where everyone has a home and family, a good job, and plenty to eat. They both believe in many, maybe all, of the same American values. Their most important difference is in how they fix responsibility. Hayes places it on the government and on the privileged. He masks his paternalistic bias with reformist rhetoric: while the wealthy and powerful should be held accountable for their decisions, those in the lower strata of the economy should not. In Fuentes's view, Hayes does not grant the homeless the dignity of reponsibility for their own behavior. Fuentes believes that responsibility must start with each individual, rich or poor. Our mistake is seeing the underclass as helpless victims, she says. Hayes is widely portrayed and celebrated as an idealist; Fuentes, often as a resistant official. It could just as easily be argued, however, that Fuentes is the idealist, based on her faith that the poor and the powerless can and must take control of their own lives and on her respect for them not as victims but as persons with a share in their own fate. Hayes can feel the pleasure of accomplishment, as the community of conscience mobilizes and as agendas, laws, programs, and the press respond to his efforts. Fuentes sees homelessness increasing, the streets getting worse, and the parks more dangerous, as society transmits the signal to many of its members that they have rights without responsibilities.

Cecil Williams, pastor of Glide Memorial Methodist Church in San Francisco, is a leading member of the community of conscience. The church operates more programs for the homeless than any other organization in the San Francisco Bay area. Williams shouts from pulpit and from podium against perceived injustice and oppression in contemporary American society more than almost anybody else in the area. He ceaselessly upbraids the government for its failure to provide adequate resources for the poor. At the same time, he raises large amounts of private money and advises others that, if a program is needed, to go ahead with the program and "the money will come, the money will come."

Williams has sponsored a conference, "Crack Cocaine, the Death of a Race,"[5] from which there emerged a dual message: the black community has to take charge of itself and deal with its problems; it must also demand that the federal government do vastly more than it is doing now.

In a recent segment on the "MacNeil/Lehrer NewsHour," Williams found himself debating others about whether more federal dollars would help solve the problems of the urban underclass. He did not say they really would or that they would not. He gave a curious answer, that we do not have "the will or the way" to solve these problems; not "the will or the way," he repeated in his rhythmic style. Perhaps his preacher's delivery caused the others to miss his significant departure from the usual community of conscience rhetoric. He said we did not have the will, but he also said we did not have the way. No one asked him if that meant that with all the will, determination, commitment, and public money that the community of conscience believes are needed, we might be no better off, because we do not have the way to solve the problem. A man of faith himself, perhaps he believes the way would come.

Would Williams grant that others of conscience might honestly believe otherwise, might think that public programs undermine private institutions, might believe that federal programs weaken local capacity, or might be suspicious that things have sometimes gotten worse not because the government has done too little but because it has done too much, with too little knowledge, from too great a distance?

Terry Teachout of the *New York Daily News* thinks that people see things strangely in some of our cities. He says,

> I'm from the Midwest. New York wrecks the way one sees the world. People where I'm from don't feel like they need to reconcile everything and make it consistent. When I got here I found the underlying assumptions of this city to be so different I didn't know what to think.
>
> We need to remind ourselves that New York, Berkeley, and Chicago are not America. This country is more like Kansas City. It is on the whole pretty sensible, pretty balanced.[6]

The community of conscience, Teachout might say, wants to reconcile everything and make it consistent, thinks all problems can be solved if the will and the commitment are there, believes that what is fair and what is unfair can be measured by ideological yardsticks, is convinced that the political "good guys" and "bad guys" can be readily determined.

My experience confirms Teachout's observation about the contrast between New York and Kansas City. Firmly drawn lines and positions define and dominate the discussion of the homeless issue at the national level and in some of our major cities, particularly the media centers. The community of conscience is influential in New York, San Francisco, and Washington, D.C., as well as in Berkeley, Cambridge, and Ann Arbor. It is influential in places where ideology is important and where information and misinformation are wholesaled out to the rest of America.

Few politicians of stature have the courage, the ego, or the brilliance to challenge directly the claims of the community of conscience. While Mayor Koch did it, often with flair, his style finally wore thin. Ronald Reagan did it with more finesse, and for many years it seems to have enhanced his appeal. As the only elected politician in America with a national constituency, he could count on the people in many other places like Teachout's Kansas City to respond from personal experience. In contrast, the community of conscience assumes that Congress fails to pass the needed legislation and appropriations for all the desirable programs because they cost money, because they offend special interests, or because there are not enough votes to override the veto of a conservative president, who is seen, variously, as mean-spirited, confused, or a toady of the right wing of his party. In this view, Congress does not have the will to do the right thing.

All this might be true. But there is, I believe, another element present as well. Quite simply, many of our leaders no longer have confidence in the glossy formulations and columns of data showing that social programs work—that a small investment in prevention now will yield vast savings later on. They have heard it before. Because they have no evidence to refute the data offered (or if they do, it is too complicated to explain), they do the safe thing and plead budgetary poverty or political stalemate. In the past, many expensive measures with little or no evidence of workability have been enacted and billions of dollars spent on them. I do not think, however, that important programs proved cost effective have been turned down simply for lack of commitment.

In the 1968 book *The Unheavenly City*, Edward C. Banfield asked about the troubled cities of that time, "What can be done?" In the years since then our leaders have had many opportunities to learn the wisdom of Banfield's answer:

> First . . . the range of feasible measures for dealing with the serious problems of the cities is much narrower than one might think, and second, . . . within this range hardly any of the measures are acceptable. If what is, in general, feasible [say, taking new babies away from long-term welfare mothers and placing them up for adoption] is not acceptable, the reverse is also true: what is acceptable [say, job training for the hard-core unemployed] is not, in general, feasible. Government seems to have a perverse tendency to choose measures that are the very opposite of those which would be recommended [based on an objective analysis of their probable outcomes]. The reasons for this perversity may be found in the nature of American political institutions and, especially, in the influence on public opinion of the upper-class cultural ideal of "service" and "responsibility to the community."[7]

Congress does not pass all the measures advocated by the community of conscience for many reasons. An important one is that a majority of the members cannot be convinced the measures will work. They have heard persuasive arguments before, enacted programs, and seen the problem get worse. They have heard Charles Murray and others argue persuasively that a program made the problem worse. They do not know who is right. When Banfield wrote his book, just about all of us were believers. Most of those with a financial stake in the now gigantic social program industry are still believers, politically if no longer personally. Banfield wrote of an "upper-class culture," the same group as Mitch Snyder's "community of conscience," and they are still believers. Most responsible officials and many Americans, still just as concerned about the poor, are not believers any longer. I do not argue that they have lost their faith or their compassion but that they have simply grown more careful.

IN SOME COMMUNITIES, consideration of the homelessness issue and other problems takes on a less rancorous tone. In Portland, Oregon, the mayor's office has become the focal point for persons with power and influence in the community to carry on a reasoned discussion about community problems and arrive at practical courses of action. When a problem or an opportunity for the city gets the attention of city hall, the mayor gathers together those who have influence over the situation. This approach has been followed for about twenty years, according to local officials I interviewed. It is partly a legacy of how the city acted during the Great Society period and partly built on earlier antecedents. In the early 1970s, U.S. mayors were given a potentially important role in the federal Model Cities program, and Portland's mayor at the time, Neil Goldschmidt, used the opportunity to improve the governance of the city. Since the original settlement of displaced New England Puritans on the shores of the Willamette River, an attitude of civic responsibility has been widely shared throughout the community. Speaking to this point, Marilyn Miller of Portland Impact, a program for homeless families, said, "We don't have to spend time in Portland convincing people there is a problem, only working on how to solve it."[8] The public has enough trust to accept the explanations of community leaders. Responsibility to one another and mutual respect have been an important current, a cultural stream that has flowed quietly and powerfully through the public life of the area. Because of Portland's historical background and its political culture of civility, high-quality individuals have been eager to assume leadership roles in Portland and Multnomah County, both formally, through election or appointment, and informally. And they have been able to succeed as leaders—that is, be regarded well in the community and treated kindly by the newspapers.

The business community sits at the table with the social service agencies and others, bringing both its economic interests and a commitment to help to the situation. The Chamber of Commerce, which set up a task force of its own on social concerns, has committed time and money. When everyone with influence over a problem participates, solutions seem to be more complete, with fewer unanticipated consequences.

"We help the poor," explained Don Clark, the city's housing director, "because it is the Christian thing to do." Sometimes the "Christian thing" has a steel edge. According to Clark,

> Two years ago I told big business representatives that we would not allow development in skid row that would drive all of the poor people from their housing. Business interests had just lost a battle over the Beaver Hotel, so they knew we had the power and they'd have to cut a deal. The deal, which came to be known as the Clark-Shields Agreement (March 30, 1987), was incorporated into the city General Plan. It established numbers of low-income housing units that were to be preserved.[9]

Mutual respect does not mean that everyone gets his way but that problems get worked out and become manageable rather than degenerating into crises or being inflated into such.

The mayor's role is critical, not so much as a commander but as a convenor: The mayor is the only public official with enough status to pull those with influence over an issue together and keep them working until they can reach agreement on a course of action. The mayor's powers of appointment and his influence over permit approvals and the allocation of city personnel and financial resources are tools that are seldom wielded overtly. Everyone knows he has them, but using them is seen as a sign of weakness. Modern Portland mayors have tended not to make the important policy decisions themselves but to help community leaders reach consensus.

When the mayor appeals to community leaders, the effort is to find a solution that incorporates the legitimate public and private interests of the participants into a framework of civic improvement. Civic improvement is implicitly defined circularly, as whatever all can agree to. There is always the danger that someone outside the group may not agree. How that danger is avoided, and how the city seems to succeed—that is, to be perceived as fair, efficient, and effective—is by being inclusive. The group ensures that everyone with an important stake in the outcome is invited to participate or to be represented in appropriate, acceptable, and manageable ways. Influential people who might criticize from outside are invited inside the circle. They tacitly accept its culture of mutual respect and feel responsibility to each other when they are included. For most, the rewards are worth it.

Marilyn Miller recalls an earlier time in America when a sense of responsibility to others was more common than today. This is what a community was about, she reflects. In a bureaucratic policy-making system, in contrast, no identifiable person is accountable for anything. The community-based model, though, founded on shared responsibility, relies on horizontal negotiation rather than top down. Leadership makes accountability work through focusing attention. Miller concedes that it helps to be in a smaller city: "You can see what is going on, in a city as small as Portland, so you can see what will work." Miller believes that it is necessary in a city of any size to experiment, to "try things on a small scale that may fail."

Referring to exaggerated claims and distortions by Mitch Snyder and an ally of his, Michael Stoops, who until recently tried to follow Snyder's strident style in Portland (he has since left the area), Miller states in different words a lament I heard later from HUD Assistant Secretary Anna Kondratas. Miller says, "We seem to have to go through such extremes of foolishness to go to work on a problem seriously." From Miller's perspective, it took the community of conscience to get the issue before the city. Complaints from local businesses about disturbances by homeless persons probably also played a part. Now that homelessness is on the agenda, though, local leaders have taken hold and are acting effectively. Snyder played a key role, she maintains, in getting the issue before the American public. But his wild claims and demands were not useful, in her view. "We need to go behind the image to see what is really going on. The real world has to be and can be exciting," she says. Fictionalized accounts and exaggerated numbers should be unnecessary.

According to Marsha Moskowitz, recently director of Portland's umbrella agency for antipoverty programs, Metropolitan Community Action Agency, the point of view in the area is becoming more pragmatic, less radical.[10] Mayors elected since Goldschmidt, although quite different in personality and even in electoral base, have shared his commitment to civility and have entered into a governing process they can see is working. In the jargon of political science, there is "an effective political infrastructure." Don Hendrix of Central City Concerned, an agency that provides low-income rental housing in Portland's old downtown, says:

Now that we've gone through the Great Society, local liberal activists have gotten more conservative. And it is possible to deal with our problems here, because the infrastructure is in place—both physical and political. We are more modest about our expectations.[11]

Tim Gallagher, special assistant to Portland's mayor, Bud Clark, reports that Portland has systematically approached housing issues over a fifteen-year period, including implementation of a specific policy to retain low-income housing.[12] Still, Portland has lost half this housing. The problem, Gallagher believes, is lack of a national housing policy directed to this objective. Portland has used federal funds in many ways differently from other communities. It has spent to save existing units and to rehabilitate rather than to construct new units. It has renovated SROs with housing authority funds. In fact, all but 1,000 of the SROs in Portland have been renovated, and the remainder are scheduled. One of several financing methods used for rehabilitation was the sale of tax-free municipal bonds. The money raised in this manner was linked to federal urban renewal funds. The same combination of financing enabled the city to develop a widely regarded new river-front park.

Gallagher describes how he and mayors Schrunk, then Clark, have worked to enroll nonprofit social services agencies in a partnership with other city institutions. Boutiques were moving into the Burnside (North Downtown) neighborhood to take advantage of lower rents there, low partly because of the street alcoholics and drug users. Because the neighborhood is adjacent to Portland's main downtown business district, whose businesses were benefiting from extensive recent redevelopment, Burnside property values would likely appreciate. The mayor's office saw in this potential escalation of values both a threat and an opportunity for the local social services agencies. The agencies could be pushed out by higher rents, or if they could gain ownership of their property, they could benefit from increases in values and continue to provide programs in the neighborhood. Gallagher and Schrunk helped nonprofit social service and housing agencies in the neighborhood to obtain title to the property where their programs were located. "Get on that escalator," Gallagher says he told them. "Amass some capital." The city arranged for loans so that as long as the property remained in its present use, no payment of principal or interest was required. Federal McKinney Act homeless funds were used for this. Loans were made through the urban renewal agency, whose head is a city council member appointed by the mayor. (Each member of the city council has a portfolio: members are in effect the chief executive officers of the departments assigned to them by the mayor.)

Even in a city such as Portland where civility is developed to a high degree, it is not unlimited. In the interests of justice, the truth may sometimes be a casualty. Gretchen Kaufory, an elected county commissioner, told me, "The visible homeless are an unattractive population. We are emphasizing both here and nationally that homeless are in the main families, Vietnam Vets, mentally ill," rather than drug and alcohol abusers.[13] Thus, desired public perceptions of the homeless are marketed in the political arena. The pill is being coated with palliatives, rather than the truth being simply told. This form of marketing does not always work, even in the short run. "Voters are schizoid about what they will pay for," said Kaufory. They say they will pay more to house the homeless, and then they turn down various ballot measures that will do this, she complained. Voters have passed many add-ons to the property tax, for example, but not a recent measure to house the homeless. Even in enlightened Portland, leaders who reach their own decisions in an environment of mutual respect sometimes consider it unrealistic to give the voters the respect of the unvarnished truth.

IN SPITE OF THE EFFORTS by Portland to protect its low-income housing supply and the presence of a reasonably full array of other human care programs and municipal services, the homeless there as in other cities have become more noticeable in recent years. A series of recessions in the building industry had led to substantial inmigrations of unemployed families from communities where logging operations had shut down. The expansion of Portland's downtown brought the long-term population of street alcoholics and marginal workers in the North Downtown, their ranks also swollen by recession in the logging industry, into conflict with new businesses. Portlanders perceived their city to have a serious problem of homelessness.

In February 1986, Portland's method of governing itself and its recent experience in working on problems of homelessness enabled the city and the county to adopt a comprehensive "12 Point Plan for the Homeless."[14] The plan included much that was already in place as well as new policies and programs. The twelve points, called "initiatives," can be summarized as follows:

1. *Comprehensive planning:* A single body with local government and private agency representation will present homelessness programs for enactment and will evaluate their results.

2. *Housing:* One body will coordinate all city and county housing programs, under a policy to "provide the opportunity for safe and decent housing for everyone in need."

3. *Person down:* "No one incapacitated by alcohol or drugs should be left untreated on the streets of Portland. . . . Anyone 'down' should be quickly assessed and taken to appropriate care [involuntarily, if necessary]."

4. *Alcohol and drug treatment system:* "Sufficient programs and capacity" will be developed, with incentives to break dependency.

5. *Involuntary commitment:* "Society has a right to compel chronic users of substance abuse detoxification services to obtain ongoing treatment." A bill will be proposed to the state legislature to make this possible.

6. *Street sanitation:* "Clean streets help create a hospitable atmosphere." Public toilets will be provided and dumpsters taken away from sidewalk areas.

7. *Jobs:* Anyone who can work should have access to a job at the minimum wage doing something useful. Public and private hiring programs for the homeless will be encouraged and training provided as necessary.

8. *Case management:* Everyone who cannot cope with the system should have a case manager.

9. *Central point of access to services:* Multiservice centers will be established where appropriate, particularly where there is low-income housing.

10. *Street safety:* "People entering the Central City are confronted by behavior and appearances they perceive to be

threatening." An environment will be provided where "people feel safe to interact with others who differ in lifestyle, age, race, socio-economic class, and appearance."

11. *Chronic mental illness treatment:* "Adequate treatment" and "sufficient programs" will be provided "in an environment that is the least restrictive and most likely to protect the individual and others from harm."

12. *Public participation:* An open forum will meet regularly to discuss and resolve the problems of homelessness. It will be led by the Office of the Mayor, and participation by top officials of city and county operating agencies will be mandatory.

Within a year of the plan's adoption, the mayor's office reported that there were

significant visual improvements in North Downtown and increased cooperation between business, government, and social services agencies. Emergency services such as shelter and case management were improved and folded into a comprehensive effort that could return individuals to self-sufficiency . . . [and] a task force . . . was developing a system for coordinating funding, planning, and delivery of emergency basic needs . . . addressing jurisdictional disputes, overlaps and gaps in service within the city and Multnomah County.[15]

After a second year, the mayor's office announced a detailed list of accomplishments. Some of them follow:

• The emergency shelter system was expanded to provide space designed for the needs of single men, women, families, and youths. *"No one* is forced to sleep in the streets."

• Permanent housing for fifty-seven homeless women with special needs was created.

• State funds were added to city and county funds in a pool for housing vouchers.

• Two SRO hotels were purchased and renovated. One of them is now a multiservice center.

- Funds were allocated to replace 750 units of downtown low-income housing lost in recent years. The Chamber of Commerce committed itself to raising $18 million for further housing.[16]

- City and county agencies reorganized themselves to conform to the recommendations by the homeless policy group set up by initiative 1.

- Two-person emergency medical teams replaced the one-person voluntary system of inebriate pickup. A van operates in the central city area from 8 A.M. until midnight and is tied to the 911 emergency system.

- Three SRO hotels now have alcohol- and drug-free floors where all clients are case managed. The sale of fortified wine was banned in some areas of the city and restricted in others.

- Public toilets were installed and more are on the way. Low-income residents were hired to sweep the downtown sidewalks. An ordinance against on-street dumpsters is now enforced and the dumpster problem is gone.

- Case management was substantially expanded, and the Chamber of Commerce committed itself to providing additional funds to complete the job.[17]

- Several new job programs for the homeless were established.

- Two multiservice locations were established.

- Police patrols in the North Downtown area were increased. A crime prevention coordinator was funded by the city to work for an association of local businesses *and residents* to coordinate about two dozen voluntary watch programs, including some in SRO hotels. A new ordinance enables police "to control aggressive street behavior." Shoppers receive cards that help them direct panhandlers to emergency services.

- The legislature passed a bill "both safeguarding personal rights and making it easier to commit chronically mentally ill individuals whose conditions were severely deteriorating." Housing suitable for over 100 seriously mentally ill individuals has been developed or is in the process.

In making urban policy on homelessness or any other issue, says homeless family program director Marilyn Miller, all the players, including the clients, must see themselves as responsible. Everyone needs to feel accountable for his own success or failure, she insists. And all of the players, again including clients, need to commit themselves fully to the plan. Miller and other Portland officials take pride and satisfaction in this model of governance. Miller says that at least some of the Portland experience "can be put in a can and sold to America."

WITHIN A YEAR of Portland's adoption of its twelve-point program, San Francisco officials visited the city to look at how it was working. They went home impressed enough to recommend that their own elected leaders adopt a similar twelve-point policy. San Francisco's Board of Supervisors, persuaded by the evidence of success they were given, did so. The policy adopted by San Francisco differed from Portland's in two important respects, however: first, it was developed without such broad participation; and second, it gave little or no recognition to the needs and concerns of the larger, nonhomeless community of businesses and residents. The San Francisco statement, for instance, contains nothing about involuntary commitment or public safety. The San Francisco policy reflected principally the interests of social services agencies and homeless advocates.

At the end of a year, the *San Francisco Examiner* carried a lead editorial headed, "The $57 Million Question: One Year after Passage of a Homeless Policy S.F.'s Costs Are High, but Has a Strategy Emerged?" The answer was no.

Some of the reason, I believe, is the difference in the way business is done in the two cities. San Francisco, of course, is part of the urban core of a much larger and more complex metropolitan area, where solving problems is more difficult. The idea of a twelve-point policy was "put in a can" and shipped to San Francisco without a necessary ingredient: the way Portland makes and implements policy. Portland has a tradition of mutual respect, a general belief that problems need to be defined honestly and solutions negotiated through give-and-take rather than fought out adversarially or imposed arbitrarily. The sounds we hear from the San Francisco city hall or from those outside the city government are more likely to be angry accusations than cooperatively reached plans. Leaders blame each other or the state government or maybe the administration in Washington. People lament the lack of resources, even though per capita expenditures for most social goods are higher in San Francisco than in most cities that govern themselves less turbulently. In Portland, program officials would like to have more money for the homeless, because they think it would really help. As they see it, money is not the main problem but, instead, the difficulty of finding and carrying out approaches that work.

In the summer of 1990, San Francisco's mayor Art Agnos announced another plan for services to the homeless and initiated a process for its public discussion. He declared that once all the homeless had a place to stay, then camping out in public areas would no longer be tolerated. San Francisco, however, did not have the necessary political infrastructure for the plan to work. Maxene Johnston, director of the Weingart Center on Los Angeles's skid row, was invited to work with San Francisco officials in developing a similar program there. Weingart is based on a broad partnership of public and private agencies and business leaders. In her talk before an audience of officials in Oakland a few months before announcement of the Agnos plan, she probably pleased some of the locals by reporting little progress in laying the groundwork for her model in San Francisco. In that city, she said, after working with its government for over a year, "Nothing has really happened yet. The problem is turf." San Francisco was like a collection of Balkan nations instead of a community.

The lesson of Portland is not that it has been able to eliminate its homelessness problem but rather that the community has joined forces to try to solve the problem in a mutually respectful manner. The problem has been reduced, and—according to an opinion widely shared—is being managed effectively. Perhaps as important, community has been strengthened.

MOST OF US have some visceral response to an issue like homelessness, either "liberal" or "conservative." Our response comes before we struggle actively with the issue, either intellectually— say, by trying to write a book about it—or politically—say, by trying to deal with it as a mayor. Mayor Agnos and I have both evolved on this issue as we have struggled with it. Agnos, starting from the Left, has moved toward the center. When he took office, he saw the homeless primarily as victims of the system who needed to be defended and assisted. Those who complained about the homeless were viewed as ungenerous or ill informed. I have moved toward the center also, on this issue at least, from the other direction. My visceral response was that homelessness was a manufactured crisis, made up by Mitch Snyder and people like him (if there is anyone quite like Mitch Snyder) to build support for social and housing programs and to attack conservative politicians. While I still believe the crisis was manufactured, I also believe that serious problems exist, both more limited and more complex than claimed by advocates. Some of these problems have gotten worse in recent years, and studying them has revealed more important problems. Policy changes and even some increases in appropriations are warranted.

Mayor Agnos has also learned, moderating his positions as he has gained on-the-job experience with this set of issues. As his public statements show, he has increasingly come to understand the point of view of San Francisco residents who want to reclaim their public places for their own enjoyment. At first, his comments dwelt almost completely on the concerns of the homeless advocates and service providers—their requests for shelter, jobs, food, and protection—and the city's published plans on homelessness continue to reflect this emphasis. But it has come home to Agnos more strongly that not all the homeless are truthful about conditions and that some are not only victims but also victimizers, of each other and others. While he has maintained his sympathy, he has also gotten tougher.

In the American political culture, those with responsibility at the local level for finding workable approaches to social problems tend to become less ideologically pure, more moderate, or, perhaps more accurately, better balanced. Liberals become more conservative on the issues they are working on, although they may stay just as liberal on other matters. Conservatives grow more liberal on the particular issues, but—like liberals—seldom extend this moderation to other issues they know less directly. Practical experience brings people toward the center and tempers their visceral responses. Only persons who maintain their distance from practical action can maintain their ideological purity.

In America, the vast majority of politically active individuals—including those I have referred to as "conservatives"—are liberals, in both the international and the historical senses of the term. Except for the small and, one assumes, dwindling number of Communists and antidemocratic socialists on one end of the political spectrum and some of the religious Right and a few nativists such as the Ku Klux Klan on the other, the rest of us share a great many assumptions about political, economic, and social life. On surveys about such things, we classify ourselves as radicals, liberals, moderates, conservatives, and reactionaries. The great center in American political life is made up of progressive liberals, moderate liberals, and conservative (or classical) liberals—progressives, moderates, and conservatives for short. We are all liberals, however, in the broader sense. All, for example, would be considered liberals in Eastern Europe or the Soviet Union and share fundamental values, differing in degree, or balance, on such values as rights and responsibilities. Few, for example, would want to curtail press freedom significantly, impose a state religion, or abolish private industrial ownership.

On the homelessness issue, and probably on most social welfare issues, what differentiates the three kinds of liberals from each other is the relative weight we give to rights and responsibilities. Often, this emphasis manifests itself in the reaction we have to a particular issue—whether it is to tell the welfare mother to go to work or to try to get her welfare check increased so she can take better care of her children. Radical liberals emphasize the determinacy of the system and the importance of individual (and even, these days, group) rights to be protected from or to gain a place in the system, seriously undervaluing the importance of individual responsibility for one's fate. Conservative liberals place the responsibility on individuals for their circumstances almost completely, except where government has gotten in their way—say, undermined natural institutions (such as the family) or usurped property rights. Moderate liberals stress both rights and responsibilities.

These days, moderates, I believe, tend to appear like, and even think they are, conservatives, because the public emphasis on rights, at the expense of responsibilities, has become unbalanced. In Berkeley, Boona Cheema, for example, thinks she has grown conservative. Rights and responsibilities may have achieved a reasonable balance in the late 1950s, theoretically at least, with the passage of the two civil rights acts, and then the emphasis on rights accelerated and responsibilities declined rapidly in the 1960s. More recently this trend has slowed. No important national leader, though, has coherently framed for political action the issue of restoring personal and family responsibilities. The homelessness issue challenges us to reconsider the balance between rights and responsibilities.[18]

George Will, in a column, "Begging, Free Speech, and Civilization," complains of a recent judicial ruling by Judge Leonard Sand of New York. Will describes the ruling as "reeking of liberal self-approval." Judge Sand ruled that panhandling in the New York subways is protected speech under the First Amendment of the Bill of Rights. Clearly a member of the community of conscience, Judge Sand is quoted by Will:

> A true test of one's commitment to constitutional principles is the extent to which recognition is given to the rights of those in our midst who are the least affluent, least powerful, and least welcome.

Will points out, "First Amendment rights do not vary inversely with the affluence of individuals." He says, "The question of what society owes in compassionate help to street people is, surely, severable from the question of what right the community has to protect a minimally civilized ambiance in public spaces." In the mentality of "severely individualistic liberalism," Will says, the "community deteriorates through [James Q. Wilson's] 'broken window' dynamic," under which one broken window in a building, left unrepaired, encourages more windows to be broken until no good ones are left. The broken window has sent a "message that no one cares." In the same way, street people begin a "destabilization process" that ends in "dead parks." Will quotes New York columnist John Leo:

> Sandboxes become urinals. Swings are broken. Every park bench seems to be owned by a dozing alcoholic or perhaps a street schizophrenic. When the cycle is complete, the community withdraws, serious druggies and criminals move in.

Beggars, Will says, are human "broken windows," many of them "deranged by alcohol or other drugs or mental illness and dangerous in fact or appearance." "But in the social analysis spawned by liberalism," Will goes on to say, "the individual is the only reality and the community is an abstraction without claims."[19]

Low-income families are those worst hit by the emphasis on individual rights over the community. In my childhood a popular song claimed, "The best things in life are free." Many of the free things are now being ruined. And those things are most important to those with the least money. The *San Francisco Chronicle* reprinted an article from the *New York Times* on changes in the life of that city identified in recent studies:

> Among more affluent New Yorkers . . . there's a tendency . . . to cut themselves off from the city's public places. On the part of people who cannot escape—the poor—there's a despair that results in people's shutting themselves up in their apartment houses.[20]

The liberals George Will writes of see themselves as champions of the poor, failing to differentiate among the poor and to notice how liberal policies in action have affected life for the working poor or those struggling to live a decent life on welfare. These liberals have sacrificed our public places for a feeling of righteous generosity.

The rest of us, though, are entitled to the enjoyment of our public places. People who pay taxes to support the streets and parks ought to be able to use them in comfort and safety. We must discover how we can define rights for the community at large without excessive abridgement of individual rights and how we can link responsibility with rights. Consideration of the applicability of the Golden Rule to civic life might be a good place to start.

The electorate in each jurisdiction can choose whether and to what extent it wishes to undertake the alternative of providing dignified, safe, and sanitary living accommodations to the destitute living in their public places. The electorate can decide whether to support their public officials in the intensive and continuous patrols and roundups required, at least for a time, to restore a satisfactory degree of safety and comfort for the general public.

What underlies effective self-governance is a principle of reciprocity. According to Ronald J. Oakerson, reciprocity is "a continuing relationship between or among persons based on mutual expectations of behavior." He continues his discussion of this idea:

> In a reciprocal relationship, each individual contributes to the welfare of others with an expectation that others will do likewise, but without a fully contingent quid pro quo.
>
> Unlike exchange, where each party's action is fully contingent upon the action of others, reciprocal relationships are exposed to the possibility of "free rider" behavior, the strategy of enjoying the contributions of others while contributing nothing oneself. "Shirking" is a form of "easy riding," where one does less than expected in a reciprocal relationship.
>
> The establishment and maintenance of reciprocity depends critically upon the properties of trust, fairness, and mutual respect. The language and precepts of moral reasoning are fundamental to reciprocity.
>
> While it is possible for exchange to occur on quite a narrow base of agreement, reciprocity requires broader agreement on the basic norms of social interaction.[21]

Oakerson's explanation of reciprocity can be seen as the application of the Golden Rule to civic life. If I treat the mentally ill the way I would want to be treated, then I have a moral right to expect a response. It is not the only right at issue, but it counts. It obligates us to act from conscience, not simply from self-interest.

As a safeguard, where quality-of-life laws are to be enacted and enforced, review committees should advise the jurisdiction on how the patrols and roundups are being managed and regularly visit and evaluate all sites to which people are taken from the parks and other public places. These committees should include professionals, members of the general public, and representatives of consumer groups—recovering alcoholics, former mental patients, and parents. They should be free to publicize their findings.

National leaders need to be more alert to this principle of reciprocity. President Reagan ignored it in a way that was, perhaps for thousands of the seriously mentally ill, disastrous. Early in his first administration, he gave an order that summarily cut off hundreds of thousands of disabled persons whose eligibility could be questioned from the SSI rolls. Most of these individuals eventually had their eligibility documented and were reinstated, but by then many had been cut loose from their natural support systems—neighbors, landlords, friends, storekeepers, and others—as they went for weeks or months without their welfare check. This action revealed the administration's apparent rejection of reciprocity and of the Golden Rule. Multitudes of fragile social arrangements, social ecologies no less complex than any other natural system, were ruptured. Many of these SSI recipients were seriously mentally ill and could not cope with this disruption. When people could not pay their rent, they lost places they had been living in for years, ending relationships with landlords, neighbors, local storekeepers, and others. By the time their eligibility had been reestablished, for many it was too late. This thoughtless action unquestionably increased the numbers of homeless, perhaps by many thousands.

How should we treat an alcoholic who is not psychotic but merely intolerable to those around him? If he is kicked out of everywhere, he is back on the street. Involuntary commitment to a dry facility seems the appropriate last resort for someone like this who will not or who cannot live freely in a manner that respects the rights of others. Because peace is a treasured good, much like money, when someone constantly robs others of their peace, he is properly isolated and restrained.

I have seen no program that holds its clients responsible for proper behavior that has faced up to the issue of what to do with clients who always fail. According to Portland's Don Hendrix, leaders increasingly realize that the solution to such problems is not always more money:

> After a certain point, spending more money is not critical. Different models will be necessary to solve the hard core of the problem. When there is shelter and case management for everyone who is "workable," that is the limit of social policy.

Hendrix expects his agency to run into that limit very soon; then a new model for "harder cases" will be needed. The new model "may need to have a correctional element in it," according to him.

Unfortunately, some individuals remain in difficulty after we have done everything we can think of. They are caught in the revolving door until they die—always homeless part of the time, as they rotate in and out of agencies and programs. If we want to reclaim our public places, what do we do with them? The mayor's office in Seattle came up with one idea for the alcoholics who repeatedly cycled through detox and treatment programs or who were too far gone to reform. The office set up a "wet house" for them, where only the minimum rules required for safety were in force. When the individuals living there are found drinking on the street, they are simply taken home. Seattle, it should be noted, has not recaptured its public places, but the city has achieved a *modus vivendi* with its derelicts in the downtown area. The city is managing the problem in a mutually respectful, reciprocal way, with participation of the downtown business community, social agencies, and other stake holders.

THE COMMUNITY OF CONSCIENCE has sometimes sacrificed the poor and working families to achieve a "higher value," as Lillian Rubin sets forth comprehensively in her book *Busing vs. Backlash*. This book shows how upperclass whites in the Richmond Unified School District pursued the laudable dream of racial integration by busing poor whites and blacks around. It did not occur to them how this program affected the white working class. (It certainly did not occur to them that it might set back public education for whites and blacks alike.) Wealthier parents in the busing areas enjoyed the resources to send their children to private schools; some of their neighborhoods were conveniently excluded from the plan anyway. This story has been repeated in hundreds of communities across the United States: upper-middle class reformers often overlook the problems and concerns of working-class Americans in their pursuit of social justice.

Consider an incident that took place in San Francisco in December 1988. I saw the first report of it in the *San Francisco Chronicle* of December 6. It was headed, "Death in S.F. Stirs Outcry over Homeless":

> In life, Joseph Eaton was just another faceless transient. In death, he has become a symbol.
>
> Eaton was found dead on the sidewalk at Seventh and Market streets in downtown San Francisco on Saturday night after a security guard ejected him from a Carl's Jr. restaurant. Eaton had no occupation. He lived nowhere. He was 38.

"Like a lot of homeless people, he was beaten down by the system," said Don Grindell, a counselor at the Tenderloin Self-Help Center, a San Francisco agency that provides mental health services for the homeless. "It's a damn shame that a person can die on the streets and nobody cares. But maybe his death will help other people."

George Waters, the guard who removed Eaton from the restaurant, said he dragged the man to the street shortly after midnight because Eaton had collapsed unconscious over his food. Waters said he thought Eaton was drunk and would eventually sober up in the chilly night air like other inebriated people he has escorted from the 24-hour restaurant.

"I was just doing my job," said Waters, who earns $5 an hour guarding Carl's Jr. "I thought he would sleep it off and wake up in the morning like the others."[22]

Guard Waters was not fired. A reprimand was placed in his personnel folder. Perhaps he managed to hang onto his job.

The coroner's report on Eaton's death pointed out that there were fresh needle marks on the man indicating that he may have died from a drug overdose. Followup articles showed Eaton to be Joseph Emerson Eaton, Jr., "the son of a wealthy business executive and grandson of a prominent financier" in Boston. He "suffered from severe alcoholism and AIDS-related complex." The very day he died his family had "tried to get him back to New England in the care of his family." His family had "loved him deeply," in spite of alcoholism, at least one drug arrest, and other problems.[23] His family and several San Francisco agencies had tried to help him many times. And the security guard? According to *San Francisco Examiner* columnist Stephanie Salter,

The security guard, who has seen a few drunk people in the 3½ years he has worked at Seventh and Market, determined Eaton was drunk.

As any city-dweller knows, there are people who drink or intravenously shoot themselves into a stupor on the streets and wake up, again and again, where they passed out.

Let those who would condemn either [the night manager of the restaurant or the security guard] first work a few all-night shifts at a Seventh and Market fast-food restaurant.[24]

A man who has wasted his life is assumed to be a homeless victim, a metaphor for our country's injustice. One who struggles responsibly to do his job for years at $5 an hour gets a reprimand in his personnel folder. The rest of us read our morning newspapers and enjoy a second cup of coffee.

Recently, I came across an article in the local section of the *Oakland Tribune* headlined, "Homeless Spark Furor in New Berkeley Park." It reported on complaints by residents in a moderate-income "flatlands" neighborhood that "homeless drinkers and drug abusers have taken over the park" and that now "residents of the area avoid the park completely": "The homeless have turned a barbecue area into an outdoor kitchen and they threaten nearby neighbors with violence, said Sharon Tiller, representing 40 members of Friends of Ohlone Park."[25] Complaints were reported by the head of the City Parks Commission about homeless people in two other flatland area parks. Residents near a fourth park, she added, in a particularly low-income area where drug dealing has been a persistent problem, have asked for increased policing of drug use and dealing there "or they want the park closed."

In an interview with the *Tribune,* Tiller explained that she had "lived in Berkeley since 1960" and was "part of the free speech movement." She said that the residents "sympathize with the plight of the homeless, but they also strongly feel that their park is being denied to them." "We want them to close the barbecue area and maybe take out the bushes where they sit and lie down," she said. "We want our park back again."

Free speech movement credentials and expressions of sympathy for the homeless, however, are not enough to get action. The city manager, asked by the city council what steps should be taken about the takeover of these parks, replied,

> This is a tough issue. I agree that parks should be used as parks for people with little kids. . . . Unfortunately, . . . Berkeley is forced to deal with what is really a national problem—homelessness. . . . [T]he federal government has reduced its expenditures for public housing from $37 billion to just $7 billion since 1980.
>
> The problem is that homeless people go into the parks because it is the only place they have to go.[26]

The drunks and druggies get the parks. Ronald Reagan's housing policies get blamed for the city's inability to manage its problems. The people who paid for the parks get excuses. Once again, the working class in particular and the broader community in general are made to pay the tab so the community of conscience can feel right about itself.

Studies by the Tax Foundation, a nonprofit Washington, D.C., organization that issues a report each year on how the tax load is distributed among the U.S. population, show that taxes fall most heavily on our lowest-income workers and our highest-income—those with money income below $10,000 and those with incomes above $90,000. Workers earning less than $10,000 contribute almost 50 percent of what they earn in taxes they pay themselves or in taxes the employer pays in relation to their employment. Sales taxes, social security taxes, excise taxes, and gasoline taxes fall most heavily on poor workers. Taxes on income and capital gains fall most heavily on the rich. Those with incomes between $30,000 and $90,000 pay on average between 31 and 32 percent of their income in taxes of one sort or another; those over $90,000 about 52 percent.[27] The working poor now pay an unfairly high share of their income to support the parks and other public places that are being turned over by the community of conscience to people who do not work.

The United States needs to find a way to support the struggle of working families at the low end of the economic scale to achieve their dreams. Now it is often the opposite. William Tucker's new book, *The Excluded Americans*, provides many examples.[28] The author shows how workers are excluded from owning homes through growth controls, exclusionary zoning, and other restrictive practices that drive up the cost of housing beyond what they can afford. In addition, in many communities extreme forms of rent control and other practices take the profit out of rental housing and cut workers off from one of the traditional ways they have been able, without higher education, to achieve higher economic status—buying a duplex or a triplex or the house next door, renting it out, managing and maintaining it themselves, and profiting from the rent and the increase in equity from appreciation. Thousands of working-class landlords have seen their equity stripped away by policies designed to help the poor. In New York City and in several other places, a whole new generation of workers has had this traditional avenue to economic improvement eliminated.

In recent decades, governmental programs may have focused on welfare issues to the exclusion of issues affecting the working poor. The perception is widespread, and with some reason, that for many Americans getting on welfare and taking advantage of the many public assistance programs that go along with it can provide a better life than working. This perception has contributed to the pressure to hold welfare payments below the rate of inflation. In fact, such payments have not kept pace with inflation for the past fifteen years or so. It has been increasingly difficult to live on AFDC, and—perhaps as a result—in recent years the number of AFDC clients has declined somewhat. While welfare and, more recently, drug dealing have been made less attractive, little has been done through public policy to make working at a job that an unskilled person can get more rewarding. Indeed, not only do unskilled workers receive low wages, perhaps unavoidably in a free economy, but also low-wage workers get to take home so little of what they earn.

In militating for housing and other programs for the homeless, advocates may inadvertently be pushing for positions that will further aggravate the position of low-income workers as they struggle to afford food, shelter, and other necessities. In many jurisdictions nonworking poor are placed ahead of the working poor in line for subsidized housing, public housing, and social services. He who needs the most because he has not taken care of himself gets the most public attention. He who struggles to succeed without public help sees others who appear less deserving getting the service from government. The system seems to favor both those who do not work and wealthier workers. The Republicans appear to favor the rich who demand special privileges; the Democrats, the poor who want special privileges. No one seems to stand behind workers of modest means who ask only that their government provide and enforce a framework of rules so they can raise their families in decency and safety. In our system of justice, we need to make certain that the rights of those who follow society's behests are protected.

Public policy should be designed to ensure that taking responsibility for oneself produces relative advantages in the economy over failing to do so. Giving everyone who drinks or drugs himself into homelessness a decent place to live before all the working families can afford such a place makes no sense. The minimal protection of a shelter is more appropriate in such a context than is a housing-for-the-homeless program. Good and fair government favors those who act responsibly over those who do not, or at least it treats them equally: it does not direct its benefits primarily to those who offend its norms. In this important respect our government is not entirely good and fair to poor workers and others of modest means.

Taxes and other public policies need to be evaluated and revised to ensure that they reward work over the choice not to work, family over individual, neighborhood and community over mere propinquity. We do not need to be punitive toward those on welfare, unrelated individuals, persons who choose not to be a part of community life, but positive and supportive of those who work and who try to take care of themselves, their families, and their neighborhoods. They are entitled to their dream, too.

9

Manufacturing a Crisis

NEWS STORIES ABOUT HOMELESSNESS in America have increased a thousandfold from ten years ago: there are not a thousand times more homeless. Objectively, it is difficult to discern whether the number of homeless has increased only marginally in recent times or whether it has perhaps more than doubled. One reason for this difficulty is that the media and social scientists did not find the homeless worthy of sustained attention until Ronald Reagan became president. The first entry in a library index of popular and academic periodicals for the word *homeless* or *homelessness* did not appear until the year after Reagan's election. Now it would be unusual to pick up the daily newspaper of most of our cities without seeing some reference to homelessness. The issue has appeared in news reports, opinion columns, gossip columns and cartoons. Everyone "knows" we have a national homeless crisis in America.

Is there really a crisis? Could one make a reasonable argument that there is no national homeless crisis today? The proportion of Americans who are homeless, according to careful estimates, has risen in the last two decades from about 1 in 800 Americans to about 1 in 400. But only a small portion of any increase in the incidence of homelessness is likely to have taken place during the first year of the Reagan administration, the time newspapers and television began to identify such a crisis.

In 1973 *Public Opinion Quarterly* reported on a study by G. Ray Funkhauser, who considered media coverage on and public concern over eight of the issues of the 1960s. Funkhauser found that the emergence of noticeable public concern corresponded almost perfectly with the incidence of high (more than median) news coverage. Furthermore, he noted . . . that media attention to problems did not covary with their actual severity. . . . [W]hen media coverage and actual severity diverged, the public's maximal response coincided with the highest point in [media coverage].[1]

As Funkhauser's research would have predicted, homelessness became a crisis to most Americans after the media introduced the term and labeled it a crisis. Before then it was not a crisis or even a problem: it was several problems, most of which were likely growing at varying rates, some for only a few years and some for much longer.

For the politician in our culture, reality perceived is reality itself. An unseen issue is not an issue at all. I recall a Latin phrase first heard in freshman philosophy at UCLA, *esse est percipe*, "to be is to be perceived"—words of Bishop George Berkeley, the Irish philosopher and cleric after whom the seat of the University of California's oldest campus is named. Bishop Berkeley argued that nothing was real unless someone was there to perceive it; the only reason objects did not continually appear and disappear was that God was always watching even when no person was. Other philosophers have pointed out the flaws in Berkeley's logic, but his argument does appear correct when applied to political crises. When the press is watching, we have a crisis. When the press stops watching, the crisis ceases to exist.

Mitch Snyder made this particular crisis happen. During the Vietnam War, Snyder and his associates at the Community for Creative Non-Violence (CCNV) in Washington, D.C., devoted most of their attention to antiwar protests. After the war, Snyder and the others, described by Snyder's authorized biographer, Victoria Rader, as "seven young radicals at Euclid House," needed a new issue. According to Rader,

> *Washington Post* columnist and CCNV friend Colman McCarthy recalled with frustration: They were all over the map. Every other week Mitch was calling me about a new issue. I told him to focus on one issue and stay with it. There are countless outrages every day, you can't respond to every one of them. And it's not effective![2]

In Rader's memory, Snyder's first homeless media event took place "at high noon on August 12, 1976." The District of Columbia had condemned a building Rader described as a "decayed residence, overgrown with weeds that curled around the plywood tacked up against the doors and windows." Snyder selected it to dramatize the fact that the city owned vacant buildings, while poor families were being evicted. Earlier in the week Snyder had threatened "all-out non-violent warfare" if the city did not agree to let an evicted family use the house. CCNV and other supporters would "storm" the place. "Clearly the media, which regularly ignores the problems of the poor, had taken the bait and arrived in good numbers to witness the battle," Rader recalls. After speaking to a crowd of reporters and other onlookers, Snyder and four colleagues used a crowbar to rip off the plywood from the front door; then they entered and occupied the house. The police, Rader reported, "stood motionless, stiffly at attention, looking silly in all their riot gear." The police inspector in charge said they could make no arrests until the housing authority filed a complaint. Hours passed, and the suspense melted under the August sun. Reporters drifted away. As told by Rader,

> The complaint was filed at 5:30 and five arrests were made for illegal entry. The officials across the street clapped and cheered as the protesters were handcuffed and led to squad cars. City police secured off the vacant old house and, ironically, began an expensive 24-hour guard duty.[3]

Some of the reporters who had left returned. More demonstrations and arrests followed at other locations.

The publicity attracted several new members to the core of seven organizers at Snyder's Euclid House. CCNV began to get frequent calls from homeless individuals in need of a place to stay. Snyder had found his issue. During the particularly cold winter of 1977, Snyder and his colleagues searched the city to find all the homeless they could. Rader claimed they "gradually discovered hundreds and hundreds of men and women—and even some children—living on the streets." She continued:

> People slept in abandoned cars in vacant lots, under the bridges near the river, behind the marble pillars and on top of the grates

of federal buildings. They wrapped up in plastic or climbed into dumpsters in the alleys, and they hid in abandoned buildings all over the city. Euclid House members felt they had discovered a hidden world that few others saw.[4]

CCNV sent 1,100 letters, to "every church, temple and synagogue in Washington, D.C.," asking for shelter space. It followed up with phone calls, at the same time continuing to drive around bringing people to Euclid House. In response to the letters and phone calls, "only Luther Place Memorial Church said Yes and CCNV helped staff the Luther Place shelter."[5]

CCNV struggled to acquire and rehabilitate a city-owned building. When the group demonstrated, it received local press coverage, some focusing on the need for shelter and some on CCNV's tactics. CCNV staged a symbolic and acrimonious public confrontation at the wealthy Holy Trinity Church in Georgetown, where the Kennedys had worshipped, over whether the church should spend money on renovating its building and acquiring a new organ when there were people sleeping without shelter in the city. In June 1978, Snyder and others began to enter the church, standing during all the weekend Masses. In late July, they began a liquid fast. News coverage, according to Rader, "clearly favored" the position of the church.

Then Snyder got the idea of demanding the historic but vacant Union Station for use as a shelter. The building had been converted into the National Visitors' Center in connection with the celebration of the bicentennial, but by 1978 it was attracting few visitors and had become a white elephant. The press had been wondering in print whether it could be put to better use. CCNV wrote to the secretary of the interior of its intention to turn the place into a nighttime shelter for the homeless. On November 16, to make their point, Snyder and Anne Splaine, a wheelchair-bound member of CCNV, "moved out onto the streets," sleeping on steam grates during the nights and talking with anyone they could during the day.[6]

Sympathetic articles began to appear in the local papers, and by his living on the streets, said Rader, Snyder gained "a new legitimacy to speak for the homeless." Department of Interior officials decided to meet with CCNV and talk about homelessness. The meeting conferred upon CCNV a new degree of credibility. The officials did not, however, agree to let Union Station be used as a shelter, citing "legal problems." CCNV said it would "open" a shelter there anyway.[7]

By then Snyder was living in Lafayette Park, across from the White House, and CCNV decided to serve there a turkey dinner with all the trimmings for the homeless of Washington, D.C. "The press loved it," wrote Rader. Pictures of bedraggled people lined up to get a meal went out across the world; the White House showed clearly in the background. In a matter of days, another meeting had been set up at the Interior Department. Rader described the scene with eloquence and candor:

> The camera crews were waiting when Snyder wheeled Anne Splaine in. . . . Anne was dressed in multiple layers of clothing and a wool watchcap, while Mitch wore his army field jacket, jeans and a red plaid tablecloth pulled around his head to keep out the cold (even though it was a fairly mild November day). It was a sweet study in contrasts: Ragged clothes in sumptuous lobbies, raw moral demands in hallways polished smooth with compromise. Snyder played the scene for all it was worth.[8]

After several meetings, the Department of Interior agreed to "let CCNV demonstrate the need for a shelter" but not to give CCNV official approval to occupy Union Station. Officials made no promises about how long the homeless could remain there. In spite of this informal permission, however, CCNV decided to stage its planned 10 P.M. opening of the Union Station homeless shelter on November 30 as an "occupation."

Standing in front of Union Station with the Capitol behind them, several hundred onlookers, including a large contingent of the press and about eighty people who planned to occupy the station, listened to Mitch Snyder "apologize to the homeless for having neglected them for so long."[9] Then he led the way into the station; it was a scene made for television. The occupation hit the networks and newspapers across the country: the homeless, and no doubt some of those who had joined them for the event, settled into Union Station for the duration.

Meanwhile, Snyder was still battling the Georgetown parish. A few weeks later, on Christmas Eve, he undertook a total fast and was "available," as the fast began, in the living room of

Euclid House. Although members of the press visited, according to Rader they "seemed confused, thrashing around for some familiar peg on which to hang the story":

> Was it a hunger strike? Blackmail and extortion? Or was this the action of a saint? One reporter dismissed Snyder as a Jim Jones on a suicide kick. (It would be different a few years later, after an Academy Award film portrayed Gandhi's fasts sympathetically to Western viewers. Bobby Sands' and Andrei Sakharov's fasts were still to come.) Young Americans regularly offered their lives in war for the love of their country; that was a "normal" sacrifice that we understood and took seriously. But Americans didn't sacrifice themselves for the poor; it seemed so melodramatic. The media could not communicate a message that had no roots in the culture.
>
> Besides, the media was disgusted with the Trinity campaign; it seemed a general affront to the established order in which they believed, and it reminded them too much of fabricated anti-war protests in the 1960's.[10]

The fast was called off after ten days, with Snyder hallucinating and in grave physical condition. The church had refused to budge. Press coverage in Washington, D.C., had been extensive and opinion divided, with most columnists opposed to the strike. Snyder recalled, "We were described as terrorists, moral terrorists."[11] At about the same time, the newspapers were tiring of the occupation of the Visitors' Center at Union Station. The story had turned into a series of attacks and counterattacks between CCNV and the Department of Interior in which the issues had gotten murky. The *Washington Star* commented that the affair had a "disconcerting odor of artificiality."[12] The *Washington Post* thought CCNV was taking things too far.[13] While CCNV received a lot of press coverage for its activity, it could not assume such coverage would be positive.

About this time Robert Hayes, a young lawyer in New York City, left a potentially lucrative and powerful position with one of Wall Street's most prestigious law firms to fill what turned out to be a less lucrative but more powerful, fame-generating position as the nation's de facto chief lawyer for the homeless. Hayes sued the city and won a "right to shelter" for all persons in the state of New York. His activities received national news coverage in the late 1970s, when Snyder was carrying out his Washington, D.C., campaigns. Between the two of them and their associates, they began to bring the issue of homelessness before the national public.

Still there was no homeless crisis. While Snyder and his friends continued to demonstrate and agitate, they also began to provide food and shelter to increasing numbers of the homeless. CCNV members slept on heating grates, sprinkled their blood on a church altar, went to jail, got out of jail, held public funerals, and demonstrated some more.

Rader reported that in early 1979, at the time of the Union Station campaign, the press generally referred to the homeless as panhandlers, vagrants, indigents, and derelicts. "It would be years," wrote Rader, "before reporters referred to people without homes as 'the homeless'."[14] It took Ronald Reagan's election to the presidency before the word *homeless* entered the American lexicon and before we faced a national "homeless crisis."

Ronald Reagan had run against the federal government (as had Carter in 1976) and against welfare spending. Most important, while Carter supported the huge bureaucracy of agencies and programs that had grown up around the War on Poverty, Reagan had long been their active enemy, first as governor of California and then as a presidential candidate. Although he was popular with the general public in those prepresidential days, and certainly as president, he was the most hated politician of the time among antipoverty bureaucrats and their organized constituencies. At least one otherwise even-tempered fellow anti-poverty official told me during Ronald Reagan's first presidential campaign that if Reagan were elected president, he would move to Canada.

After Reagan was inaugurated, one of his first moves was to call for domestic budget cuts, including the abolition of the federal War on Poverty agency for which my colleague and I worked. Reagan proposed turning the agency's functions over to state governments, with funding somewhat reduced. He succeeded in relocating the bureaucracy but not in diminishing either the size or the political effectiveness of the structure that was relocated.

The homeless crisis was born as part of the strategy to protect antipoverty agencies and budgets from further damage. Home-lessness was attributed to Reagan's budget cuts before they had been enacted by Congress, let alone taken effect. The first mention of the homeless or of homelessness appeared in the *Social Sciences Readers' Index* in 1981, the first year of Reagan's presidency, and in 1982 in the more general *Readers' Guide to Periodic Literature.* After that, each year the number of references has increased, until today homelessness stories are among the most common items appearing in the press.

IN 1981, HOMELESSNESS MOVED from rare mention in the recesses of the paper, or late in the television newscast, to frequent coverage close to the front page. The difference was its "news peg." Instead of being defined by editors as a local human interest, social justice, or politics story, homelessness came to be seen as an element in a big national story, the page-one story of Reagan's budget cuts. National and local reporters were assigned to find out what the effects of the proposed cuts would be, including their effects on the poor. Local antipoverty agencies were a natural source for interviews about how the poor would be affected. Some of these agencies had observed increases in homelessness in their communities in recent years, and all officials who read their national newsletters knew about Snyder's demonstrations and Hayes's successful lawsuit. They knew the word *homeless* and they knew how to use it.

The Reagan administration played into the hands of the advocates. The "Reaganauts" allowed themselves to look like cold, uncaring budget cutters. They could show no alternative explanation for the apparent increase in homelessness. They tried to deny the crisis, instead insisting the number of homeless was insignificantly small. While increasing numbers of reports and pictures from all over the country seemed to prove there was a crisis, the Reagan administration continued to downplay it. They had no factual basis for their denial, no evidence to which they could point. Nonetheless, they insisted no crisis existed. These denials further piqued the interest of the press, rather than discouraging it. Edward Jay Epstein, in *News from Nowhere,* observes that network correspondents believe that government officials are mired in a routine until confronted with the "glare of exposure." Only then do they act.[15] On such a basis, the press saw a critical role for itself in this issue.

The press could photograph the homeless and show them on television. Homeless women and children could be found—without much effort. Homeless professionals could be found too—with considerably more effort. Statistics could be inflated and purified to make the problem look big, growing, and primarily economic.

Reporters and editors were ready to use the stories and play them large and often: they filled all the needs of their news process and fit within their political biases. Moreover, no credible opposition arose—the administration's claims could be dismissed as self-serving—and every special interest group that could perceive a stake in the issue stood to benefit by it rather than suffer.

The media's ready acceptance of advocates' claims about homelessness raises a longstanding argument about a shared media bias—particularly whether the bias runs counter to the beliefs of most Americans. David Brinkley, a network television editor and an "anchorman" long before the term came into popular use, was once asked for the criteria employed in news selection. He replied, with the droll candor that has become his trademark, "News is what I say it is. It's something worth knowing by *my* standards."[16] Edith Efron, in *The News Twisters*, has accepted the truth of Brinkley's comment, writing that news is "entirely *chosen*." This process, she maintains, is "an entirely *selective* operation" that involves "culling out from all the events in the universe . . . those events which the editors believe to be of the greatest importance and interest to *most* people."[17]

If Brinkley and Efron are correct, the ideological or partisan biases of editors and reporters are important, particularly biases of which they are unaware—and share. In *The Media Elite,* S. Robert Lichter, Stanley Rothman, and Linda S. Lichter report on an early 1980s survey they conducted of a random sample of 238 journalists, editors, and news executives at "America's most influential media outlets," the *New York Times,* the *Washington Post,* the *Wall Street Journal, Time, Newsweek, U.S. News and World Report,* and the television news staffs of ABC, CBS, NBC, and PBS.[18] The results showed dramatic differences between these journalists and most Americans in background, political candidates they support, and positions on a selection of social and economic issues. Over the sixteen-year span covered by the interviews, fewer than one in five supported any Republican presidential candidate. Notably, 81 percent voted for George McGovern against Richard Nixon in the year of Nixon's landslide.[19]

Rothman and the Lichters carefully point out that while the media elite vote overwhelmingly for Democrats and take positions on policy issues commonly identified as liberal, "Most are anything but socialists":

> For example, they overwhelmingly reject the proposition that major corporations should be publicly owned. . . . [T]wo thirds declare themselves strongly opposed. . . . [T]hey overwhelmingly support . . . people with greater ability earn[ing] higher wages than those with less ability. Most also believe that free enterprise gives workers a fair shake, and that some deregulation of business would serve the national interest. [They] accept an essentially capitalist framework, even as they endorse the welfare state.
>
> In contrast to their acceptance of the economic order, many leading journalists voice discontent with the social system. [They] are united in rejecting social conservatism and traditional norms.[20]

BENJAMIN BRADLEE does not believe that the Rothman and Lichter figures demonstrate an ideological bias. Bradlee, the former executive editor of the *Washington Post,* believes instead that the news business draws young people to it who have "some vague feeling" that the newsroom has been a place "where injustices could be found and put right . . . where truth could be pursued against tough, tough odds and every so often could actually emerge and set men free . . . the brave . . . memorialized, the pompous deflated, the arrogant held to account, the innocent warned, the difficult explained."[21] Bradlee's statement reflects an assumption that in America people in power typically oppress others. The desire to remedy such oppression—deflate the pompous, set men free, protect the innocent—through public revelation may indeed be the reason many choose a career in journalism. Professor Michael Massing of the Columbia University School of Journalism has reflected the same view, saying that he believes in "the old dictum: the role of the press is to comfort the afflicted and afflict the comfortable."[22] Aaron Wildavsky, founder of the Graduate School of Public Policy at the University of California at Berkeley, would insist that even if Bradlee's statement is correct, it does not refute the notion of ideological bias. The description is implicit with ideology—an ideology Wildavsky calls "American egalitarianism."[23] In this egalitarian view, the main problems in society are caused by inequalities of economic wealth or social position.

Questions of ideology aside, most of the statements just cited suggest that the press is oriented toward negative news. Howard K. Smith, one of the great broadcasters of radio and of the early days of television, noted,

> The tradition, deeply engrained, of American journalism is negative. We are attracted mostly to what goes wrong in a nation where we must be doing something right. The emigration figures of people trying to get out of this country are few. The immigration figures are high. They must know something we are not adequately reporting.[24]

Irving Kristol has observed that American journalists have always had a populist bias that has reflected the deep and continuing distrust of government shared by most Americans. Kristol believes that among some contemporary journalists this bias has deepened in recent years. Referring to a "new journalism of advocacy," he quoted national television correspondent Roger Mudd's remark that the national media, especially the television networks, see their "chief duty" to be to "put before the nation its unfinished business: pollution, the Vietnam War, discrimination, continuing violence, motor traffic, slums." Kristol says this view represents a change in the nature of journalistic populism. While the older populist press looked at management of "the public's actual business," they now are more interested in "the composition of the political agenda—the latter being a traditional prerogative of the politician" rather than of the press. Kristol writes:

> The new journalism of "advocacy" is just as populist in mind and spirit as the old—only its populace is the college-educated middle class, out of which it emerges [today, though not in earlier times] and which is, at this time, the most discontented, restless, and dissatisfied of all our classes.[25]

The new populism seems animated by a hostility . . . to the institutions of the republic itself. Instead of "shoot the piano player," now it is "shoot the piano." Soon it may be shooting up the whole saloon.[26]

Kristol believes that the media have become "insatiable critics" who simply will not be satisfied by any government or policy.[27]

Edith Efron sees such journalistic attitudes as part of a more broadly based deterioration in the humanities and social sciences. She writes:

In all branches of the humanities and the social sciences, there has been a rejection of the criteria and disciplines of the field and a slide into subjectivity which serves as a vehicle, overt or covert, for ideological values. . . . It is a manifestation of a much larger cultural problem—an insidious assault on reason, science, and the value of objectivity which has taken place in every field of scholarship since the 1960s.[28]

Journalists are egalitarians: they oppose hierarchy. They want to bring the top down and the bottom up, although, say Wildavsky and the Lichters and Rothman, not completely. Working journalists, who dislike and distrust authority, want to see vertical distinctions reduced, and power and wealth distributed more evenly.

Although journalists seek to weaken hierarchical distinctions, they increasingly demonstrate a cultural bias. According to Robert L. Bartley, the editorial page editor of the *Wall Street Journal*, people go into journalism instead of, say, business because they are idealistic. He has said this choice represents a cultural crisis. Within the American middle and upper classes, he sees a gap between idealists and people of a more practical bent. Self-selection of journalists from among the idealists means "that there is a powerful tendency for all the[ir] mistakes to cut in the same direction."[29] Not only is the press biased against authority and wealth, he says, but it is also biased against people seen to lack vision.

What Bartley describes as a cultural gap between the idealistic and the practical is similar to what others have described as the emergence of a "new class." Peter Berger has called it "the knowledge class."[30] It might be seen as "post-industrial," in sociologist Daniel Bell's phrase. A. Lawrence Chickering of the Institute for Contemporary Studies has called it "the new information elite."[31]

Members of this new class establish their occupational qualifications with formal education rather than through practical experience. In their daily work, words are usually more important to them than numbers. The product of their work is likely to be an image, concept, or feeling rather than a thing. Their social prestige increasingly depends on cultural rather than on physical consumption. In their emphasis on quality rather than quantity, they particularly distrust individuals who have derived wealth or position from the production of traditional goods and services and see them as uncultured, the postindustrial intellectual equivalent of a country bumpkin. Members of the new class feel estranged from members of the old.

Even though both crafts are of ancient lineage, business is seen as old class and journalism as new. Reporters see the business side of journalism—advertising, circulation, finance—as "old," want nothing to do with it, and sometimes think it impedes their mission, whereas the editorial side is "new." Journalists have decided not to go into business, although it may pay better, and feel superior: going into business is for ordinary people, not for those with a calling. It is only natural that those who specifically avoid commercial business would think there is something wrong with it; otherwise, they would probably have gone into business: it pays better after all.

Extended, a hostile attitude toward business enterprises manifests itself in a hostile attitude toward the American economic system, a system based on business. The Lichters and Rothman have shown that only about one in eight journalists believes that big corporations should be publicly owned,[32] but a journalist need not be a Socialist to blame problems in society on industrial elites (old class), government officials, and other people in authority (the comfortable). A journalist will tend not to attribute to the poor, "the afflicted," much responsibility for their condition. Efron has said, for example, that a journalist will say in a story that "poverty causes crime . . . unaware that he is proselytizing for an unproved theory." She attributes this oversight to both insufficient education and bias.[33]

Perhaps any of the above biases would fit with the media's coverage of homelessness since the election of Ronald Reagan.

On the basis of ideology—liberal, left-wing, negative, or egal-itarian—none of the media critics I have quoted would be surprised at the press's treatment of this issue. It is also easy to entertain the notion that the press responded to the issue from a perspective that was specifically pro-Democrat, anti-Republican, or at least anti-Reagan, inasmuch as the issue did not catch on until Reagan had become president—did not catch on despite the hard work of Snyder, Hayes, and others to put it before the public.

Any of these biases could have played a role, but none was sufficient without a good news peg to hang the story on. Indeed, the story might have played differently had the administration not botched its response. Apparently well-documented claims by national and local advocacy groups, including networks of self-interested community action and social service agencies, con-trasted sharply with the Reagan administration's quibbles and feeble denials. Modern American journalism, wrote Paul H. Weaver, is "a moralizing form" as Aristotle defined the term in *Rhetoric*. It is not primarily "deliberative"—concerned with costs, benefits, cause and effect, and future impact; it is not "forensic"—aimed at finding out what actually happened; it is "epidiectic"—aimed at setting praise or blame. Its method is amplification—taking things out of context and highlighting them.[34] The Reagan administration's defensiveness provided an excellent opportunity for the press to exercise any propensity it might have had at the time for epidiecticity.

Ironically, as time has passed the press has begun to find a story in the public's reaction to exaggerations about the homeless in which the media have participated. In the late summer of 1991 the *New York Times* reports that the public's sympathy for the homeless is wearing thin. " 'They have heard all the solutions for the last 10 years,' " says an advocate, " 'but it doesn't seem to make a dent in the problem.' "[35]

The importance of an issue sometimes bears little relation-ship to its media coverage. The press did not notice the savings and loan crisis until the financial losses were estimated in the hundreds of billions of dollars. Blowing the whistle on the banks could have been of monumental benefit. The story fit the same press biases as did the homeless story, and it was much larger on any objective basis. Yet the press helped elevate the small number of homeless in America to major status while overlooking completely the impending fiscal disaster. Manifestly, all of the factors discussed so far—negativism, anti-hierarchical bias, political partisanship, alienation from the business class, cultural elitism—are, without someone blowing a very loud whistle, not sufficient to get the press to discover a crisis, even where the moral significance of an issue and the magnitude of its impact are colossal.

THE PRIMARY DETERMINANT of what gets covered by the news media and how it is covered is called the "news process." The way the news process works is another piece in the puzzle of under-standing why homelessness got so much coverage and why the savings and loan crisis had to get so big before it made page one. Looking at this process, we may accept news bias as a fact and still argue that it was not an important factor in making homeless-ness the big media issue it is. Possibly the news process—rather than bias—gets an issue covered and then bias influences *how* it is reported. Edward Jay Epstein believes that "the tendency of network news to focus on certain causes" stems mostly from the established process of news selection.[36] After more than a year of on-site observation at NBC News, Epstein came up with a list of six informal criteria for story selection: *newsworthiness, predic-tability* (the limited number of news crews need to recognize that a story is about to happen to be there to cover it), *film value* (bat-tlefield correspondents were instructed to "shoot bloody"), *pictures with "instant meaning"* (which might or might not accurately reflect their "real" meaning), *geographic balance* (as a national network of local affiliates, a mixture of stories from around the country is essential), and *time considerations* (late-breaking stories on the West Coast cannot be presented to eastern viewers on the same day; the reverse is not true).[37] Epstein attributes some of the reputa-tion of California for eccentricity to the fact that items making the evening news are likely to be relatively timeless features rather than hard news, irrelevant a day later, and eccentric occurrences make good features. Moreover, an editor or producer's preference for certain correspondents is significant: if a favored correspon-dent is available to cover a story, it is more likely to be covered; if the assignment falls to a disliked correspondent, it has a strike against its coverage.[38]

I believe that judgments of newsworthiness could be influenced by ideology. According to the bias of negativism, for example, a scandal is newsworthy, whereas an organization's taking steps to ensure it is free of scandal is not. The criterion of correspondent preference could also be influenced by ideology: the producer may, for example, anticipate that he and the correspondent will agree on how the story should play. Epstein makes a good case for the importance of the news process, but he does not convince me that ideological bias is unimportant in news selection and news interpretation.

Longer items selected for coverage become "stories." At CBS's "60 Minutes," Axel Madsen has written, to make the show a story must have "hook," "pipe," and "topspin": hook is the dramatic premise, pipe is the history of the characters, and topspin is how each scene and observation propels the viewer into the next scene.[39] Had the news not learned from advocates—and had we not learned from the news—to see homelessness as a "story," with hook, pipe, and topspin, we could just as well have gone on seeing it as an unconnected set of local issues, given its multiplicity of causes and circumstances.

Another factor is the media's tendency to "nationalize" stories. "Network news *is* national news," Epstein quotes an NBC executive as saying. Networks can nationalize any issue by editing around a theme. If the Cleveland subway system has a problem, the network will nationalize the story or will not put it on the national news. When it ran the Cleveland story, there were only six subway systems in the United States. The producer sought two other communities that were having problems with the subways to make the story national.[40] If a story plays often enough, in time a national problem or crisis will be perceived. The incidents may be confined to a few places, vary greatly from place to place, but the problem begins through media coverage to look like a single, unified national trend or phenomenon. Epstein concludes that "many of the trend stories," he cited transportation, urban decay, and national crime problems, "derive from the need to nationalize local stories."[41] Later in the book he continues this theme: "A dramatic event, though limited in time and location, is . . . commonly presumed to be an indicator of a national trend or illustration of a national malaise."[42]

I am convinced that bias helped to make the homeless story big, but more significantly that it has contributed to the failure of the press to understand the story or report it analytically and objectively. Instead, the story has been sensationalized, perhaps more in the national than in the local media. The media typically report in a tone that reflects a sense of mission. They offer little or no critical evaluation of claims by advocates about matters such as numbers and characteristics of the homeless and the purported causes of homelessness. They give no attention to possible adverse effects of the remedies being pushed. Epstein reported that the networks undertake media research on any issue only when they can see how it will give them an advantage over a competitor—for instance, in predicting election results.[43] He also noted that standard editorial controls designed to avoid bias tend to be omitted when the executives, producers, and correspondents share the same perspective and believe their view is accepted by all thoughtful persons. Epstein offered as examples pollution, poor health care, racial discrimination, and poverty. In these cases, he said, the press will "openly advocate eradication" and may put an issue in the terms of a crusade. Controls designed to ensure fairness are activated only when local network affiliates or other important constituencies appear likely to complain.[44]

Jerry Mildner of the Manhattan Institute thinks that to turn the attention of the American public to an issue a *causus belli* is needed, a dramatic event such as the bombing of Pearl Harbor.[45] Epstein says the networks do their job "by exposing to the public the visually shocking moments and dramatic contradictions of the news,"[46] not through obtaining information and making it public. Reagan's 1981 budget proposals felt like Pearl Harbor to many people in the antipoverty business: they went to war and the media signed on.

Through all the debate about homelessness, no interest has emerged to take the other side. Home is, of course, "mother and apple pie." All the special interests concerned with homelessness argue that there is a national crisis that needs more money. Only politicians and budget cutters have a vested interest in saying that the problem is smaller than believed, that treatment often does not work, that housing will not solve the problem, that government programs have side effects, and that we do not really know what to do for some of the homeless no matter how much we spend. Although such understanding may be in the interest of the administration and in the general interest, there is no agency a reporter might think to call that is devoted to this point of view. The only widely known reason for being opposed to social program spending is saving money, and it is generally assumed that such savings are at the expense of the poor.

NOT ONLY WAS THERE no institutionalized interest opposed to the notion of the homelessness crisis at the time the issue became front page news, but also little or no academic work was under way on contemporary homelessness—neither in universities nor in research institutes. Reporters who might have sought a critical analysis of claims by advocates had nowhere to turn. Academics were working on many if not all components of the problem— alcoholism, drug addiction, mental illness, housing policy, unemployment, family breakdown, and the like—but not on homelessness as such. Academic experts on contemporary home- lessness did not exist, nor did a body of contemporary data or analysis on the subject. A political invention of the moment, the concept of homelessness had not been defined as an issue for social science research.

Most academic social scientists begin from the same biases as the national media. Ronald Reagan has long been particularly disliked by academics. Not only was the idea that a movie star could succeed in politics galling, but Reagan was the governor of California who called in troops to quell student demonstrations at Berkeley in the 1960s. Politically, the social science and liberal arts faculties at U.S. colleges and universites are overwhelmingly on the Left. "When we send our sons and daughters to college," writes Irving Kristol, "we may expect that by the time they are graduated they are likely to have a lower opinion of our social and economic order than when they entered."[47] Both by ideology and by economic interest, these academics support increased government funding for social programs. Such funding often means consultant fees and research grants for them. It means jobs as caseworkers and program administrators for their students. Economically, they are part of the public sector, even those who work at private universities, which are nonprofit educational institutions that have grown heavily dependent on public funding for student scholarships and loans, research grants, and other important budget components.

Because of their ideological biases, their political biases, and their financial interests, most social scientists would be of little use in helping journalists delve deeper into issues of homelessness. Even those able to do good work in spite of such biases (Peter H. Rossi was the earliest to do so on homelessness and is the most notable), or those having biases that cut differently from the majority of their colleagues, proved not really useful in bringing critical perspectives to bear for several years after homelessness became a crisis.

I HAVE FOUND my local papers generally to be more informative on homelessness than national television. It is not that printed stories take more news space. San Francisco Bay area newspapers are not the *New York Times,* the *Washington Post,* or the *Los Angeles Times;* their stories are frustratingly brief (rather than annoyingly long). Because these papers cover the homelessness story day after day and because their reporters talk with homeless people as well as with officials, small business people, and residents, they live with the story and grow in their understanding. They learn what the homeless are actually like just by contact with them. They do not often come to conclusions in their stories—that is left to the op-ed writers. But they do describe what is going on.

Local reporters hold more moderate views on a great many issues than do national ones. A. Lawrence Chickering's new information elite is in fact an elite, and the more elite the member, the more his views reflect the views of *the* elite. Writers and editors at the leading papers in the country, the national television networks, the wire services, and *Time, Newsweek,* and *U.S. News and World Report* are disproportionately from the highest economic classes and the best colleges and universities.[48] Locals come from humbler family backgrounds and schools, although still well respected. They are more in touch with, or at least less removed from, the common sense of daily experience and less firmly embedded in the new information elite.

Reading the *San Francisco Chronicle,* I did not have to wait for national advocate Robert Hayes to get around to telling me that most of the San Francisco homeless had serious problems other than lack of housing. The local papers did not formally draw that conclusion, but it did come across in interviews with and descriptions of the homeless. The relationship of homelessness to alcohol and drug abuse, mental illness, and criminal behavior was clear. The information allowed me to confirm what I suspected from my experience as an antipoverty administrator and from what I had seen for myself in public places.

The commercial news networks—ABC, CBS, and NBC—did not do as well as the major California newspapers.[49] The Center for Media and Public Affairs tracked the homelessness issue on the national networks and in the major news magazines—*Time, Newsweek,* and *U.S. News and World Report*—from November 1986 through February 1989. First, the national media overwhelmingly portrayed the homeless as more like the general population than they were. They made no mention of substance abuse in the vast majority of cases, and a mere 7 percent were "identified as drug or alcohol users."[50] Where employment was considered, a majority of the homeless described were said to be currently employed. Only one person was identified as a criminal from a total of 103 television and 26 magazine stories, although more than a quarter of homeless individuals have served time in state or federal prisons. Second, the national media almost completely blamed homelessness on the "system." Only 4 percent of the stories assigned the difficulties of the homeless to personal problems, "such as mental illness, lack of motivation, or drug and alcohol abuse." Blamed most often were housing market forces (44 percent), government inaction (26 percent), and unemployment, low wage scales, and deinstitutionalization (26 percent among them).[51]

Showing the strength of the consensus on homelessness in the news community, journalists usually provided their own conclusions on the reasons for homelessness (71 percent of the time) rather than relying on officials or experts, as the media traditionally do on complex matters. When asking for a judgment, the media chose homeless persons or advocates, not academics or government officials. The organization quoted most often was the National Coalition for the Homeless, cited twice as often as the federal Departments of Housing and Urban Development (HUD) and Health and Human Services (HHS) taken together.[52]

I have collected twenty-two transcripts representing most of the special broadcasts or segments done on homelessness by the major television networks from the time the story broke through 1988. Few of the broadcasts are balanced, penetrating, and informative. Most of the best were done by "60 Minutes" (CBS), which did six shows on the subject, all of them competent. "Nightline" (ABC) aired eight shows on the subject; they were uneven in quality and generally took the role of holding the government accountable and trying to force it to act. "20-20" (ABC) did a revealing broadcast on panhandling in New York City, but "West 57th Street" (CBS) did two segments that reinforced advocate propaganda. There was a weak CBS "48 Hours" segment. I found no record of NBC news specials on the homeless during this period.

The best source of information and understanding about homelessness in this decade has been the signed opinion columns. Although the so-called news has often been slanted, usually by selection and omission rather than by how the material is presented, the argument on the opinion pages has typically been more representative, open, lively, and helpful. Perhaps editors of the news pages should experiment with signed articles on complex issues, encouraging their reporters to interpret the information they are given and raise questions about it.

"Discovering a crisis" should be an oxymoron, and "manufacturing" one a Machiavellian outrage. But our media seem to work this way, and it is probably better than the alternative: not recognizing the problem at all. Our banking system, for example, is fairly described as in crisis and has been for about a decade, but only in the latter years of the period have we been aware of it. The homeless crisis, manufactured for various motives, is not, per se, a true crisis like the one the banking industry is experiencing. There may be a larger crisis of our natural institutions, of which homelessness is a part; there may be a crisis of the seriously mentally ill, who are a part of homelessness; there is no national housing shortage at all, for low-income persons or any other group, although there are local housing crises: but the homelessness crisis is a creation by advocates and our news process. It has gotten several issues onto the national agenda that deserve to be there. This does not mean that lying, exaggeration, and lawbreaking help our governing process—they corrupt it. Because these techniques have been employed so extravagently to arouse concern about homelessness, we may lose interest in it before needed changes are made. And our trust has been further eroded. We should seek better ways to set our national agenda.

UNSOLICITED CAVEATS FOR THE PRESS

1. Treat the claims made by social advocates and nonprofit organizations with the same skepticism as those made by business or government leaders.
2. Put anyone's claims about numbers to the test of experience. Advocates often exaggerate by a factor of ten.
3. Where verifiable claims are made, verify them. If an official says all the shelters are full, for instance, ask to see shelters or records.
4. Respect the poor and other ordinary people enough to allow them to have some control over their own condition and bear some of the responsibility for it.
5. Question the assumption that more government action necessarily helps to alleviate social problems.
6. Examine critically any claim about how outside intervention might solve a problem or even that anyone knows how to solve it at all.
7. Consider that reservations expressed by average Americans about programs for the homeless, or others thought to be victims of the "system," may not be based wholly on meanspiritedness but at least in part on independent thinking and life experience.
8. Stop approaching stories as though there is some big problem in America that could be dealt with effectively if only we got serious and spent more money.
9. Call both poor and rich people to account for blaming their bad decisions on everyone else.
10. Stop using every unsolved social problem to disparage the system or those in authority.

III

Community

10

America Unraveling

NO SINGLE CAUSE explains the increase of homelessness in America over the past two decades. Differing sets of factors are behind the homelessness of each group—substance abusers, the seriously mentally ill, economically displaced families, families that have fallen through the bottom of the underclass, and so forth. Clearly, explaining homelessness as simply a housing problem does not pass muster. Alan Sutherland of Travelers Aid has described the complex of problems resulting in homelessness as "a hundred ugly threads coming together into a single horrible tapestry."[1]

A common theme does seem to tie these problems together. Homelessness seems to be one thing as well as many things. Homelessness strikes us so emotionally and confronts us with so many social and political dilemmas that it suggests itself as a metaphor for something larger.

Perhaps we can see the answer if we turn Sutherland's metaphor around: what is happening is not so much the weaving of a horrible tapestry as the unweaving of a good one, a good one with imperfections, like any fine handmade rug. Society is coming unraveled. The underlying problem, common to all the manifestations of homelessness, is a diminution in strength and scope of the fundamental institutions of social cohesion—the self-governing institutions of family and place. Around the turn of the century, pioneering sociologist Charles Horton Cooley coined the term *primary groups* to refer to such institutions: "By primary groups I mean those characterized by intimate face-to-face association and cooperation. They are primary in several senses, but

245

chiefly in that they are fundamental in forming the social nature and ideals of the individual."[2]

As observed by social historians, these institutions, based as they are on nonrational premises, have been under challenge since the dawn of Enlightenment rationalism, under increasing challenge with the advance of industrialization and urbanization. Writing in 1909, Cooley commented on the situation as it appeared then:

> In our own cities the crowded tenements and the general economic and social confusion have sorely wounded the family and the neighborhood, but it is remarkable, in view of these conditions, what vitality they show; and there is nothing upon which the conscience of the time is more determined than upon restoring them to health.[3]

In the past few decades our primary institutions have come under a barrage of pressures. The authority and functions of interpersonal arrangements that have developed naturally from living together and depending on one another—that is, *ecologically*—are not just being disrupted. They are being industrialized—taken over by purposely and rationally created institutions, governments or other bureaucracies, whose authority is based on presumed efficiency rather than on naturally developed mutual obligation. Often the intention of assuming the functions or prerogatives formerly reserved to private exchange relationships is to advance social justice. Whether that aim has been, on balance, served well by such bureaucratic intervention is beyond the purview of this book. A by-product of this intervention, however, has been a sharp acceleration in the weakening of the ability of the family and other natural institutions to do what they have done naturally in the past: to tie us together, thereby enabling us to govern ourselves and maintain productive social order, without requiring a continuously expanding outside structure for support and supervision.

While on the one hand bureaucracies have been absorbing functions of the family and other informal institutions, on the other the concept of individual rights has been greatly expanded. This process too has been with a view to correct or prevent social injustice—and it too has occurred at the expense of family, thereby at the expense of our capacity for self-governance. Rights alone are antisocial: one gets something without giving anything. Social life, though, focuses around exchange. The work of social psychologists, beginning from theories set forth by Cooley's contemporary, philosopher George Herbert Mead, tells us that human identity is first developed in the interaction between infants and their parents. This identity grows out of a two-way process of gesture and response. The idea children acquire of themselves is shaped significantly by the responses of others to what they do.[4] To function in society the child learns to play a set of social roles—daughter, friend, worker, student, and so on. Each of these, following the interaction process begun between infants and parents, has a two-way character. What was, in the immediate setting of a preverbal parent-child relationship, simply gesture and response becomes in a more developed and time-extended setting a matter of expectation and realization. Now the two-way process is no longer merely gesture and response but claim and obligation, in the words of the social psychologist: this concept translates without too much loss of precision into the broader social notions of right and responsibility.[5] Unless rights—expectations about what one is due from others—are balanced by a sense of obligation, they undermine individual identity and weaken social connection.

Sutherland's metaphor of the "horrible tapestry" derives from the craft of weaving. To borrow one from ecology, our roots are being destroyed. And homelessness itself is a metaphor for what is happening to all our human systems.

A century and a half ago, before our industrialization had advanced very far, Alexis de Tocqueville, for one, believed that American family life and sense of place were actually too strong. He described us as family-centered individualists and predicted that our bonds of family and community might become a serious liability. Tocqueville cautioned readers in both Europe and the United States about

> a mature and calm feeling, which disposes each member of the community to sever himself from the mass of his fellows and to draw apart with his family and friends, so that after he has thus created a little circle of his own, he willingly leaves society at large to itself.[6]

On this one issue, at least, the renowned commentator appears in the very long run to have been wrong. Before the Industrial

Revolution the family was clearly the strongest unit in our society, strong enough at least to perform its basic functions. Tocqueville saw this very strength as a threat to the integration of the larger society. Sometimes today families and neighborhoods act as he predicted they would, standing against the system. Such events are unusual enough to be newsworthy: Christian Science parents' insistence on keeping their children away from doctors, resistance of some parents to busing for school integration, and a strong preference for home education, are some examples. When we see these issues covered on the evening news, such stands often appear to the rest of us as reactionary and retrograde, and probably some of them are. Looking back on these disputes later on, however, sometimes we notice a wisdom in their position that we did not see at the time. Whether these families and neighborhoods are right or wrong, however, each time they lose a fight for what they perceive to be their way of life, society— while perhaps winning on some matter of principle—may also lose something by reducing the ability of its primary institutions to communicate and enforce norms of behavior.

The traditional family was weakened first by the separation of work from home that accompanied industrialization. It has been further weakened by the increasing social mobility, by liberalization of attitudes toward marriage of persons from widely different backgrounds, by relaxed divorce laws, by conflicting values communicated in primary and secondary schools, by mass media onslaught, and by higher education, which is increasingly necessary for economic success and increasingly dominated by points of view counter to many traditional American values. Many of these developments have a positive side and may even be on balance positive, in that they free our economy to improve the provision of goods and services and enable individuals to have more freedom to choose and pursue their own dreams. This progress, though, has been at the expense of our self-governing institutions. More and more they are unable to do what we have expected of them in the past. According to Robert Nisbet,

> Our present crisis lies in the fact that whereas small traditional associations, founded upon kinship, faith, or locality, are still expected to communicate to individuals the principal moral

ends and psychological gratifications of society, they have manifestly become detached from positions of functional relevance to the larger economic and political decisions of our society. Family, local community, church, and the whole network of informal interpersonal relationships have ceased to play a determining role in our institutional system of mutual aid, welfare, education, recreation, and economic production and distribution.[7]

HOMELESSNESS IS MODERN, and, in a sense, the more modern we allow ourselves to become, the more homelessness we will have. Individual rights and economic rationalism are twin nemeses of the traditional institutions that have been home. In earlier industrial days, swings in the economy left fathers unemployed and placed a strain on families when fathers could not find a way to carry out their responsibilities. Some men traveled in search of work, returning home from time to time when they had earned enough. (This pattern is still common for many Mexican citizens, who come to the United States as migratory farm workers each year and winter in Mexico with their families.) Some men did not marry, because they could not afford to, and followed mining and construction where it took them, staying in residential hotels and other low-rent downtown living accommodations. But mines and mills would close down, displacing whole communities when the ore or the timber was gone. Nowadays, leveraged buyouts, mergers, acquisitions, and relocations of facilities undertaken in response to rational economic calculations often result in massive disruption of primary institutions such as families, neighborhoods, churches, landlord-tenant arrangements, and friendships, including friendships at work. With increased rationality, the whole economy becomes more turbulent. Even when prosperity is fairly general, the social structure is increasingly likely to be disrupted and then disrupted again.

Loyalty is a traditional, nonrational virtue. When life moved more slowly, a company was likely to see itself as a family. Many still do, but they clearly do not represent the future. As work life becomes more competitive, relationships become increasingly disposable. Managers may sincerely care about one another and their workers, but they must, to keep their own jobs, defend the company in a hostile world where everything and everyone is temporary and replaceable. That means relocations, layoffs, pay cuts, and plant closings. Sometimes whole towns and even regions of the country are disposed of.

The process of removing functions from family and place is much less advanced in rural areas and small towns than in larger cities. Rural areas have very little homelessness, not just because the homeless move to the cities with services but because urbanization and industrialization have not yet overcome the strengths of natural institutions in that more settled environment. Divorce is less frequent, and the schools and the police are run by the community. People do not become homeless there even when income is low. It is instructive that Utah, one of the lowest-income states in the country, has very few homeless. The low average family income reflects the fact that in most families only the father works. The divorce rate is very low, nearly everyone goes to church, and those in trouble can count on their neighbors and the church to help get them on their feet. The idea is still uncommon that people have a right to anything without working for it. These rural areas show a relative lack of social dysfunction because they are "behind the times," less modern, and less affected by the growth of economic rationalism and individualism.

Even in major cities, ethnic groups that still maintain strong traditional values show little homelessness and low rates of social dysfunction generally. In Chicago, researchers found low birth weight in 17 percent of black babies from low-income families and only 6 percent of the babies from economically similar Hispanic families and tried to explain the difference by "cultural patterns and lifestyles." "Mexican-American mothers," they noted, "tended to be older, married, less educated, and less likely to be recipients of welfare or food stamps. . . . There was no significant difference in income during the pregnancy." Unlike the black families, the Mexican-Americans were "not culturally urban—rather they are representative of individuals who were raised in a rural, somewhat preindustrial, social milieu."[8]

Examining public health statistics and other demographic data for California, David Hayes-Bautista and associates at the University of California at Los Angeles have discovered that Latinos, whose income is lower on the average than Asians', Anglos', or blacks'—show rates of welfare use, joblessness, and crime comparable to Asians, lower than Anglos and greatly lower than blacks. Latinos live almost as long as Asians, longer than Anglos or blacks,[9] and have lower rates of prenatal and infant mortality,[10] adult illness, accidental death, and death by violence.[11] The explanation for these surprising findings lies in the Latin culture of family primacy. Latinos are twice as likely to have a family that consists of a married couple with children: almost half of U.S. Latinos live in such families, as opposed to fewer than a quarter of Anglos or blacks. Latinos have larger households, a higher rate of male labor-force participation[12] and lower rates of welfare participation.[13]

As Latinos are exposed to American ways, traditional values and patterns erode. Consequently, health and social functioning do not rise in parallel with education and income. Hayes-Bautista's data show that while both immigrant and native-born Latinos demonstrate better health and social behavior than Anglos or blacks,[14] the immigrants, although they are poorer and less educated, actually have significantly better health and social statistics than Latinos born in the United States. For instance, immigrant Latinas (females) drink less, smoke less, and use drugs less.[15] Most Latinos rise on the educational and social ladder, and as they rise from poverty into the middle classes, their health and social functioning decline toward the Anglo rates. Among those who do not make a successful transition, rates deteriorate dramatically, as the old healthy ways are lost in the modern context and are not replaced by the wealth, knowledge, and contacts needed to develop a new support system to take the place of the traditional family and its values. According to Hayes-Bautista,

> The disturbing picture that is emerging is that the Latin population begins its sojourn in the U.S. as a fairly active, healthy, vigorous group. Over time, we notice that these traits seem to erode somewhat, by generation and assimilation. While there is still enough of these traits to lift the Latino population head and shoulders above other populations in terms of health, family, work, we are very disturbed by the constant erosion and loss of strengths.[16]

The National Science Foundation is supporting a study led by Lisandro Perez at Florida International University that should determine whether such findings hold true as well for blacks immigrating to Florida from the West Indies and Caribbean islands.[17]

The longer one is exposed to modernity the more the traditional ways are eroded. Most find new ways that work for them and achieve success and presumably happiness. But with each passing generation a few more families and individuals lose their traditional connections without achieving integration into an adequate new set of supportive institutions. The old institutions are no longer there to catch them when they fall, or they may now be too strange to the partially modernized for them to go back.

All along, economic and technological change have strained the family-centered individualism that Tocqueville observed. The precipitate expansion in the role of government over the past two decades, however, has greatly accelerated this process. The very nature of American individualism is changing. According to sociologist Amitai Etzioni, "The rise of ego-centered individualism has paralleled the rise of big government. *Both* constitute a retreat from community, from family, schools, and neighborhoods, and from a viable and effective self."[18]

THE FAMILY does society's most important work: it socializes the young. The biological and psychological ties that bind a family together are so fundamental that it will survive almost anything in some condition. To do its work most effectively, however, it needs not just the love of parent for child and the physical necessities of survival. Two parents are generally better than one. Parents who have a place of respect in the community and respect themselves and each other can communicate society's values better than parents who do not. Parents who work can communicate the value of work. Parents who plan for the future can communicate the value of looking ahead. Parents who are dealt with respectfully and deal with others the same way can communicate the value of civilized living.

As the family-centered individualism remarked by Tocqueville gives way to a more self-centered version, an array of social consequences follows. "Many Americans," according to Etzioni, "are no longer willing to take care of themselves, and each other." In his metaphor, this deterioration is a "hollowing of America," where community has been "whittled down."

He says that increased dependence on government has been accompanied by "me-ism."[19]

The family is most weakened among the poor on welfare. There most families have only one parent instead of two, and the responsibility of providing food and shelter has shifted from the parents to government. These families have little leverage in their outside relationships. When they do, the leverage often comes from exercising "rights," where they reduce someone else's authority, and therefore responsibility, rather than through empowerment, where they acquire the means to exercise responsibility themselves.

Where low-status families try in the face of serious odds to communicate values to their children, they are often contradicted not just by what their children see inadequately socialized people doing in the neighborhood and at school but by permissive policies imposed by judges and administrators who espouse attitudes current in the larger society. The weakening of dress standards is an example with which I am personally familiar. Several years ago when serving on a Berkeley school-parent committee, I learned of some black parents' strong support for a dress code. They did not want their daughters and their daughters' peers "dressing like prostitutes." Their fears were real that their daughters might *become* prostitutes. We white upper-middle class parents were not worried about any such thing. Some of us supported our children's freedom to make their own decisions on such things, even thought it ought to be a "right"; some enjoyed the variety of dress; some thought the matter unimportant; and some remembered their own high school days of petty rules and were glad to see fewer of them. Were the issue ever seriously brought up, the schools would not have dared to enforce very much of a code. White upper-middle class students, with the support of their parents, would have made it an issue for all kinds of protest. Without the support of these parents, the school would not be able to make the code stick. Thus, conscientious lower-income black families lost their ability to insist on what they saw as proper dress for their children.

The most important value that families can instill is responsibility. From it, many other values are derived. Responsibility is communicated by the very act of getting up and going to work. Having a "place" in society, through work, home ownership, labor union, church, or other associations, leads to activities that further demonstrate responsibility. People who live on welfare tend not to maintain such networks, and when they do, it is often focused around rights with respect to the welfare system, the schools, landlord-tenant relations, and public safety, rather than responsibility. Most do take a great deal of responsibility within their families, struggling mightily to see that their children are properly fed and clothed and are safe. Neighbors may look out for each other's children, and sisters and friends typically baby-sit for each other, without charge. But little sense of responsibility develops beyond these personal relationships because public bureaucracies do not require anything from those they serve except to be poor, hungry, or homeless. William Donohue, in his book *The New Freedom*, complains of what he calls the "socialization of responsibility," from individuals and families to public institutions.[20]

Welfare may be a way of keeping people alive, but few are happy on welfare. As the system relieves individuals of responsibility for their own condition, their self-respect erodes. The children are not insulated from these indignities. Many learn to value their lives very little, an evaluation reflected in youth homicide rates of our inner cities. Instead of taking practical steps to make sure that families are able to form, stay together, and take responsibility for themselves, government has absorbed family functions and advanced individual rights. Where parents once banded together to recruit a teacher and set up a school, for instance, the schools have been turned into government bureaucracies of tenured professionals and administrators only marginally responsive to locally elected school boards.

In recent years the courts have awarded to students rights against invasion of the privacy of their lockers and the like. The parents can help greatly in their children's education, but they no longer have much control over it. Before, when it could be assumed that school officials reflected the desires of parents, searching the lockers of students, if there had been any need for it, would likely have been supported by the parents, as would the occasional application of "the rod" to a small backside. Today, in areas of high drug use, parents might still support locker searches, but the ability of school officials to make such searches without proving a reason to suspect drugs in a particular locker has been challenged successfully by lawyers purporting to represent the rights of students. This combination of absorbing the authority of parents for choosing schools and teachers into the educational bureaucracy and then limiting what that bureaucracy can do by reference to the individual rights of students illustrates the simultaneous absorption of the functions of natural groups such as the family and the extension of individual rights.

The school example applies not only to the poor but also to the majority of American families. For the poor on welfare there are many more institutional relationships that place them in a subservient role. Their traditional self-determinative functions—their authority and responsibility—are eroded by their dependence on the beneficence of government for the goods and services they need. The family's ability to convey values is weakened, a tragic result, as in Etzioni's words, "There is no adequate substitute for the family in forming the basic character of the young."[21]

Hundreds of thousands of people are reaching adulthood in families where no one has ever earned a dollar by working and in communities where they have learned much about rights and little about personal responsibility. According to Donohue,

> The problems of the ghetto—illegitimacy, single-parent families, poor school performance, drugs, violence—are problems of impoverished character, the kinds of individual moral failings that have been socially produced and nourished. It cannot be said too strongly that these are not maladies rooted in race. On the contrary, these are ailments directly traceable to an enfeebled environment, one that was created in the 1960s and sustained in subsequent decades.
>
> What happened in the 1960s was that the same government that awarded blacks their long-overdue rights, simultaneously socialized responsibilities for them as well, thus uncoupling the traditional relationship between rights and responsibilities. Within the space of just a few years, a large segment of the black population went from a position of many responsibilities and few rights to many rights and few responsibilities.[22]

At root, these problems reflect a flight from personal and family responsibility. This flight is manifested in the growth of institutions that absorb our duties in exchange for cash—either directly from us as consumers or, in the case of welfare programs, after it has been laundered by the government. Some have remarked that Americans have become excessively materialistic, trying to get all the money they can to buy things. A preoccupation with things, though, is not the real problem, which is that we buy our way out of our fundamental human responsibilities. Responsibility begins and centers in the family, extending from there to neighbors, friends, church, school, and community. To the extent that the principals in the family, usually the parents, forsake their responsibilities or have them usurped, the family itself is weakened, and the seams of society begin to unravel. I believe that Donohue is correct in attributing the public greed and narcissism observed in recent years not to capitalism but to irresponsibility. "The sleaze on Wall Street that has been so apparent in recent years," he says, "and the profiteering that former government insiders traffic in so casually, is more a function of a culture gone wild with irresponsibility than of market economics."[23]

As problems manifest themselves, our solution is increasingly to fund programs and hire experts; yet this approach only aggravates our problems, for as functions are absorbed elsewhere, the family is further diminished. "To think that bureaucracy can answer the problems of community," Donohue says in criticizing solutions offered by Robert Bellah and associates in *Habits of the Heart*, "after the painful lessons of the twentieth century are considered, is astounding."[24]

Although it is logically possible that we could decide to set up institutions and give them cash to take over all the functions of the family, we know intuitively that this would be dehumanizing. This insight suggests that we are already partly dehumanized to the extent that we have delegated our fundamentally human responsibilities to outside institutions. Hiring people to help us is one thing; paying them to make our decisions and transmit our love is another.

UNTIL THE 1970s, the homeless on skid row were predominantly alcoholic white males. Then they were joined by increasing numbers of black males, many of them left unemployed by the deindustrialization of the inner cities. These single males are the counterparts of unmarried mothers still living in the ghetto. Most single men and women even in the inner city are not homeless, though: single mothers rent a place for themselves and their children with income from AFDC or (less often) work, and single men live with their own parents, their girlfriends (on AFDC), or alone. But the story of growing homelessness is often the story of homeless men not working and not married and of women with children in shelters not working and not married. A homeless single male is likely to be matched somewhere by one or more single black females whose children he has fathered. These women, without a mate to help support and raise their children, are vulnerable to becoming homeless too. Sequentially, first perhaps as teenagers, these young women bear babies without marrying the fathers—unemployed young men are, after all, "unmarriageable"—continue to live in their parents' home for a while, then live with friends, and then move into a homeless shelter. The women and children live in homeless shelters; the men are on skid row or in other homeless shelters. In another time and place they would be married to each other, the husband would have a job or both would, and they would have their own place.

What happened? Deindustrialization of the inner cities sneaked up on us: high-paying unionized jobs were replaced by lower-paying office and service jobs. Although a partial explanation was a changing economy, that was not all. The nature of life in the inner city and the quality of its workforce were changing as well. Hard-working parents of black youths in the inner city were losing out in the debate over values to a post-Martin Luther King generation of civil rights leaders and other community activists. These leaders and advocates defined the problem as racial oppression, surely true historically and to some extent true still; but oppression is only a starting point for understanding the problem. Taking advantage of the opening up of better neighborhoods to blacks through the enforcement of antidiscrimination laws, many parents who could afford to moved their families out of the inner city.

The people who remained heard repeatedly that they were victims of injustice and would get what they deserved only if they demanded and took it. Many got jobs in antipoverty programs, and—as described so well in *The World of Patience Gromes*—seemed to others to get paid for not working. Values that had survived in black communities of America through the years of slavery, reconstruction, repression, recession, depression, and war—the values of work, family, and faith (the phrase is George Gilder's)—took their worst beating from bad ideas.[25]

In the face of all this, manufacturers did what many black families were doing: they moved out. Instead of modernizing their existing plants, they pulled up stakes and relocated their operations away from the rioting to areas where workers were better educated, less troublesome, harder working, and not (yet) unionized.

The position of black men in the labor market was further diminished when the manufacturing jobs that remained were opened to women. A combination of affirmative action policies and, perhaps, better work habits resulted in women's getting most of those jobs. Federally funded community organizers argued that welfare, in the form of AFDC, which paid money to women without men, was a right, and antipoverty lawyers followed with lawsuits. A program originally intended as temporary support for widows with small children became the principal and long-term source of income in many neighborhoods.

HOMELESSNESS INCREASES as the family weakens and as greater numbers of individuals become alienated from their families and neighborhoods. These individuals do not need rights so much as they need roots. Reportedly, most of those released from mental hospitals in the early years of deinstitutionalization did not become homeless because they had families and friends to help them relocate and to see that they were cared for. Only when patients without supporting relatives began coming out of the hospitals in significant numbers did we begin noticing mentally ill individuals on the streets. A recent study shows the "degree of estrangement from family and community" to be significantly more pronounced among the homeless mentally ill than among the nonhomeless.[26]

The expansion of personal rights is an important underlying factor in homelessness because it attenuates social connection. Each personal right is defined or expanded at the expense of some prerogative that existed before—a tradition of some sort. Traditions, which inhere in groups, hold groups together and defend them from the outside world. They were born in important life experiences shared by the group. Values based on common experiences that extended beyond one group to another help to bond our groups together. Deciding that common values cannot override rights "inherent" in persons as individuals destroys our essence as humans, our humanness, and our value-generating capacity. We seem to have decided that only very limited and clearly defined and restricted nationally or internationally held values may predominate over personal prerogatives. When we restrict the exclusivity of groups and limit their ability to make decisions based on mutual obligation rather than by the mere reason that a person exists, we weaken the fabric of our society.

Society comprises many groups bonded internally and then bonded to other groups based on what they share. If the values that define a group are continuously attacked, or a group is continuously restricted in its ability to teach and enforce its values, the group is weakened, and its ability to care for its members is reduced. One big group will not work: it cannot include everyone. Groups take care of the people they value. If they cannot value anyone more than anyone else, they will not take care of them. The homeless are those most visibly excluded as we move toward homogenization in the interest of personal rights, for personal rights are fundamentally at variance with group values.

People who will take care of one another in difficult times need to feel something special toward each other. They will not perform extraordinary deeds for just anyone. When they are told repeatedly in other connections they can no longer regard some people as special, when they are required to treat everyone the same, regardless of differences in background and values, the ability of groups to take care of their own is diminished. Then we find it necessary to substitute government or bureaucratic programs to do this—programs based on rationality rather than on affective bonds.

EVELYN SMITH of Chico, California, is in a group that believes that couples should not live together unless they are married. The group she is in believes other things too, of course, and holds most of these beliefs in common with many other groups, generally called Christian churches. These groups give their members strength and take care of them. Studies show that church-going Americans do better than others on indexes of social well-being, economic achievement, and so forth.[27] Fewer become homeless. Evelyn Smith and her group's values, however, are under attack by the government. She has been told that under California state law and the right to privacy implied in the U.S. Constitution, she cannot refuse to rent an apartment in her duplex to an unmarried couple.[28]

Apparently, the argument that not renting to this couple interferes with their privacy can be proved legally, but it is not readily grasped through common sense. Common sense is the understanding that people who agree on a set of values or have undergone a particular set of experiences (a history) would share in common when faced with a new set of facts. "Common" does not mean just ordinary, although it does include that meaning in the sense that ordinary people may be more open to a mutual understanding than people who are trained not to be. It also means shared—what we perceive because we live together, practically, day to day, and not in some world of theory. What ordinary people sense in common is under attack by ideologues and legal theorists. They will be able to win every argument, for the rules of argument are logical and the position of the opposition is based on logic. What holds us all together is not primarily logic, but affection, which is not rational. If our social cohesion has to be rational, it will be destroyed.

The extension of personal rights, such as that at issue between Evelyn Smith and the young unmarried couple, contributes to homelessness in at least three ways. The first, least obvious, and most fundamental way is by weakening nongovernmental institutions as a class. They are the knots that make up the weave of society, and they are reduced in strength whenever they cannot apply their values within their environment. When these knots weaken, people come loose. The second way is through diminishing the particular institution, in this case the institution "landlord." If a landlord cannot decide to whom to rent, the informal role of landlords in social control and determination of neighborhood quality is eroded, and the neighborhood deteriorates. If it is a low-income neighborhood, after a while the government becomes involved, maybe taking it over or bulldozing it. The third way is through the effect on the issue itself, in this case marriage. Even if it is desirable for the government to be neutral on a particular value, like marriage, does that mean that government, on behalf of society, should require everyone making an economic decision to be neutral on the value? A value is maintained only through people's actions in supporting it. If they do not support it, it will die. Should all values on which government is neutral die? The indefinite extension of personal rights implies that they should.

Ironically, the government is not neutral on marriage and the family as a specific value. Government, on this, as on many values, is inconsistent. Marriage is favored, for instance, in our tax system. But contradictorily, it appears through a process of evolutionary emergence of issue after issue that it is the de facto policy of government to expand the rights of persons to engage in activities or lifestyles outside of or counter to marriage that are both generally disapproved and disapproved passionately by groups within the society, and even to require the cooperation of those who find these practices expensive, offensive, or even abhorrent. Tradition is oppression, according to this line of reasoning, and oppression must be overcome—unless, it seems sometimes, the tradition is that of a group defined as oppressed, such as women who want to maintain a single-sex college but would deny men the ability to do so. When a group that has succeeded in defining itself as traditionally oppressed wants prerogatives, then all bets are off.

The suggestion is not that the definition, enforcement, and even expansion of personal rights is necessarily bad. But it is possible to go too far too fast. We need to be aware that there are always costs in weakened social cohesion whenever new values are forcibly laid upon old and, in this context, that homelessness results fundamentally from declining social cohesion.

Whether one accepts my argument from common sense that homelessness is a significant *indirect* effect of the expansion of individual liberties, the fact that so many people are living in the streets is certainly a *direct* effect. First, the expansion of civil liberties law and of public attitudes toward civil liberties has made it more difficult for the authorities to remove people from the streets. Vagrancy statutes were found to be unconstitutional in the early 1970s when the U.S. Supreme Court decided in *Papachristu* v. *United States* that it was unconstitutional to punish people for a status rather than a crime.[29] Until then it had been possible for the police to arrest someone for just being on the street without means of support. While it is difficult to take logical issue with this decision, an effect of it and of many subsequent decisions is to let people live on the streets, including people who might have some choice in the matter and would not have chosen to do so before the decision.

In New York City, panhandling has been protected as free speech. One after another, civil rights decisions, both reasonable and unreasonable, have taken away our ability to maintain order in public places and to enjoy those places that we have all paid for. More and more we are turning them over to people who take no responsibility for them at all or even for themselves.

Donohue says that we make a mistake by "defining rights as the sine qua non of liberty." In so doing, "We have been driven to conclude that the more rights an individual has, the freer he is." He continues:

> So the pattern has been to pile one right on top of another, as if the higher the stack, the greater the degree of freedom. It is precisely this logic that motivates civil libertarians to lobby for a new round of rights each time they score a victory in the courts. To them, rights are a sufficient cause of freedom.
>
> Ironic as it might seem to some, a value is not enhanced when it is maximized. It is corrupted. Take rights. Push one person's rights too far and the result is the emasculation of someone else's rights. Elevate rights to the status of an absolute and the result is the destruction of other values. Expand the definition of rights to include all desirable ends and the result is a diminution of interest in rights that really matter. Extend the concept of rights to every conceivable animate and inanimate object and the result is a depreciation of human rights. In short, attempts to maximize rights insure their minimization.[30]

Donohue says that we have come to "make a fetish" of individual rights and that doing so inevitably leads us to view individual responsibilities as an unfair burden. He concludes from this that "the quality of public life seems to be eviscerated with the awarding of additional individual rights."[31]

Unquestionably, street persons are becoming more brazen and offensive. More of them have the idea that they have been offended by society and that each person who passes them owes them something. Sarah Ferguson, a writer for the *San Francisco Chronicle*, commented on this issue in a recent column:

The stereotypical image of the old skid row bum meekly extending his palm for change has been replaced by young African-American and Hispanic men, angry at the lack of well-paying jobs, often taking drugs or selling them—or demanding money with a sense of entitlement that passers-by find enraging.[32]

The director of City Union Mission in Kansas City, the Reverend Maurice Vandenberg, says that today there is "a much greater sense of entitlement and consequently [the street people] seem much more violent. If we don't have enough desserts to go around at dinner time there's likely to be a fight."[33]

The homeless used to think they were homeless because they had in some way failed. They were generally correct that the problem was at least partly their own doing, the mentally ill being a notable exception. Now, because of what they hear in protest songs, read in the newspapers, see on television, hear from advocates, or learn from the social service system, they think their condition is someone else's fault. Some act as if they think they are morally superior to people who work and raise a family. Popular culture and popular politics, so much of which centers on oppression and corruption, obviously imparts that idea.

Public policy studies should focus on how we can protect the liberties of individual citizens and unpopular groups without damaging the quality of life for everyone, including those specifically being protected. The key lies in attaching the concept of personal responsibility to notions of personal right. Donohue believes that our law schools are a good place to start because they have been promoting the concept of rights to the exclusion of responsibilities: "The notion of the common good, the public weal" should be unearthed and emphasized alongside the notion of individual rights in constitutional law classes, he believes. Students should graduate with the same degree of respect for one as for the other.[34]

The American Civil Liberties Union and other civil rights advocates have shown no interest in the problem of relating rights to responsibilities. Yet their interest in the homeless has gone far beyond trying to ensure that established constitutional rights are protected. In the words of Martha Fleetwood and Laura Schulkind of Public Advocates, Inc./Homebase, civil libertarians are interested in establishing, either by legislation or litigation, "the right of every American to decent and adequate food, health care, education, and employment" and hope that around the homeless issue they have "begun to build the groundswell for these principles."[35] It puzzles me that people who are intelligent enough to graduate from good law schools are not intelligent enough to discern that simply establishing rights for people and appropriating funds for programs will not cure all social problems. But then as sociologist Peter Berger observes, "Intellectuals have not fewer but *different* superstitions, and they are capable of the most mindless fanaticisms."[36]

In the winter of 1990, journalists reported that local governments are "turning heartless" about the homeless.[37] These governments had not turned cold: they simply saw no solutions. Whatever governments do, the problem seems to grow larger—and then they are asked to turn over their treasure to social pleaders. Intuitively, some suspect that if governments do less, the problem may grow less. There *are* solutions, though; some of them will cost a lot of money, some will actually save money, and some will provide wonderful opportunities to exercise leadership. But it is time to stop lying to each other, to get off advocacy binges, and get to work.

Two homeless shelters: in 1930 (top), crowded, run-down, and dirty; in 1985, still crowded and run-down (note the loose tiles), but clean—and there are signs of caring in the donated quilts.

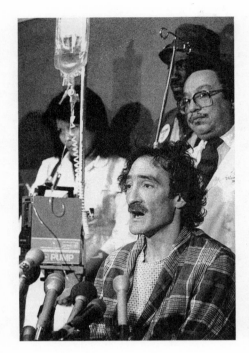

Mitch Snyder, being fed intravenously, holds a press conference at Howard University Hospital after ending a fifty-one-day hunger strike.

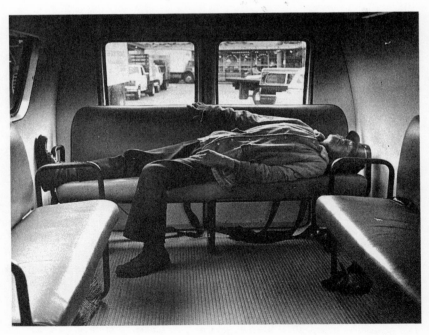

Sleeping it off in the back of Dutch Shisler's van in downtown Seattle. Shortly the van will be full.

11

Building Self-Governance

THE ARGUMENT OVER domestic social policy needs to be recast. For many years it has consisted mainly in a debate about how, or—in the extreme—whether, to put resources into social agencies and programs, into building and improving a service bureacracy, a "welfare state." The Left has held that we need more of this, and the Right has answered that we need less or none.

This book argues that we could take another way, a way emerging from a broad range of policy ideas but not yet clearly articulated as a different direction, a way of the center. With the Left, it carries an active role for our government in the welfare of its citizens, and with the Right, it insists on the primacy of traditional institutions and of personal responsibility. Some call this approach empowerment; it can also be called self-governance. Fundamentally, instead of continuing to emphasize building a service bureaucracy, this new approach would turn toward building—or, perhaps, rebuilding—our social infrastructure, our web of natural institutions. We should enact laws to facilitate and allocate funds to nourish not *government*, but *self-governance*.

PRINCIPLE: *Government policy should be aimed at restoring the social, educational, and cultural functions and resources of daily life to the institutions of family and place—neighborhood, work site, voluntary grouping, informal association, friendship group, religious assembly, and other spontaneous and natural communities.*

Advocates for increased services may confuse this distinction between more government and self-governance by asking for programs that they believe will strengthen the family or other primary institutions. A current example is the pressure for a federally funded system of child care centers that would meet quality standards set by experts. Under a self-governance approach, policies would be aimed at empowering families either to take care of their own children or to make their own arrangements for child care. If they decide to place their child in a program, it would be a program of their own choosing, and the agency providing it would receive its income not from the government, but from the family itself. The distinction is crucial. In the federally funded program the powers of the family are given by government to a cadre of outsiders, excellent as they may be. In the self-governance approach, the importance of the family in raising its children is recognized, and its capacity strengthened. This capacity would probably enhance its ability to play a larger role in the community as well.

Listen carefully to what a politician says about health and welfare issues. If he or she asserts that we need to provide for the needs of our people, that is an expression of the welfare state approach. Diane Feinstein used such language in her recent gubernatorial campaign in California. Her successful opponent instead supported ways of making it so that people could take responsibility for their own lives. Both are moderates, but this distinction is decisive.

Consider, as an example, substance abuse. Substance abusers have decided through their actions not to take responsibility for themselves or anyone else. The rest of us have decided not to hold them responsible for themselves. Instead, we have interpreted their behavior as evidence of a disease. Although we pay cash to the government to avail them of what has come to be called "treatment," somehow we leave them their "rights." The substance abusers are out on our streets and in our parks, increasingly visible as their individual rights are expanded and governmental and other programs enable them to continue in their condition.

How can we solve this problem? First, we will never know how to get people to make good decisions all the time, and must accept the fact that we will never eradicate drug abuse completely. Second, we need to stop thinking that we know of effective medical or scientific treatment for either alcoholism or drug abuse. We do not, at least not yet. We can only help people make and keep to a decision. And that is better done by people who love them—with "tough-love"—than by people who do not. Third, research should be increased to find a biological means to end the craving for alcohol or drugs or to end the adverse effects of these substances when ingested. Fourth, and most important, we need to restore our family life so that each person feels important and responsible there and has sufficiently persuasive reasons not to drink or take drugs. Fifth, we need to insist on responsible behavior in our public places and give our officials the tools they need to enforce it.

Charles Murray thinks that we can make a difference on some of these problems rather easily and inexpensively in just this way. Principals and teachers, he says, could control the schools if they had "a free hand to oversee, discipline, suspend, and expel, 1950s-style."[1] He asks if we are willing to return that level of authority to school officials. If so, he says, "It is easy to run schools so they have [a] drug problem . . . no worse than the alcohol problem in the typical 1950s high school."[2]

Murray believes that too often in making public policy we ask the wrong question. We wonder how to help society as a whole instead of how individuals and families can pursue their own happiness more effectively—take responsibility for their own situation. In the case of public education, we ask, for example, how we can make education of high quality available to everyone, and we get twisted into pretzels trying to find a solution. The problem, posed that way, probably cannot be solved. If it could, we would have done it by now; we have certainly put enough effort into it. If we look at the situation faced by families or individuals one at a time, however, questions arise that may be possible to answer, and the answers may add up to something that works broadly. For this reason Murray supports a program of unrestricted educational vouchers. Then a parent whose priority is a drug-free school, for instance, can enroll a child in a school with strict enforcement policies—unannounced locker searches, policed hallways, drug testing, and first-violation expulsion. Another family more concerned about the civil liberties of youths can send their child to a school that is somewhat more relaxed. Schools, to get the funding they need to survive and grow, will have to develop a set of policies attractive to enough parents. Each parent can get something closer than now to what he or she wants. If parents are getting what they want for their children, are we "making education of high quality available to everyone?" Do we need to ask that question?

Under a voucher system, not only is it possible to straighten out our schools, but also in letting the families decide where their children will attend school, the role of the parents has been strengthened. We have built "self-governance." Parents are empowered with a function that restores importance to the family within the social system, thereby enhancing their ability to communicate values to children. A nexus is created for families to join with teachers, administrators, and other parents around the values to be pursued in the schools. The family becomes a true partner in the educational process, not just a unit for reinforcing what the school asks of children or, more often, fails to ask. Parents decide where to send their children and therefore have a serious say in how the school will operate. Right now, low-income parents have the responsibility to see that their children are educated but not the authority to make it happen. Vouchers will give that authority to those who care to take the trouble. Over time, this empowerment should improve the schools, the families themselves, and life in the community. Everything, as Daniel Patrick Moynihan says, is related to everything.

Characteristically, supporters of school vouchers and other "choice" programs in education believe their approach will improve the schools through taking away monopoly control held by the educational establishment and subjecting the schools to competition in the market. The schools will have to perform, or parents will take their children elsewhere. I agree that choice will make the schools better, but I disagree on how it will happen. Recent educational research is close to unanimous that the most important factor in the education of children is the homes they come from, not the quality of the educational experience provided by the school. Academically successful children come from homes where the educational experience is valued and the efforts of the school supported. Schools with high average test scores are schools where most of the students come from supportive homes. Parents who choose where to send their children and are accorded respect and participation based on their control of the funds will take a greater interest in the process and support their children's learning more effectively. Moreover, as they gain power and respect in their community through controlling this important resource, their children will do better in school *whether the school does a better job or not.* But the school *will* do a better job, partly because it will be subject to market forces but even more because the students will come to school better prepared to learn. Their parents will understand and support the process instead of feeling angry and helpless.

PRINCIPLE: *All who can should be expected to behave in a civilized manner. The exercise of individual rights in public places is not unlimited but contingent on the maintenance of public order so that others are free to enjoy the commons in comfort and safety.*

Serious attention should be given to the idea of a community rights act that would reestablish the rights of citizens to the enjoyment of their public places while still protecting the civil rights of individuals. Part of the problem of drugs in the schools is that the hands of responsible school officials have been tied by the expansion of civil liberties. Admittedly, we have a drug problem, and a serious one, but our problem is also that rights have been extended so far that irresponsible behavior has been allowed to take over and rule the setting. If people want to destroy their minds in private and let other people alone, that is one thing. When their behavior interferes with the ability of others to carry on normal business, though, that is something else. To maximize liberty is seldom to optimize it; at some point, liberty degenerates into license. We need to find a balance between the rights of some to due process and privacy and the rights of others to pursue their lives in peace and safety. Our goal should not be the continuous extension of our liberties but a balance that enables us to pursue happiness. This does not, of course, mean the wholesale repeal of civil liberties for those suspected of wrongdoing. As Donohue writes in the last paragraph of *The New Freedom,*

> What it comes down to is that we have been living a lie. We have been acting as though we can have maximum freedom for the individual and sense of community and civility in society as well. We have come to believe that psychological and social

disorders can be mitigated without making personal sacrifices. We have convinced ourselves that the only alternative to the new freedom is moral despotism. But it is fatuous to pretend that we are stuck with only two choices; in between the two extremes is a great big middle area, and it is in this gray area that ordered liberty has been and can be found. We do not need to shove this pendulum between individual liberty and social well-being full force—a gentle push will do just fine.[3]

Parents, with a voucher in their hands, will insist that a way be found to reconcile individual rights with social peace in their children's schools.

PRINCIPLE: *Governments should discontinue the practice of providing cash welfare grants to known substance abusers.*

Local governments are beginning to question making uncontrolled cash payments to general assistance recipients believed to be substance abusers and are providing vouchers or services instead or entrusting management of the cash to a third party "protective payee." Seattle has found that most street drunks are not on general assistance, but they are often on SSI, SSDI, aid through the Bureau of Indian Affairs, or other government welfare funding. The U.S. Department of Health and Human Services and other federal agencies should join local governments in considering whether means could be tried to help appropriate local agencies to place substance-abusing homeless clients under protective-payee arrangements like Seattle's.

PRINCIPLE: *Mental illness is a disease. Insofar as possible, the mentally ill should be cared for by those who love them. In doing this, they are carrying out the work of society and should not have to carry an excessive financial burden for it.*

Mentally ill individuals do not choose their condition. Whatever the verdict on substance abusers, the mentally ill are victims of a set of diseases that are almost surely and almost always organic. These diseases strike arbitrarily, and ways are not known to avoid them. Public policy should be to support families in caring for their mentally ill. Whatever the abstract arguments might be about the rights of the mentally ill, both as an element in empowering the family to take responsibility for its own mentally ill members and as part of a general policy to restore functions to the family, we need to take the side of the family in the argument about rights of the mentally ill.

Families that will accept and carry out the responsibility should be given a voucher to purchase the needed services, including institutional residence if they determine it to be appropriate and a judge agrees. Although they may not always make the right decision, they care more than the government does. Where there is no family that will take responsibility, the state will need to and probably should do so through purchase of services by an appointed guardian, much as the family would have done through use of a voucher. U.S. policy should provide every mentally ill individual a guardian, either a family member or a court appointee, who is legally empowered and appropriately funded or vouchered to see that he or she gets proper care and is not a threat or a nuisance to the public.

The psychiatric profession should examine itself, as should the psychologists, social workers, and others who practice in the field of mental health, particularly the majority who got government help in financing their education. Most of the professionals working with the seriously mentally ill are badly qualified for what they are doing, especially those working in public psychiatric hospitals. A large proportion of them are foreign born, and many have not even passed the qualification examinations to practice. Mental health professionals should arrange to work with the seriously mentally ill at least some of the time.

Some local programs, such as the Goddard-Riverside Center in New York City, have succeeded in enrolling psychiatrists as volunteers to work with their mentally ill clients. The American Psychiatric Association and other such associations should take the lead in promoting such volunteer work.

PRINCIPLE: *No working family in America should fall below a decent subsistence level. Families are carrying out the fundamental social functions of our society. The difference between what they can earn in the labor market and a minimum adequate income should be provided as social income, through the tax system. This is not a matter of entitlement, but of social justice—our collective belief in what is best for our society.*

For homeless families that have fallen through the bottom of the underclass, the answer again is to assign responsibility to the principals—to enable them to govern themselves. The most useful policy ideas have come from David T. Ellwood and Mary Jo Bane. Ellwood has complained that until now there has been "no serious policy that encourages family formation."[4] The welfare system has taken this incentive away, and it needs to be given back. First, AFDC should be eliminated, say, over a period of two or three years. Parents raising their children responsibly gain from this widely available natural activity the greatest joy that human life has to offer. At the same time, they are doing society's most important work. If children are to grow up as productive citizens, as youngsters they need to see the link between having a family and providing for its support. Through working, parents are carrying out both an economic function and a social function. It should be our national policy that no working family live below the poverty level. The difference between what they earn in the labor market and what is needed to bring them up to the poverty level should be provided to them through the tax system as earned social income, not as welfare, and there should be no trace of stigma attached to it. It makes sense morally and economically: the price of labor to the employer in a free market must be determined by what the employer can sell his product for, not by the value society places on a worker's off-the-job contributions.

The best way to provide the social component of a family's income is probably through increasing the present Earned Income Tax Credit (EITC) for working families. It should be raised to a level so that when child care tax credits are added, no family with the equivalent of one full-time worker would fall below the poverty level.[5] The projected tax credit would be added into the paycheck by the employer just as he withholds taxes for employees earning more.

Absent fathers would not get the EITC but would be required to pay a fixed percentage of their own earnings to support their children. Wisconsin is currently testing a policy of deducting the required amount directly from the man's paycheck. Where such funds prove uncollectable or inadequate, the parent raising the children should receive an added tax credit from the government.

Any single parent could, therefore, reach at least the poverty level by working half time at the minimum wage.

This plan assumes that the parent can get and hold a job paying at least the minimum wage. Where this is not the case and where state or local governments are willing to pay 50 percent of the cost, government-funded jobs, administered locally, should be made available at the minimum wage. Such jobs would result in eligibility for the child care tax credit but not the added social income of the EITC. Working in these special jobs would not ensure an income above the poverty level. Only a job in the economic mainstream would do that.

It is essential that a cash match be required of the local government in a public employment program to ensure that the jobs created are seen as transitional, involve productive work, and are administered effectively. If the money is free, these goals are unlikely to be achieved.

Examples of worthwhile public jobs under this program could include childcare aides, school safety patrols, neighborhood patrols, crossing guards, bus stop monitors, playground monitors, and human care aides in nonprofit care facilities.

I expect that most people would stay in such employment only for a short time, because the money elsewhere would be so much better. The program should be administered to achieve that objective. With tax credits and other supports that will be available to those who find employment in the private sector and the potential for promotion there, few should be content to remain in minimum-wage employment-of-last-resort jobs.

This policy would replace AFDC, Medicaid, food stamps, and parts of several other federal programs for those now on AFDC. The savings from these other programs would pay for it. The toughest adjustment is that once families were cut loose from AFDC, they would no longer be eligible for Medicaid. Those taking government minimum-wage jobs would have no health insurance and would need to bear their own health costs or depend on state and local health services. Those who go to work in the private sector would have whatever health insurance their employers provide any other employee, just as the millions of low-income workers not on welfare have at present. The problem we currently face of what to do about the 37 million Americans not now covered by health insurance would be expanded to include the 11 million now on AFDC. How to solve that problem is beyond the scope of this book, and I do not pretend to have the answer.[6]

Such an employment program makes the most sense when combined with a program to stimulate the creation of private sector jobs in locations where those who will be moving off welfare live. Enterprise zones should provide that stimulation. The problem of making each of these programs work—and getting them and related programs to support each other—is the kind of political and administrative challenge just difficult enough to make government work interesting again. Perhaps some real talent could be recruited into the ranks; for the past several decades many of the most able employees have been leaving government work.

Food stamps, a stigmatizing form of welfare, are subject to extensive abuse and should be ended. Employment and training services funded by the federal government should be refocused on job development, training, and placement for AFDC recipients moving into private employment.

The new employment policy would not cover unattached individuals. Our national policy would not encourage unattached living or provide a social income to families without children. Programs for the aged and disabled, other than substance abusers and the seriously mentally ill, would be unchanged.

Homeless shelters should continue to be a local option. Since it has been shown that the residents of shelters more often come from housing than from the streets, the United States should adopt the European practice of not counting those in shelters as homeless. Instead, the shelter count should be maintained as a separate index of social shortfall. With families earning at least a poverty-level income, the need for family shelters should be quite limited except in booming cities with bad housing policies. Many of the homeless could have rented a place to live and not been on the streets or in shelters were it not for a combination of increasing urban land values and bad local government policies. Communities will need to decide how they want to manage the homeless who still remain after the adoption of effective housing and employment policies for those who should support themselves and choose to do so. These communities will also need an adequate program for the seriously mentally ill.

We have no way of knowing how many other expenses might be reduced by replacing welfare with employment and how much all our lives would be improved. In a society where responsibility and authority reside in the family and the social, health, and tax systems are designed to help it function, the difference would be so great as to be unpredictable.

PRINCIPLE: *Alcohol and drug abuse are not best understood as diseases in the classic medical sense. They are in significant measure symptoms of a breakdown in productive community and individual responsibility. Treatment, while it may often be helpful, should not be substituted for a recognition of the responsibility of the individual and the need to strengthen natural institutions of support such as family and community.*

I believe that, based on the results so far, we may never develop large-scale effective alcoholism or drug treatment policies that are not biologically based. If we could do it, it is my intuition that by now we would have. It appears that when present programs work, a combination of intelligent practice and ineffable factors such as inspiration, faith, or love has been the cause. The ineffable cannot be reproduced on a large scale: we must build or rebuild will in individuals, one by one. Some local programs have what this effort takes, for a while, as long as the magic is there—a particular combination of staff, volunteers, and administrative or political circumstances. In such places, friendship and love may develop in spite of the fact that cash exchanges hands. Alcoholics Anonymous, an entirely volunteer program, often seems to work locally, but evaluations fail to confirm that it works as a large-scale policy. No one knows how to administer the ineffable. Personnel, structures, regulations, certifications, and procedures cannot do it.

PRINCIPLE: *Housing can only be produced efficiently by the private market. States should set local housing goals and follow these with appropriate rewards and penalties. Because economic isolation is not in the best interest of society, land use policies should be administered so that a significant amount of person-to-person interaction across income levels will take place naturally.*

Federal law should place the responsibility firmly upon state governments to establish and enforce rules that require local populations either to accept their fair share of needed new housing units or to compensate others nearby for doing so. San Diego, with its SRO housing, has proved that privately developed housing for low-income singles and couples can be made profitable through the purposeful design of zoning and building codes. For this, the only needed government subsidy is mortgage insurance, and the Bush administration is expanding FHA regulations to cover it.

One of the ways in which the government has taken functions away from the community is through what it has done to the landlord-tenant relationship in many cities, particulary cities with high rates of homelessness. William Tucker has made the case persuasively in *The Excluded Americans*.[7] Charles Murray explores this problem when writing of the difference between Harlem in the 1940s and the present. Landlords, he says, "whatever their faults," have "one undoubted virtue: they want responsible tenants." They are a force for responsibility in society, in that they seek tenants who take care of the property and pay their rent on time. "Given their way, they tend to let good tenants be and to evict bad ones, and this is one of the most efficient forms of socialization known to a free society," he says. The whole process by which landlords and tenants find each other is rich in its social functions. A neighborhood evolves "a set of norms" and attracts "a certain kind of person." Money is not especially important in telling one neighborhood from another:

> The difference between the scruffy, hustling blocks and the exactingly neat and orderly working-class blocks was not a vast difference in income among the tenants, but vast differences in norms and values. In the working-class neighborhoods, unless you presented yourself as being a certain kind of person, you weren't going to get in, even if you could pay the rent. In the scruffy neighborhoods, you could get in, but the landlords charged a premium to compensate for the damage they expected you to cause.
>
> In the rush to rid society of the socially disapproved reasons for discriminating among applicants, starting with race, we threw out as well all the ways in which landlords performed a neighborhood formation function.[8]

Then we tore down neighborhoods "in the name of urban renewal, threw up public housing in the middle of other such neighborhoods," and otherwise made it difficult for neighborhoods "to define and defend themselves."[9] Each time a function internal to the neighborhood was weakened, and the functions of landlords were an important part of this mixture, natural bonds between people were weakened, social discipline was eroded, and social problems increased.

Landlords should be seen as contributors to the life of the community instead of as gougers. Housing assistance to communities with forms of rent control that discourage the development of new housing and lead to the removal of existing units of housing from the rental market should be discontinued immediately. "Moderate" forms of rent control should also be phased out as housing supply rises to meet demand. Localities may need to design transitional arrangements to lessen the severity of rent increases for low-income renters as a result of this change in policy. State tax codes that make it more profitable to local governments to approve shopping centers and office buildings than housing should be changed.

Murray recommends that even if we cannot roll back the clock to 1940, and in some respects probably should not, we could "free up the housing market in black neighborhoods in the same way that the many 'enterprise zone' proposals seek to free up business investment." Without doing away with public interference in the landlord-tenant relationship everywhere, we could identify and set aside areas where racial discrimination is not an issue and let the market operate there. Middle-class people are often able to choose what kind of neighborhood they want to live in, but the poor live in neighborhoods shaped by a government-administered relationship between landlords and tenants. It is difficult to find a place where the poor can assume their neighbors' values will correspond to their own. Murray suggests landlords in his special zones be able to set any rules they wish— no unemployed, no welfare mothers, or no unmarried couples, for example—and instant eviction for any reason the landlord wants. Murray calls this plan making it possible to "make a buck by renting to responsible low-income people." He says,

> These reforms will permit the creation of neighborhoods of likeminded people in low-income areas. . . . For practical purposes, most white neighborhoods already enjoy the same

freedoms to form neighborhoods that I propose giving to black neighborhoods. . . . The laws and regulations are really effective in breaking up neighborhoods only when people are poor and where a large proportion of the people rent rather than own. . . . Give hardworking, low-income black people the same freedom to segregate themselves into enclaves, using their nonmonetary assets that landlords prize.[10]

Murray views this situation from the standpoint of an individual or family, not from a societywide perspective. His policy goal is to improve life for each, and that should lead in time to improvement for all. When it comes to neighborhoods, work places, and drug policy, for instance, his purpose is not to end drug dealing in America but to enable the rich and poor alike to live and work in places that drug dealers stay away from. It should come to the same thing and enable responsible families to raise their children in an environment of responsibility so they will not become homeless. Murray says:

Let us stop fixating on the worst-of-the-worst part of the problem, begin to recognize how badly we have ignored those who are already trying to do everything right. . . .

The most profoundly important truth about drugs is not that drugs are evil but that drugs are unsatisfying. . . . [T]he choice faced by many inner-city youths is limited to life in their streets, drab and dispiriting, compared to life they see on their television screens, unimaginably glamorous and unattainable. What they badly need are some options closer to home—a neighborhood a few blocks away, not on the other side of town—where the families have fathers as well as mothers, where the streets aren't strewn with garbage, where the playgrounds are safe from gangs and drug dealers. . . . [T]he kinds of qualities I am talking about do not depend on having much money. They depend on the ability of like-minded people to control and shape their small worlds . . . to the way of life they prefer.

To win the war on drugs it is not necessary that drug abusers become criminals, only that they be made outcasts. In the natural course of events, schools, employe[rs], and communities will do this. Let them.[11]

AS A MASS DEMOCRACY, America has passed the point of diminishing returns. Continuing our pursuit of the values of the nation's founding requires that we reject the exhausted idea that we can solve our social problems nationally and turn our attention more fully to the potential of our pluralistic cultural institutions. Our vision should be to create a community of communities.

To achieve such a vision requires that we rebuild traditional institutions such as the family, neighborhood, church, and school—arrangements that predate mass society. In doing so, it is necessary both to emphasize older values and to recognize and incorporate the progress we have made in achieving social justice.

Institution-building calls for leadership. The mass media have led us to believe that politicians are our primary leaders and that government is the solution to our problems. Their emphasis on politics and government action ignores how the real work of American society gets done: through vast numbers of self-governing associations across the country. Our real leaders are the individuals who create and nurture these entities.

Leadership in a self-governing society helps people take care of themselves and each other, rather than teaching them to fight for an ever-expanding welfare state. We need more leaders in the self-governance mold. Many Americans feel leaderless. According to a recent book, *The Day America Told the Truth*, "More than half" of a very large number of individuals surveyed replied that they "would be interested in volunteer work or in donating money to help, if they believed in the leadership."[12]

More and better leaders will help the rest of us to see what it is that we can do together, understand it, and believe in it. Yet the nature and the importance of leadership for self-governance has received little research attention. To generate more leaders and support them better we will need to learn about such leadership—and tell each other about it.

Currently, most of the political discussion about domestic social needs and programs is dominated by advocates for individual rights and by bureaucratic collectivists. A bureaucratic collectivist's view of human nature, usually unstated, is that people won't take care of matters for themselves and therefore need someone else to do it for them. Advocates for expanding individual rights tend to leave any problem caused by their action for someone else to solve—usually the bureaucratic collectivist.

We need to draw a distinction between *self-governing* leadership and the kind of leadership that moves us toward the proliferation of "rights" and a benign form of bureaucratic collectivism. Advocates of self-governance call for control to move from the professional politicians and bureaucrats and into the hands of communities, families, and individuals—those affected by what happens.

In June 1991, as chapters of this book pass back and forth between the writer and his editor, a rancorous debate about civil rights and employment quotas dominates the national news. As in so many of the arguments in our contemporary politics, both sides in this one miss the point. There is still race and gender discrimination in America, and it should cease. But discrimination is no longer the primary cause of our social malaise. On the contrary, write the editors of the *New Republic,* preoccupation with this issue "is a fatal distraction from the matter at hand." The matter at hand for many black Americans, who make up an increasing proportion of our homeless,

> is the collapse of the black family, the inner city drug epidemic, the violent crime that now besieges a central part of black America, and the decline of public education. . . .[13]

In a spring 1991 book, *Why Americans Hate Politics,* the *Washington Post* columnist E. J. Dionne, Jr., writes that "politics these days is not about finding solutions. It is about discovering postures that offer short-term benefits."[14] In many of our cities, he says, politics "has been reduced to a crude battle of resources. . . ."[15] The politician who convinces a working plurality of special interest groups that he will deliver on "their issues" succeeds in holding power. Dionne points to the replacement in our public discourse of the old word "problems" by the word "issues" as evidence that we are no longer properly focused.[16]

A civil rights bill offers a forum for posturing, requires all politicians to "take a stand," and ensures that there will be both winners and losers. Success requires impressive presence, political cleverness, and forensic skill. It does not call so much for courage as it does for derring-do. It does not help us to change the way we feel about ourselves as a society and the way we do things. That requires something more: leadership—not derring-do, but courage. Dionne calls for "a resurgence of the language of common citizenship that animated the early civil rights movement." In those days, the conservative values of self-help and hard work, he says, were joined to the liberal values of generosity and tolerance.[17] We have gotten off course. We need leadership to get back on it.

In his book, for many of the same reasons as I have done, Dionne calls for the creation of a new political center. He credits the idea, as one must so many, to Daniel Patrick Moynihan. In *Family and Nation,* Moynihan wrote:

> The central conservative truth is that it is culture, not politics, that determines the success of a society. The central liberal truth is that politics can change a culture and save it from itself.[18]

To open one's mind to the power of this phrase, I believe, is to understand that the whole truth about contemporary American society can be grasped only at the political center. Dionne says that with some conservatives discovering a "new paradigm" of government and actively pursuing an agenda of decentralization and empowerment, and liberals "rediscovering the virtues of 'virtue' "—the value of the intact family of mother, father, and children, for instance—Moynihan's hope of bringing about a new political center that is "at once generous and sensible" no longer appears unrealistic, as it did just five years ago.[19]

Conservatives have made a grievous error in concluding that the public is tired of government and wants less of it. The public wants a government that governs instead of trying to take care of us or run our lives. We would like to take these responsibilities ourselves, and believe that we can do it better. But we do need an orderly public framework in which to do it. Healthy personalities and productive social groups only develop where there is a stable setting. The main role of government is to help provide it.

Recent Democratic administrations have supported domestic government agencies well, administered most of their programs with reasonable competence if not always strategic judgment, and have used their programs effectively in the pursuit of political support. Republicans, often disagreeing with these programs, mostly created by Democrats, and also seeing a government bureaucracy whose members are overwhelmingly registered in the other party, have attempted, sometimes successfully, to cut back the programs and have sometimes administered the agencies in an unfriendly manner. This has hastened the departure of many of their most talented employees and made the government a less desirable place to work.

Both of these approaches are wrong: government should not be a tool for one party or an enemy of the other. Executive leadership is needed that will restore a sense of pride and professionalism to government. No amount of pay awarded by a legislature controlled by the other party can do this. The civil service needs not to be put in charge, nor to be put in its place, but to be made a partner in our effort to weave our natural institutions and our liberal traditions into a mutually supportive structure of social civility.

The president and the cabinet have a profound effect on life in the civil service. When they articulate a vision of the good society and define for each agency a specific and positive role in achieving this vision, the government does its job better and cheaper. The need to rebuild our traditional institutions could be seen as an opportunity to weaken the government—a course of action that I believe would be a grievous error—or to change what government does and how government does it. That is a job for bipartisan leadership at a vital political center.

The words "civil servant" as I have used them here sound anachronistic. The most common term these days is probably "bureaucrat," and not infrequently the negative tone it conveys is warranted. Let us, however, enlist the millions of federal, state, and local employees in a program to restore and help sustain the self-governing of American families and communities. Government workers can communicate an optimistic, productive, and publicly responsible attitude throughout the public sector. Strongly improved results are likely to follow.

This book opened with two goals: to learn something about homelessness and to learn something about ourselves. As the book closes, it becomes difficult for me to make a distinction between the two. The homeless crisis is our crisis. It tells us quite a few things about ourselves and our society that we need to hear. The most important of these is about the need for leadership from all of us in whatever situation we find ourselves: in facing and telling the truth, both about what we know and about how little we know; in finding a balance between rights and responsibilities; in developing mutual respect among the diverse groups in our society; in achieving excellence; in caring for our loved ones; in the faith that America can and will achieve its promise.

Appendix

Model Programs

FAMILY FULL EMPLOYMENT ACT. The AFDC program should be phased out over a period of two to three years. Tax policy should be designed so that no family with the equivalent of one full-time worker employed in an unsubsidized position will earn less than a decent subsistence wage. Heads of families with children should receive an Earned Income Tax Credit (EITC) of half the difference between their hourly wage in private employment and an hourly rate to be determined. They also should receive child care tax credits. Absent fathers (or mothers) should have a payroll deduction of a fixed percentage of their earnings sent to help support their children. Where the father cannot be identified, or his earnings are below a certain level, the shortfall should be made up by the federal government.

Parents unable to obtain or hold a job in the private sector should be offered local public or nonprofit employment at the minimum wage. There should be no EITC for such employment, but the other provisions should apply.

Existing federal employment and training programs should be focused on job assistance, education, and training to help family heads find and hold jobs in the private sector or unsubsidized sector jobs.

None of the above tax benefits or services should be available except to the heads of families with children.

SOCIAL SERVICES. Generally, public social services for the able population should be administered not by offices and individuals responsible to distant bureaucracies but by volunteers or persons hired by and responsible to agencies and organizations in the neighborhoods, such as churches or schools.

PROGRAMS FOR THE PERMANENTLY INCAPACITATED. Generally, such programs as SSI, SSDI, and others directed to those whose ability to work is impaired should be continued.

MENTAL ILLNESS TREATMENT AND SUPPORT ACT. Federal funds for mental health services aimed at the general public should be placed into a block grant to states and restricted to serving individuals diagnosed as seriously mentally ill—generally schizophrenics and persons suffering from bipolar disorder (manic-depressive psychosis). Allocation of such funds should be contingent on a state plan that includes the following:

- A guardian to be named for each mentally ill person found to be living outside frequently or continuously. Where it is feasible, the guardian should be a member of the patient's family or a friend.
- Guardian to be allocated a budget (voucher) at a preestablished level based on the nature and severity of the patient's condition. The level should be determined by a designated psychiatrist or panel including a psychiatrist.
- Guardian to assume responsibility for the patient's care, contracting for living support and treatment and sending the bills to a designated public agency for payment.
- Guardian to have the options of contracting for a case manager, contracting with public or private vendors, and entering into arrangements with other guardians to ensure the delivery and effective treatment and support but not to receive funds himself from the voucher.
- Guardian services to be audited and evaluated by an independent panel of patients, family, and professionals, but there will be no day-to-day bureaucratic supervision of the guardian's activity or prior approval of expenses.

PUBLIC ASSISTANCE REFORM ACTS. All levels of government should stop making uncontrolled cash payments to alcohol and drug abusers under their general assistance programs. Vouchers or protective payee programs should be used instead.

HOUSING ACT. All federal cash subsidies for housing construction or rehabilitation should be ended or incorporated into block grants to the states. Mortgage insurance and tax policies should be continued and adjusted as appropriate to facilitate the construction of affordable rental units and particularly home ownership. All federal housing assistance, including mortgage insurance, within a state should be contingent on a state housing policy that meets the following conditions:

- Rents to be based on the market unless the landlord wishes to do otherwise. (In some areas this will necessitate transition programs for low-income renters.)
- Landlords to have the right to screen tenants on any basis they wish except where this is specifically prohibited by federal statute.
- Within a federal standard to be established, state governments to set fair-share goals for each jurisdiction concerning housing for low-income working families and individuals. Cities and counties to see that this housing is built within their borders or contract with a nearby jurisdiction to do so. Failure to do so should result in taxation of the jurisdiction by the state and allocation of the resulting revenue to other jurisdictions for low-income housing.
- State tax policies to be modified as necessary to favor the construction and rehabilitation of housing at least equally with shopping centers, office buildings, and other projects that increase the demand for housing.

If there is to be public housing, it should be reserved for families that have earned it in some way, and the standards of behavior there should be a model for the community. Tenants who live in public housing should be able to earn the privilege of buying their apartments and assisted in financing the transaction.

COMMUNITY SCHOOLS ACT. The public schools in most cities have been turned from community-based institutions into instruments of the new class and the bureaucratic state. They are more properly called "government schools." School vouchers will turn the system on its head and put the schools back in the hands of families and communities. All parents should receive a voucher for each school-aged child and have complete freedom to enroll the child in any school, public, private, or religious, that will accept him. Schools accepting vouchers would not be permitted to apply unconstitutional standards for admission, affirmatively or negatively. Achieving racial balance, if any, would be up to the parents.

SHELTER ADMINISTRATION. Shelters should not be provided as something for nothing. All shelters should charge rent, either by cash or voucher. The rent could either be used to cover expenses or be saved for the client to use in acquiring more permanent shelter. Vouchers could be provided by churches and other community organizations after an interview with the client. There should be no free and unrestricted shelter to attract people away from other housing arrangements.

PUBLIC ORDER. Responsible taxpaying citizens have a right to expect order in their public places. It is time for those who object to their takeover by the irresponsible and the demented to demand them back. The ballot box and the courts are both appropriate places for this battle to be fought. It is important not to buy the idea that a person is selfish for demanding unharassed use of facilities that he has already paid for.

IMPLEMENTATION. Although these proposals contain much that is new, no program recommended here would be run directly by the federal government. Changes in the federal role are to take place through the tax system primarily—Earned Income Tax Credits, tax forgiveness, child care credits, child support payments, and the like; through changes in mortgage insurance; through placing some existing programs into block grants; through setting some new standards; and, very important, through heightened political leadership. The federal government will be putting in a lot of money through the tax system and therefore will have the moral basis for encouraging and sometimes requiring others to do the rest.

Interviews

Andrews, Heather	Sacramento (Tel.)	10 March 1989
Armat, Virginia C.	Washington, D.C. (Tel.)	24 April 1989
Armor, David J.	Washington, D.C.	17 May 1989
Baillargeon, Diane	New York City	16 May 1989
Barker, John	Buhl, Idaho	24 June 1988
Biderman, Fran	Berkeley (Tel.)	13 March 1989
Blau, Joel	New York City	11 May 1989
Brady, Byron	Seattle	14 April 1989
Break, George	Berkeley	7 September 1988
Broeder, Lynn	St. Louis (Tel.)	19 June 1990
Brown, Roger	Concord, California	9 June 1988
Bushey, Gisela B.	Hayward, California	5 May 1989
Butler, Stuart	Washington, D.C.	17 May 1989
Carey, Tim	Montrose, New York (Tel.)	24 May 1989
Carlisle, Marcia	Seattle	13 April 1989
Casey, D. Anne Larson	Portland, Oregon	18 April 1989
Cheema, Boona	Berkeley	31 July 1989
Chickering, A. Lawrence	San Francisco	1 December 1988
Clark, Benton R.	Sacramento	2 March 1989
Clark, Donald E.	Portland, Oregon	19 April 1989
Cohen, Jonathan R.	New York City	16 May 1989
Colton, George H.	Berkeley	22 March 1989
Cook, Tom	San Francisco	20 April 1990
Curreri, Cynthia	Seattle	14 April 1989
DeBow, Margaret E.	Sacramento	2 March 1989
DeMaster, Jean	Portland, Oregon	18 April 1989
Destine, Joe	San Francisco (Tel.)	17 April 1990
Dickey, John	New York City	16 May 1989
Diodato, James	Napa, California	25 January 1990
Edelman, Bernard	New York City (Tel.)	4 May 1989
Fleetwood, Martha	San Francisco	25 April 1990
Foreman, Clay	Napa, California	25 January 1990

Freng, Steven	Seattle	12 April 1989
Fuentes, Alberta	San Francisco	19 May 1989
Gale, Michael L.	Berkeley	11 April 1988
Gallagher, Timothy L.	Portland, Oregon	19 April 1989
Goldfarb, Alan	Berkeley	7 June 1988
Goodwin, Sandra	Sacramento (Tel.)	16 August 1990
Greene, Elouise	Berkeley	4 August 1988
Harp, Howie	Oakland	16 June 1988
Hawkins, Robert B., Jr.	San Francisco	1 December 1988
Hayes, Robert M.	New York City	15 May 1989
Hayes-Bautista, David E.	Los Angeles	15 April 1991
Hendrix, Donald	Portland, Oregon	18 April 1989
Hobson, Bill	Seattle	14 April 1989
Horowitz, Carl	Washington, D.C. (Tel.)	16 August 1990
Huebner, Robert B.	Rockville, Maryland	17 May 1989
Imislund, Clancy	Los Angeles (Tel.)	13 February 1990
Inman, Bradley	Oakland	8 May 1989
Johnson, Will	Berkeley	2 January 1991
Johnston, Mark	Washington, D.C. (Tel.)	10 September 1990
Kaufory, Gretchen	Portland, Oregon	18 April 1989
Kern, Bruce	Oakland	11 July 1988
Koegel, Paul	Santa Monica (Tel.)	27 November 1990
Kondratas, Anna	Washington, D.C.	10 May 1989
Kunzig, William B.	San Francisco	3 October 1989
LeCount, David	Madison (Tel.)	24 April 1989
Leiby, James	Berkeley	13 September 1988
Lenske, Larry	New York City	11 May 1989
Levine, Irene Shifren	Rockville, Maryland	17 May 1989
LoFaso, Robert G.	Walnut Creek, California	14 July 1988
Lucas, Dean	Martinez, California	18 August 1988
Maisel, Sherman	Berkeley	12 April 1990
Marsh, Spencer	Portland, Oregon	17 April 1989
Mathews, Joe	New York City	12 May 1989
McCullough, Barbara Bunn	Berkeley	14 January 1989
McCullough, Stuart	Napa, California	25 January 1990
Medved, Mary	Portland, Oregon	19 April 1989
Mildner, Jerry	New York City	16 May 1989
Miller, Marilyn	Portland, Oregon	19 April 1989
Moskowitz, Marsha	Portland, Oregon	19 April 1989
Nakamatsu, John	Los Angeles (Tel.)	4 October 1989
Neely, Mike	Los Angeles	2 November 1989
Nicolson, A. Gordon, Jr.	Orinda, California	14 July 1988
O'Connell, Tim	San Diego (Tel.)	25 April 1990
O'Connor, Theron	Oakland	12 December 1988
O'Keefe, Pat	El Cerrito, California	11 July 1988
Paskowitz, Steve	Berkeley	8 June 1988
Perez, Lisandro	Miami (Tel.)	19 April 1991
Polich, J. Michael	Santa Monica (Tel.)	1 June 1990
Pickus, Robert	Berkeley	19 June 1989

Pomeroy, Miles	San Diego (Tel.)	18 April 1990
Pritchard, Pearl	Oakland	4 May 1989
Pruger, Robert	Berkeley	26 August 1988
Quigley, John	Berkeley	15 September 1988
Reischauer, Robert D.	Berkeley	30 March 1991
Robeson, Andy	Los Angeles (Tel.)	4 October 1989
Rossi, Peter H.	Amherst (Tel.)	8 May 1991
Ruffin, Holt	Seattle (Tel.)	21 April 1989
Salem, Deborah	Rockville, Maryland	17 May 1989
Sanders, Barbara	Walnut Creek, California	14 July 1988
Scheinman, Steve	Berkeley	28 July 1988
Schindler, Stella	New York City	12 May 1989
Schwartz, Rita I.	San Francisco	19 May 1989
Schwartz, Stephen	San Francisco	25 September 1989
Segal, Steven	Berkeley	14 November 1989
Severin, Carol	Concord, California	9 June 1988
Shapiro, Robert J.	Washington, D.C. (Tel.)	26 March 1990
Shenfil, Suzanne	Berkeley	12 August 1988
Shisler, Dutch	Seattle	12 April 1989
Siri, Jean	El Cerrito, California	2 August 1988
Snyder, Mitch	Richmond, California	14 August 1988
Sonde, Diane	New York City	10 May 1989
Starr, Roger	New York City	12 May 1989
Steffey, Daniel	Portland, Oregon	17 April 1989
Stewart, Julie A.	Sacramento	2 March 1989
Stewart, Ruth	San Diego (Tel.)	21 May 1988
Stout, Kathy	Portland, Oregon	18 April 1989
Strachan, Margaret	Portland, Oregon	18 April 1989
Sutherland, Alan R.	Washington, D.C.	10 May 1989
Teachout, Terry	New York City	15 May 1989
Terrell, Paul	Berkeley	26 August 1988
Throne, Lloyd	Eureka, California (Tel.)	17 August 1988
Torrey, E. Fuller	Washington, D.C.	18 May 1989
Tretton, Mike	Seattle	13 April 1989
Trezoff, Suzanne	New York City (Tel.)	15 May 1989
Valory, Kay	San Francisco	17 August 1988
Villarreal, Perfecto	Martinez, California	18 August 1988
Vilmur, Robert	San Francisco	16 September 1988
Walker, Dennis	Seattle	13 April 1989
Weicher, Chris	Berkeley	20 May 1990
Wildavsky, Aaron	Berkeley	2 February 1988
Wohl, Bernie	New York City	10 May 1989
Wolfe, Phyllis	Washington, D.C.	18 May 1989

Notes

PREFACE

1. Lisbeth B. Schorr, *Within Our Reach: Breaking the Cycle of Disadvantage* (New York: Doubleday, 1989), pp. xix, xxi; James D. Wright, "Science, Passion, and Polemics," *Society*, May–June 1989, pp. 21–23.
2. Randall K. Filer and Marjorie Honig, *Policy Issues in Homelessness: Current Understanding and Directions for Research* (New York: Manhattan Institute, 1990), pp. 73, 74; Daniel Patrick Moynihan, *Family and Nation* (New York: Harcourt, Brace, Jovanovich, 1986), p. 184.

CHAPTER 1 *Lying for Justice*

1. "Nightline," ABC News, 17 May 1984.
2. Benjamin F. Bobo, *A Report to the Secretary on the Homeless and Emergency Shelters* (Washington, D.C.: U.S. Department of Housing and Urban Development, Office of Policy Development and Research, May 1984), foreword by HUD secretary Samuel R. Pierce, Jr.
3. Jay Matthews, *Washington Post* (weekly edition), 9 September 1985, p. 6.
4. Peter H. Rossi, "No Good Applied Social Science Research Goes Unpunished," *Society*, November/December 1987, p. 78.
5. Ibid.
6. Ibid.
7. In the summer of 1988 I witnessed a similar example of advocacy exaggeration while examining records and interviewing public and private officials in largely suburban Contra Costa County, California.

Figures on homelessness were gathered by a private agency, which asked all agencies in the county to tally and report all client contacts under programs that were aimed at preventing or alleviating homelessness. These programs included such services as cash payments for motel rooms to help families make uninterrupted transitions from one apartment to another and cash grants to families to pay the rent so that they would not be evicted.

Records I examined and statements by officials indicated that most of the 1,035 clients counted were not actually homeless. But in "Homelessness—The Facts," a mailer announcing the results of the one-week survey, the private agency's "estimated numbers" of homeless were "5,000 in Contra Costa County" and "3 million nationwide." Here we see the "millions of homeless" claim again, while the figure for Contra Costa County is twice Rossi's count in four-times larger Chicago. The Contra Costa figure is a *multiple* of a count that *itself* included mostly persons not homeless.

8. Richard B. Freeman and Brian Hall, *Permanent Homelessness in America?* Cambridge, Mass.: National Bureau of Economic Research, Working Paper No. 2013, September 1986, p. 6.

9. Martha R. Burt and Barbara E. Cohen, *Feeding the Homeless: Does the Prepared Meals Provision Help?*, 2 vols., prepared for U.S. Department of Agriculture, Food and Nutrition Service (Washington, D.C.: Urban Institute, rev. 28 March 1989), vol. 1, p. 38.

10. Assistant Secretary Anna Kondratas (U.S. Department of Housing and Urban Development), interview with the author, 10 May 1989. Earlier Kondratas directed the Food and Nutrition Service, where she commissioned the Urban Institute study. Kondratas saw she could use the study to develop the best estimate to date of the homeless population.

11. Anyone hoping that the 1990 census would settle the question of how many Americans are homeless was handed a disappointment in the spring of 1991, when the Bureau of the Census released the results of its special homeless count. The surveyors found 178,828 persons in homeless shelters on the night of March 20–21, 1991, and 49,793 persons "visible at pre-identified street locations," a total of 228,621. Bureau officials gave several reasons why this figure "will not be considered as a count of the U.S. 'homeless' population." Most of these reasons suggest the count erred on the low side, but there was no reason to conclude that a true result would have been hugely different—certainly not in the millions. U.S. Department of Commerce, Bureau of the Census, "Census Bureau Releases 1990 Decennial Counts for Persons Enumerated in Emergency Shelters and Observed on Streets," press release CB91-117, 12 April 1991.

12. Peter H. Rossi, *Without Shelter: Homelessness in the 1980s* (New York: Priority Press Publications, 1989), p. v.

13. George F. Will, appearance on "This Week with David Brinkley," ABC News, 26 November 1989.

14. S. Robert Lichter, Stanley Rothman, and Linda S. Lichter, *The Media Elite* (Bethesda, Md.: Adler & Adler, 1986), p. 58.

15. Edward Jay Epstein, *News from Nowhere* (New York: Vintage Books, Random House, 1974), p. 21.

16. Michael Isikoff, "Lafayette Park Purchase: How George Bush Got a Bag of Crack," *San Francisco Chronicle*, 22 September 1989.

17. Robert Pruger, interview with the author, 26 August 1988.

18. Burt and Cohen, *Feeding the Homeless*, vol. 2, p. 44. It appears that both advocates and independent researchers agree that about one-third of the homeless suffer from serious mental illness. For an advocate view, see the "briefing paper for presidential candidates," *Homelessness in the United States: Background and Federal Response* (Washington, D.C.: National Coalition for the Homeless, May 1987), p. 4; for a federal government view, see testimony of Dr. Harvey R. Vieth, Chairman, Federal Task Force on the Homeless, in *Homelessness in America* (U.S. Congress, Hearing before the Subcommittee on Housing and Urban Affairs of the Senate Committee on Banking, Housing, and Urban Affairs, 100th Congress, 1st session, 29 January 1987), p. 126. For the views of independent researchers, see Rossi's summary of seventeen studies in *Without Shelter*, p. 24.

19. See Vieth, testimony.

20. Institute of Medicine, *Homelessness, Health, and Human Needs* (Washington, D.C.: National Academy Press, 1988), p. 138.

21. James D. Wright, *Address Unknown: The Homeless in America* (New York: Aldyne de Gruyter, 1989), p. 109.

22. Pamela J. Fischer, *Alcohol, Drug Abuse and Mental Health Problems Among Homeless Persons: A Review of the Literature, 1980–1990 (Executive Summary)*, (Rockville, Md.: U.S. Department of Health and Human Services—Alcohol, Drug Abuse and Mental Health Administration, March 1991), pp. xiii, xxii; Rossi, *Without Shelter*, p. 25.

23. George S. Vernez et al., *Review of California's Program for the Homeless Mentally Disabled* (Santa Monica, Calif.: The Rand Corporation, 1988).

24. Burt and Cohen, *Feeding the Homeless*, vol. 2, p. 40.

25. Wright, *Address Unknown*, pp. 98, 106.

26. Ibid.

27. *New York Times*, 22 May 1989.

28. Boona Cheema, file copy of letter.

29. Freeman and Hall, *Permanent Homeless*, p. 11.
30. Randall K. Filer and Marjorie Honig, *Policy Issues in Homelessness: Current Understanding and Directions for Research* (New York: Manhattan Institute, March 1990), p. 43.
31. Boona Cheema, interview with the author, 31 July 1989.
32. Rossi, *Without Shelter*, p. 24.
33. Freeman and Hall, *Permanent Homeless*, pp. 11–12.
34. Institute of Medicine, *Homelessness, Health, and Human Needs*, p. 51.
35. David Whitman, "Who's Who Among the Homeless," *New Republic*, 6 June 1988, p. 19.
36. The population of the homeless typically differs from the general U.S. population in other ways as well: they are more often Vietnam veterans, less often white than black, even less often Hispanic than white, and still less often Asian than Hispanic. There are few homeless in most rural areas; people do not become homeless where families are strong. When they do, either they are helped quickly by local agencies, often church related, or they move to cities where there are assumed to be jobs, housing, and services. See Wright, *Address Unknown*, pp. 64, 66–67.
37. Whitman, "Who's Who Among the Homeless," p. 19.
38. My estimate is based on figures provided me by the Human Resources Agency of New York City.
39. Rossi, "No Good Social Science," p. 78.
40. Filer and Honig, *Policy Issues in Homelessness*, pp. 41–42.
41. Rita Schwartz, *The Homeless: Impact on the Transportation Industry*, 2 vols. (New York: The Port Authority of New York and New Jersey, 1989), vol. 1, p. 23.
42. Burt and Cohen, *Feeding the Homeless*, vol. 1, p. 48.
43. Based on unpublished shelter-by-shelter data from February 1989 survey provided me by Emergency Services Network of Alameda County.
44. David Wood et al., *Over the Brink: Homeless Families in Los Angeles* (Sacramento, Calif.: Assembly Office Research, August 1989), p. 7.
45. Burt and Cohen, *Feeding the Homeless*, vol. 1, p. 48.
46. See, for example, Vernez et al., *Review of California's Program*.
47. Perfecto Villarreal, interview with the author, 27 August 1988.
48. San Francisco's mayor Art Agnos speaks of the homeless in his city who have "dropped out to pursue life along the edges" (*Beyond Shelter: A Homeless Plan for San Francisco*, 1990). A small but sometimes quite visible minority of the homeless is the voluntary homeless. Just as in a few places economically displaced two-parent homeless families are not uncommon, in some others there are concentrations of individuals for whom the condition of homelessness

is primarily a personal choice. Perhaps it is a form of social protest or at least a way of rejecting values held by the larger society.

Jeff Louie, for example, is a Canadian-born mountain climbing guide who calls himself an "outdoor survivalist." In seminars on urban survival for the homeless, he teaches people how to exist outdoors on very little, using what is available—cardboard, paper, or whatever can provide insulation. Joe Destine, a San Francisco film maker, attended such a seminar recently at Pt. Reyes National Seashore, some distance from San Francisco or any concentration of homeless persons. Destine tells me that Louie confers the honorary title "edgemaster" on individuals who can survive with a three-pound sack.

Louie encourages people to try living on as little as they can as a way of saving the world. He stays in San Francisco's Civic Center Plaza from time to time himself and reports that quite a few urban survivalists camp there in the winter and spring, heading for Europe in the summer. He estimates that 30 to 40 percent of the homeless in the downtown park are persons who have elected a survivalist lifestyle. Another 30 to 40 percent are employable people down on their luck (this group turns over rapidly), and the remainder, the core of the plaza's overnight population, are alcoholics, drug abusers, and the seriously mentally ill. He believes the proportions are the same among the homeless population of Marin County, where the seminar took place.

I made a visit to the plaza to look more closely at the people there and to talk with them. I found groups of young men and women camped out, young children coming and going, the scene in general resembling a summer youth camp, but without cabins and lodges. In one area of the park about three dozen young people—most of them Anglos, some of them females—were gathered in groups of six to ten with their effects. One man had the collected works of J.R.R. Tolkien with him; another was studying a book on strategy for the game of "Dungeons and Dragons." Several were playing "Trivial Pursuit," a contemporary board game, while others played chess and cards.

Some in the park told me of jobs they had held until recently at very high pay in the film industry, electronics, or computers. They had either been laid off or gotten tired of working. They were not interested in taking lesser jobs to earn a living. They offered various theories about what was wrong with the American economy or culture that led them to feel detached from it, much of it sounding like left-wing ramblings in coffee bars at the local universities. Other youths told of problems with drugs or alcohol and sometimes jail.

Most were waiting for a bus that was supposed to arrive in the next few days to take them to Washington, D.C., for a big homeless demonstration. I would not have called this group "urban survivalists," but most of them were there by choice, and their other choices seemed better than those available to many working Americans.

No one knows exactly what proportion of the homeless are edgemasters of one sort or another who choose this condition over ways of living ordinarily considered more desirable. Likely they make up a significant portion in some of our university cities and bohemian enclaves. Nevertheless, they probably do not make up more than a percent or two of the homeless nationally. Those that are homeless by choice are certainly not typical of the homeless population, but are probably no more unusual than the much-publicized advocate example of the homeless family with a husband, wife, and children.

49. Marcia N. Carlisle, interview with the author, 12 April 1989. The State of Washington program is discussed in Chapter 3.
50. Conference, "Crack Cocaine and the Death of a Race," San Francisco, 11–14 April 1989.
51. Pearl Pritchard, interview with the author, 5 May 1989.
52. Gisela Bushey, interview with the author, 5 May 1989.

CHAPTER 2   *"We Have Met the Enemy . . . "*

1. E. Fuller Torrey and Sidney M. Wolfe, *Care of the Seriously Mentally Ill: A Rating of State Programs* (Washington, D.C.: Public Citizen Health Research Group, 1986), p. 9. Figures I have seen elsewhere show the same general magnitude.
2. E. Fuller Torrey, *Nowhere to Go: The Tragic Odyssey of the Homeless Mentally Ill* (New York: Harper & Row, 1988), p. 199.
3. Ibid., pp. 55–58.
4. Ibid., p. 59.
5. Ibid., p. 61.
6. Ibid., pp. 85, 89.
7. Ibid., p. 91.
8. Ibid., p. 93.
9. Ibid., pp. 94–95.
10. Ibid., pp. 98–101.
11. Ibid., p. 97.
12. Ibid., p. 108.

13. Ibid., p. 117.
14. Ibid., p. 122.
15. Ibid., p. 124.
16. Ibid., p. 139.
17. Ibid., p. 152.
18. Ibid., p. 150.
19. Ibid., pp. 153–154.
20. Alan Sutherland, interview with the author, 10 May 1989.
21. Torrey, p. 152.
22. Rael Jean Isaac and Virginia C. Armat, *Madness in the Streets: How Psychiatry and the Law Abandoned the Mentally Ill* (New York: The Free Press, 1990).
23. H. Richard Lamb, ed., *The Homeless Mentally Ill: A Task Force Report of the American Psychiatric Association* (Washington, D.C.: 1984), p. 262.
24. Ibid., p. 263.
25. Isaac and Armat, *Madness in the Streets*, p. 111.
26. Ibid., p. 271.
27. Ibid., p. 272.
28. Ibid., p. 116.
29. Ibid., p. 110.
30. Ibid., p. 126.
31. Ibid., p. 132.
32. Ibid., p. 139.
33. Ibid., p. 151.
34. Ibid., p. 139.
35. Ibid., p. 160.
36. E. Fuller Torrey, et al., *Care of the Seriously Mentally Ill*, 2d ed. (Washington, D.C.: Public Citizen Health Research Group and National Alliance for the Mentally Ill, 1988), p. 5.
37. W. Robert Curtis, "The Deinstitutionalization Story," *Public Interest*, Fall 1986, p. 38.
38. *Oakland Tribune*, 22 May 1988.
39. Erica E. Goode, "When Mental Illness Hits Home," *U.S. News and World Report*, 24 April 1989, p. 63.
40. Charles Krauthammer, "How to Save the Homeless Mentally Ill," *New Republic*, 8 February 1988, pp. 23–24.
41. Catherine Maclay, "A Conversation with Steven Segal," *California Monthly*, February 1989, p. 10.
42. Howie Harp, interview with the author, 17 June 1988.
43. Leonard I. Stein, "A Systems Approach in Caring for Persons with Serious, Long-Term Mental Illness," unpublished, 1985.

44. Ibid., p. 9.
45. Blake Fleetwood, "Once 'Wacko,' Now Homeless," *San Francisco Chronicle*, 17 January 1989.
46. Ellen L. Bassuk and Alison Lauriat, "Are Emergency Shelters the Solution?" *International Journal of Mental Health*, Winter 1985–86, pp. 126–127.
47. Dane County Mental Health Task Force, *Final Report*, Madison, Wis., 13 December 1988, p. 5.
48. Leonard I. Stein, "Funding a System of Care for Schizophrenia," *Psychiatric Annals*, September 1987, pp. 596–597.
49. Krauthammer, "How to Save the Homeless Mentally Ill," p. 24.
50. H. Richard Lamb, *The Homeless Mentally Ill*, pp. 8–9.
51. Isaac and Armat, *Madness in the Streets*, pp. 329–333.
52. This was formerly referred to as "aggressive outreach," and now, in an apparent lexicographical spillover from women's assertiveness training, it is called "assertive outreach."
53. Bernie Wohl, interview with the author, 15 May 1989.
54. Lamb, *The Homeless Mentally Ill*, p. 7.
55. Diane Sonde, interview with the author, 15 May 1989.
56. Irene Shifren Levine et al., "Community Support Systems for the Homeless Mentally Ill," in Ellen L. Bassuk, ed., *The Mental Health Needs of Homeless Persons* (San Francisco: Jossey-Bass, 1986), p. 34.
57. Irene Shifren Levine, interview with the author, 17 May 1989.
58. Curtis, "The Deinstitutionalization Story."
59. Levine, interview.
60. Torrey, *Nowhere to Go*, appendix B, sets forth Torrey's reasoning and the figure $17 billion (1988). This was updated to $20 billion in Torrey et al., *Care of the Seriously Mentally Ill*, 3d ed. (1990), p. 1. Veterans Administration funds and patients have been excluded.
61. Stein, "Funding a System of Care."
62. Isaac and Armat, *Madness in the Streets*, p. 311.
63. Ibid.
64. Torrey, *Nowhere to Go*, p. 34.
65. Torrey and Wolfe, *Care of the Seriously Mentally Ill* (1986), p. 33.
66. Thomas R. Vischi, *Financing Community Services for Persons with Severe and Disabling Mental Illness: A Technical Assistance Manual* (Washington, D.C.: U.S. Department of Health and Human Services—Alcohol, Drug Abuse, and Mental Health Administration, June 1988), p. 51.
67. Thomas Deiker, "How to Ensure that the Money Follows the Patient: A Strategy for Funding Community Services," *Hospital and Community Psychiatry*, March 1986.
68. Torrey and Wolfe, *Care of the Seriously Mentally Ill* (1986), p. 71.

69. Ibid., p. 46.
70. E. Fuller Torrey, "Economic Barriers to Widespread Implementation of Model Programs for the Seriously Mentally Ill, *Hospital and Community Psychiatry,* May 1990, pp. 528, 530.
71. Ibid., pp. 528–529.
72. Torrey et al., *Care of the Seriously Mentally Ill* (1988), p. 35.
73. Torrey, "Economic Barriers," p. 530.
74. E. Fuller Torrey, "Thirty Years of Shame: The Scandalous Neglect of the Mentally Ill Homeless," *Policy Review,* Spring 1989, p. 14.

CHAPTER 3 *Lucky to Be Alive*

1. In an Urban Institute study commissioned by the U.S. Food and Nutrition Service, 35 percent of 1,408 homeless single adults nationwide were admitted to inpatient treatment for chemical dependency. Self-reporting has likely biased this figure downward. My own guess, and that of some professionals I have talked with, is that almost twice as many individuals abuse alcohol or other drugs seriously enough to experience an adverse effect on their social and economic circumstances as are ever actually institutionalized for this behavior. Martha R. Burt and Barbara E. Cohen, *Feeding the Homeless: Does the Prepared Meals Provision Help?* (Washington, D.C.: Urban Institute, rev. 28 March 1989), vol. 2, p. 44.
2. Excepting perhaps schizophrenics. Donald M. Gallant has observed that very few alcoholics are schizophrenic, although many are antisocial or depressive, which is, he says, often resolved with extended abstinence. Letter to the editor, *New England Journal of Medicine,* 9 February 1989.
3. Burt and Cohen, *Feeding the Homeless,* p. 44.
4. Surveys based on self-reporting by clients do not fully support this statement. James D. Wright, for instance, found 23 percent in his New York City survey for health care for the homeless to be "multiple-diagnosis." *Address Unknown: The Homeless in America,* (New York: Aldyne de Gruyter, 1989), pp. 108–109. I stand by my impression.
5. Paul Koegel and M. Audrey Burnham, *The Epidemiology of Alcohol Abuse and Dependency among Homeless Individuals: Findings from the Inner City of Los Angeles* (Rockville, Md.: National Institute of Alcoholism and Alcohol Abuse, 1987), p. 131. The authors go on to say they find it "noteworthy" that although four-fifths were already alcoholics, one-fifth were not, and may indeed have taken to drinking "as a way of coping with the stresses" of homelessness,

and that this group may include individuals "who are already suffering from mental illness but who use alcohol to treat their psychotic symptoms" (p. 132).

6. Judy Ronningen, *Oakland Tribune,* 13 June 1990.
7. *Oakland Tribune,* 15 June 1990.
8. Steven Freng, interview with the author, 12 April 1989.
9. Mike Tretton, interview with the author, 12 April 1989.
10. A lawsuit, *Bedford et al.* v. *Sugarman,* was brought by Evergreen Legal Services. The court upheld the plaintiff that the state could not require GA-U recipients to live in barracks as a condition of receiving assistance. This "violated their privacy." As barracks living had been the original plan, cost savings from ADATSA were further reduced through the need to pay outside rent. This decision was reversed by the state supreme court on 4 May 1989.
11. Kathy Stout, interview with the author, 18 April 1989.
12. Robert B. Huebner, interview with the author, 17 May 1989.
13. The U.S. Indian Health Service tells this story in an hour-long documentary film.
14. Cynthia Curreri, deputy mayor, interview with the author, 14 April 1989.
15. The "80–20 Rule" is a broader application of the economist Vilfredo Pareto's observation that the distribution of income in different economies appears to vary little, regardless of the nature of the economic system.
16. Marcia Carlisle, interview with the author, 13 April 1989.
17. The study was done by Marian Merkle.
18. William Breakey, "Treating the Homeless," *Alcohol Health and Research World,* Spring 1987, p. 45.
19. Jean DeMaster, interview with the author, 18 April 1989.
20. David J. Armor, J. Michael Polich, and Harriet B. Stambul, *Alcoholism and Treatment* (New York: John Wiley & Sons, 1978).
21. John J. Goldman, "Neglected Weapon in Drug War," *Los Angeles Times,* 6 April 1990.
22. Ibid.
23. J. Michael Polich, David J. Armor, and Harriet B. Braiker, *The Course of Alcoholism: Four Years After Treatment* (New York: John Wiley & Sons, 1981), p. 176.
24. J. Michael Polich, David J. Armor, and Harriet B. Braiker, "Patterns of Alcoholism over Four Years," *Journal of Studies on Alcohol,* May 1980, p. 414.
25. Polich et al., *The Course of Alcoholism,* p. 182.
26. Ibid., p. 177.
27. Polich et al., "Patterns of Alcoholism," p. 414.
28. Polich et al., *The Course of Alcoholism,* p. 120.

29. Ibid.
30. Polich et al., in *The Course of Alcoholism*, p. 174, point out that only the survivors are included in the cohort that showed no change. Those who died took some of what would have been shown as decline out of the sample, probably less of what would have been called improvements. So my point is not made so cleanly as I would like.
31. *The Effectiveness and Costs of Alcoholism Treatment* (Washington, D.C.: U.S. Congress, Office of Technology Assessment, March 1983), p. 66.
32. Ibid., p. 5.
33. M.A. Hayashida et al., "Comparative Effectiveness and Costs of Inpatient and Outpatient Medical Alcohol Detoxification," *New England Journal of Medicine*, 9 February 1989, pp. 358–365. My statement on cost escalation is based on Mary Jane England's letter of reply, 10 August 1989.
34. A. Preston West, letter of reply to Hayashida et al., ibid.
35. Gunter Krampen, "Brief Report: Motivation in the Treatment of Alcoholism," *Addictive Behaviors* 14 (1989), pp. 197–200.
36. Peter H. Rossi, quoted in Daniel P. Moynihan, *Family and Nation* (New York: Harcourt, Brace, Jovanovich, 1986), p. 74.
37. Alcohol, Drugs, and Mental Health Administration, *News Supplement*, vol. 16, no. 1, (January–February 1990).
38. "MacNeil/Lehrer NewsHour," 26 July 1989.
39. Alan Sutherland, telephone conversation with the author, August 1990.
40. Pearl Pritchard, interview with the author, 5 May 1989.
41. Donald E. Clark, interview with the author, 19 April 1989.
42. Nathan Glazer, *The Limits of Social Policy* (Cambridge, Mass.: Harvard University Press, 1988).
43. Robert L. Woodson, "Self-Help Steps Best for Poor Neighborhoods," Memphis, Tennessee, *Commercial Appeal*, 4 March 1986.
44. "The Barry Bust," *New Republic*, 12 February 1990, pp. 8–9.
45. Beny Primm, Director, Office of Treatment Improvement, "Dear Colleague" form letter received by the author, 8 May 1990.
46. For a concise and lively discussion of the research, see Robert Bazell, "The Drink Link," *New Republic*, 7 May 1990, p. 13.

CHAPTER 4   *Falling Through the Bottom of the Underclass*

1. Kim Hopper, testimony, House Committee on Banking, Finance, and Urban Affairs, *Homelessness in America: Hearing before the Subcommittee on Housing and Community Development*, 15 December 1982, p. 24.

2. Mike Neely, interview with the author, 2 November 1989.
3. Clancy Imislund, telephone interview with the author, 3 November 1989.
4. Charles Murray, "No, Welfare Isn't Really the Problem," *Public Interest*, Summer 1986, p. 9.
5. Charles Murray, "In Search of the Working Poor," *Public Interest*, Fall 1987, p. 17.
6. Cited in Isabel V. Sawhill, "The Underclass: An Overview," *Public Interest*, Summer 1989, p. 9.
7. Murray, "In Search," p. 17. Murray cautions that this does not mean that most ill-educated persons are poor. On the contrary, he writes, 90 percent are not. He points out in a footnote that in recent years there has been some deterioration in the relationship between high school graduation and low poverty: "The persons now drawn into the high school degree pool are not acquiring the same level of protection against poverty that a high school degree used to represent," he writes, "a combination of trends with intriguing implications that are too complicated to explore here."
8. William Julius Wilson, *The Truly Disavantaged: The Inner City, the Underclass, and Public Policy* (Chicago: University of Chicago Press, 1987), pp. 60, 144.
9. Sawhill, "The Underclass," p. 11.
10. Barbara Sanders, interview with the author, 14 July 1988.
11. Gisela Bushey, interview with the author, 5 May 1989.
12. Wilson, *The Truly Disadvantaged*, pp. 90–92.
13. Charles Murray, *Losing Ground: American Social Policy, 1950–1980* (New York: Basic Books, 1984), pp. 160–162.
14. Robert D. Plotnick, "Welfare and Out-of-Wedlock Childbearing: Evidence from the 1980s," *Journal of Marriage and the Family*, 1990, pp. 735-746, discussed in *The Family in America*, November 1990.
15. Murray, "No, Welfare Isn't Really the Problem," p. 8.
16. Alan Sutherland, interview with the author, 16 May 1989.
17. Pearl Pritchard, interview with the author, 5 May 1989.
18. Gretchen Kaufory, interview with the author, 18 April 1989.
19. Boona Cheema, interview with the author, 31 July 1989.
20. Stella Schindler, interview with the author, 15 May 1989.
21. Alberta Fuentes, interview with the author, 23 May 1989, and Phyllis Wolfe, interview with the author, 18 May 1989.
22. James Leiby, interview with the author, 13 September 1988.
23. Steven Freng, interview with the author, 12 April 1989.
24. Daniel Patrick Moynihan, "Toward a Post-Industrial Social Policy," *Public Interest*, Summer 1989, p. 25.
25. Jean DeMaster, interview with the author, 18 April 1989.

26. Elouise Greene, interview with the author, 4 August 1988.
27. Robert Vilmur, Homeless Projects Coordinator, City of Los Angeles, discussion with the author, 16 September 1988.
28. Roger Starr, interview with the author, 15 May 1989.
29. Moynihan, "Toward a Post-Industrial Social Policy," p. 24.
30. Mary Ellen Hombs and Mitch Snyder, *Homelessness in America: A Forced March to Nowhere*, rev. ed. (Washington, D.C.: Community for Creative Non-Violence, 1986), p. 7.
31. Art Agnos, *Beyond Shelter: A Homeless Plan for San Francisco* (San Francisco: Office of the Mayor, November 1990), p. 22.
32. *Oakland Tribune*, 7 July 1989.
33. See Jay W. Forrester, *Urban Dynamics* (Cambridge, Mass.: M.I.T. Press, 1969), for the classic discussion of the counterintuitive nature of complex systems.
34. Daniel P. Moynihan, *Family and Nation* (New York: Harcourt, Brace, Jovanovich, 1986), p. 165.
35. Wilson, *The Truly Disadvantaged*, pp. 67–70.
36. David T. Ellwood, *Poor Support: Poverty in the American Family* (New York: Basic Books, 1988), p. 61.
37. Bane and Ellwood cited in Moynihan, *Family and Nation*, p. 136.
38. Ellwood, *Poor Support*, p. 61.
39. Wilson, *The Truly Disadvantaged*, p. 61.
40. Ibid.
41. Charles Murray, "No, Welfare Isn't Really the Problem," p. 5.
42. Ibid., p. 9.
43. Ibid., pp. 7–8.
44. Ibid., pp. 8–9.
45. Wilson, *The Truly Disadvantaged*, p. 164.
46. In *Preferential Policies: An International Perspective* (New York: William Morrow, 1990), Thomas Sowell reports on his studies of such strategies as they have been implemented in the United States and several other countries under varying conditions. He concludes that such approaches disproportionately tend to benefit those already well off, generate hostility ranging from political backlash to violence in nonpreferred groups, and persist and expand even though designed to be temporary.
47. Wilson, *The Truly Disadvantaged*, p. 163.
48. Ellwood, *Poor Support*, p. 218.
49. Ibid., p. 23
50. Ibid., pp. 26–27.
51. Ibid., p. 100.
52. Ibid., p. 237.
53. Richard B. Freeman and Harry J. Holzer, "Young Blacks and Jobs— What We Now Know," *Public Interest*, Winter 1985, p. 18.

54. See, for example, Wilson, *The Truly Disadvantaged,* p. 42, quoting John Kasarda.
55. Cited by David T. Ellwood and Lawrence H. Summers, "Poverty in America: Is Welfare the Answer or the Problem?" in *Fighting Poverty: What Works and What Doesn't,* ed. Sheldon H. Danziger and Daniel H. Weinberg (Cambridge, Mass.: Harvard University Press, 1986), p. 101.
56. Bernard J. Frieden, "The Downtown Job Puzzle," *Public Interest,* Fall 1989, pp. 76–77.
57. Ibid., pp. 79, 86.
58. Lawrence M. Mead, "The Hidden Jobs Debate," *Public Interest,* Spring 1988, pp. 53, 54–55, 56.
59. Ibid., pp. 56–57.
60. Ellwood, *Poor Support,* p. 238; Phoebe H. Cottingham and David T. Ellwood, eds., *Welfare Policy for the 1990s* (Cambridge, Mass.: Harvard University Press, 1989), pp. 280–281.
61. Wilson tells how this works. *The Truly Disadvantaged,* p. 152.
62. Ellwood, *Poor Support,* p. 241.
63. Moynihan, *Family and Nation,* p. 145.
64. *Midwest Assembly on the Future of Social Welfare in America: Final Report* (Madison, Wisc.: The Robert M. LaFollette Institute of Public Affairs, 1990).
65. Robert J. Schapiro, *An American Working Wage: Ending Poverty in Working Families* (Washington, D.C.: Progressive Policy Institute, February 1990), and telephone conversation with the author, 26 March 1990.
66. Robert J. Kuttner, "What's the Beef?" *New Republic,* 2 March 1990, p. 18.
67. Robert D. Reischauer, "The Welfare Reform Legislation: Directions for the Future," in *Welfare Policy for the 1990s,* ed. Cottingham and Ellwood, p. 39.
68. Dan Desmond, *San Francisco Chronicle,* 30 December 1989.
69. *HOPE: Homeownership and Opportunity for People Everywhere,* U.S. Department of Housing and Urban Development, HUD-PDR1246 (1), March 1990, pp. 18–19.
70. David Osborne, "The Kemp Cure-All: Why Enterprise Zones Don't Work," *New Republic,* 3 April 1989, p. 25.
71. At this writing, 4 July 1991, the bipartisan National Commission on Children, with West Virginia Senator John D. Rockefeller IV, a liberal Democrat, as chairman and Allan C. Carlson, of the conservative Rockford Institute, as vice-chairman, has released a report whose many unanimous recommedations for government policies on the family constitute new dramatic evidence that an active center is forming in our domestic policy arena.

CHAPTER 5   *Housing, Housing, Housing*

1. Robert M. Hayes, *Current Biography,* April 1989, p. 21.
2. Charles Hoch and Robert A. Slayton, *New Homeless and Old* (Philadelphia: Temple University Press, 1989), pp. 7, 9.
3. Ibid., pp. 62–64.
4. Ibid., p. 70.
5. Ibid.
6. Ibid., p. 73.
7. Ibid.
8. Ibid., p. 74.
9. Ibid., p. 115.
10. Ibid., p. 117.
11. Martin Anderson, *The Federal Bulldozer: A Critical Analysis of Urban Renewal Policies, 1949–1962* (Cambridge, Mass.: The M.I.T. Press, 1964), p. 67.
12. Ibid., p. 54.
13. E. Fuller Torrey, *Nowhere to Go: The Tragic Odyssey of the Homeless Mentally Ill* (New York: Harper & Row, 1988), p. 141.
14. More recently, it is not so much a matter of patients being discharged as there being no space for the newly mentally ill. Generally the psychiatric hospitals have been emptied out about as much as they will be.
15. Hoch and Slayton, *New Homeless and Old,* p. 182.
16. Phyllis Wolfe, interview with the author, 18 May 1989.
17. Mike Tretton, interview with the author, 12 April 1989.
18. Bill Hobson, interview with the author, 14 April 1989.
19. Filer and Honig report in their survey of literature on homelessness that there "appears to be little basis for a widely quoted estimate of a nationwide decline of 1 million single room occupancy (SRO) units during the 1970s," noting that this figure "is cited in a number of studies with references to various articles by Cynthia B. Green, who has disclaimed the references." Randall K. Filer and Marjorie Honig, *Policy Issues in Homelessness: Current Understanding and Directions for Research* (New York: Manhattan Institute, March 1990), p. 27.
20. Hoch and Slayton, *New Homeless and Old,* p. 175.
21. Ibid., p. 184.
22. Ibid., pp. 183–185.
23. Ibid., p. 127.
24. Ibid., p. 156, 161.
25. Ibid., p. 33.
26. *Los Angeles Times,* 31 October 1989.

27. Scott C. Davis, *The World of Patience Gromes: Making and Unmaking a Black Community* (Lexington, Ky.: The University Press of Kentucky, 1988), p. 1.
28. Ibid., p. 12.
29. Ibid., p. 135.
30. Ibid., p. 35.
31. Ibid., p. 10.
32. Ibid., p. 41.
33. Ibid., p. 144.
34. Ibid., p. 122.
35. Ibid., p. 189.
36. Ibid., p. 7.
37. Ibid., pp. 210–212.
38. Jonathan Kozol, *Rachel and her Children: Homeless Families in America* (New York: Crown, 1988.) The city stopped placing people in the Martinique in 1989. By mid-1990 the city had ended the last such hotel arrangement.
39. *Scapegoating Rent Control: Masking the Causes of Homelessness* (Washington, D.C.: Economic Policy Institute, 1990).
40. John M. Quigley, *Does Rent Control Cause Homelessness? Taking the Claim Seriously,* University of California, Berkeley: Graduate School of Public Policy, Working Paper No. 166, May 1989.
41. Economic Policy Institute, *Scapegoating Rent Control,* pp. 3, 4.
42. Ibid., pp. 14–15.
43. Bradley Inman, interview with the author, 26 April 1990. He notes that some real estate investors figured this out on their own.
44. These cities tend to be prosperous otherwise, or else rents would not have been rising and rent control would not have been enacted.
45. Inman, telephone conversation with the author, August 1990.
46. Other adverse effects are likely, however, including the removal of traditional opportunities for lower-income families and individuals to achieve upward economic mobility through investing in small numbers of units, improving them, and selling them at a good profit.
47. "Bay Area Housing Forecast," *San Francisco Examiner,* 18 March 1990.
48. Hans Queisser, *The Conquest of the Microchip* (Cambridge, Mass.: Harvard University Press, 1988), p. 83.
49. *San Francisco Examiner,* 26 March 1989.
50. Eric Goplerud, quoted in Patricia Davis, "Tent Cities for Our Modern Migrants: High-Paying Jobs in the Cities are Creating New Hoovervilles," *San Francisco Chronicle,* 21 August 1988.
51. *Projections 90* (Oakland: Association of Bay Area Governments, 1989), pp. 50–53.

52. Stuart Butler, interview with the author, 17 May 1989.
53. William Tucker, *The Excluded Americans: Homelessness and Housing Policies* (Washington: Regnery Gateway, 1990), p. 79.
54. Such pratices are falling before lawsuits in some parts of the country.
55. Tucker, *Excluded Americans,* p. 143.
56. James G. Wright and Eleanor Weber, *Homelessness and Health* (New York: McGraw-Hill, 1987), p. 166.
57. For an informative and lively discussion of Say's Law, see George Gilder, *Wealth and Poverty* (New York: Basic Books, 1981), pp. 23, 31–35, 38–40.
58. Robert C. Ellickson, "The Homelessness Muddle," *Public Interest,* Spring 1990, p. 47. Cites data from James R. Knickerman and Beth C. Weitzman, *A Study of Homeless Families in New York City,* New York University Health Research Program, September 1989.
59. Boona Cheema, interview with the author, 31 July 1989.
60. Ellickson, "Homelessness Muddle," p. 48.
61. Filer and Honig, *Policy Issues in Homelessness,* p. 67.
62. Alan Sutherland, telephone conversation, August 1990.
63. Filer and Honig, *Policy Issues in Homelessness,* p. 69.
64. Pearl Pritchard, interview with the author, 4 May 1989.
65. Stephanie Chavez, "72 Percent Fewer Homeless Use New Shelter," *Los Angeles Times,* 11 February 1990.
66. Cited in Filer and Honig, pp. 65–71.
67. Anna Kondratas, interview with the author, 10 May 1989.
68. Peter L. Berger, "Worldly Wisdom, Christian Foolishness," *First Things,* August/September 1990, p. 21.

CHAPTER 6   *Blueprints*

1. Madeline Landau, *Race, Poverty and the Cities: Hyperinnovation in Complex Policy Systems* (Berkeley, Calif.: University of California Institute for Governmental Studies, 1988).
2. Chester Hartman, *America's Housing Crisis: What Is To Be Done?* (Boston: Routledge & Kegan Paul, 1985), p. 57.
3. *Safety Network,* October 1989, p. 2.
4. Ibid.
5. Community Ownership Organizing Project, *The Cities' Wealth: Programs for Community Economic Control in Berkeley, California* (Washington, D.C.: Institute for Policy Studies, 1976), p. 19.
6. Jill Hamberg, *Under Construction: Housing Policy in Revolutionary Cuba* (New York: Center for Cuban Studies, 1986), originally published

in *Critical Perspectives on Housing* (Philadelphia: Temple University Press, 1986), p. 25.

7. William Tucker, *The Excluded Americans: Homelessness and Housing Policies* (Washington, D.C.: Regnery Gateway, 1990), p. 190.

8. Ibid., p. 202.

9. Ibid., p. 219.

10. Ibid., p. 214.

11. Ibid., pp. 120–121.

12. Michael Carliner, "Homelessness: A Housing Problem?" in *The Homeless in Contemporary Society*, ed. Richard D. Bingham et al. (Beverly Hills: Sage Publications, 1987), p. 127.

13. Tucker, *Excluded Americans*, p. 81.

14. "A Gold-Plated Dream: Why Can't the Middle Class Buy a House Anymore?" *San Francisco Examiner*, 26 August 1990.

15. Edward B. Lazere, *A Place to Call Home: The Crisis in Housing for the Poor—San Francisco–Oakland, California* (Washington, D.C.: Center on Budget and Policy Priorities, 1990), p. 78.

16. Tucker, *Excluded Americans*, p. 348.

17. Stuart Butler cautions, by the way, that the infusion of such large additional amounts of cash into the New York City housing industry will so increase the local demand for both labor and materials as to cause a huge increase in expenses unless some action is taken to avoid it. He suggests one idea would be for the U.S. secretary of housing and urban development to be given legislative authority to suspend the terms of the Davis-Bacon Act in areas where construction employment is high already. (Davis-Bacon requires that on federally funded projects workers be paid no less than the prevailing wage in the area.) Interview with the author, 17 May 1989.

18. Tucker, *Excluded Americans*, p. 349.

19. Ibid., p. 347.

20. I take this position, as Alfred North Whitehead liked to say, "without any confusing research." Page Smith, *San Francisco Chronicle*, 18 March 1990.

21. Stuart Butler, interview with the author, 17 May 1989.

22. Daniel P. Moynihan, "The United States in Opposition," *Commentary*, March 1975.

23. Except where noted, the information about San Diego was provided to me by Tim O'Connell and Miles Pomeroy in April 1990, through telephone interviews and unpublished material.

24. *San Francisco Examiner*, 20 May 1990.

25. Bradley Inman, "Money Starting to Pour in for Low-Cost Housing," *San Francisco Examiner*, 10 June 1990.

26. Lynn Broeder, telephone interview with the author, 19 June 1990.
27. Ibid. Except where noted, the material on EHPC is from publicity handouts and file documents provided me by the organization.
28. Lynn Broeder, quoted in George Hickenlooper, "Hands On, Hands Up," *Saint Louis Home*, April 1989, p. 15.
29. Ibid. I have presented the figures differently.
30. Irving Welfeld, *Where We Live: The American Home and the Social, Political, and Economic Landscape, from Slums to Suburbs* (New York: Simon and Schuster, 1988), p. 14. Welfeld cites U.S. Census, *Current Housing Reports, Housing Vacancies*, 3rd Quarter 1987.
31. *Oakland Tribune*, 6 November 1988.
32. Welfeld, *Where We Live*, p. 151.
33. Timothy L. Gallagher, interview with the author, 19 April 1989.
34. Robert B. Hawkins, Jr., interview with the author, 4 October 1990.
35. Welfeld, *Where We Live*, p. 256. The "housing homeless" do not include, for example, persons homeless because of their mental illness, advanced alcoholism, or drug addiction.
36. Bridge Housing Corporation, *1988 Annual Report*, San Francisco.
37. *Builder* (May 1989), p. 185.
38. Bridge Housing Corporation, *1988 Annual Report*.
39. Ibid. and *Ford Foundation Letter*, August 1988, p. 2.
40. Editorial, "The Cost of Affordable Housing," *San Francisco Examiner*, 19 March 1990. To discourage profiteering, stiff penalties are levied on buyers who sell within a few years, writes Frank Viviano, "Making Housing Affordable," *San Francisco Chronicle*, 6 February 1989.
41. Steven A. Chin, "Home, Sweet Home in Hunters Point: New Townhouses for 110,000 Delighted Buyers," *San Francisco Examiner*, 28 April 1989.
42. Mike McKissick, president of MSM Developments in Pleasant Hill, California, quoted in Laura Evenson, "Help for S&Ls and the Poor," *San Francisco Chronicle*, 25 April 1989.
43. Donald Hendrix, interview with the author, 18 April 1989.
44. Kathy Stout, interview with the author, 18 April 1989.
45. Oregon has not had a generous assistance program such as that of neighboring Washington. General assistance in Oregon is carefully limited to those with temporary disabilities that prevent them from working. Oregon, in other words, has no "drunk check" such as that in Seattle or other communities. Based on my interviews, I conclude that most program officials in Oregon are unaware that general assistance exists in the state.
46. Jean DeMaster, interview with the author, 18 April 1989.

CHAPTER 7   *The Big Argument*

1. I must admit here that I am concluding a lot from only several dozen interviews, but a strong and consistent pattern did seem to emerge. I challenge others to confirm these observations more systematically.
2. In discussing social workers and the profession, I have spent no time at all on the very large number of persons trained in schools of social work and social welfare to practice psychotherapy or counseling not much different from that carried out by psychiatrists and clinical psychologists. I do not consider such individuals to be social workers, and neither do the few with whom I have discussed this point.
3. Leiby wrote me the following in August 1990: "I think the notion of personal responsibility comes out in the notion of self-determination. It is true that many social workers think of self-determination as a sort of liberty that is frustrated by oppression (discrimination, for example), but as a practical matter (as a principle of helping) it derives from the insight that if you want to help somebody or some group it is important to find out where they are coming from and what they want—to work with the grain so far as you can— and in that way to get them to take responsibility."
4. The textbooks are Winifred Bell, *Contemporary Social Welfare,* 2d ed. (New York: Macmillan, 1987); Naomi I. Brill, *Working with People: The Helping Process,* 3d ed. (New York: Longman, 1985); Diana M. DiNitto and Thomas R. Dye, *Social Welfare: Politics & Public Policy* (Englewood Cliffs, N.J.: Prentice Hall, 1983); Neil Gilbert, Henry Miller, and Harry Specht, *An Introduction to Social Work Practice* (Englewood Cliffs, N.J.: Prentice Hall, 1980); W. Joseph Heffernan, *Introduction to Social Welfare Policy: Power, Scarcity and Common Human Needs* (Itasca, Ill.: F. E. Peacock, 1979); Bruce S. Jansson, *Theory and Practice of Social Welfare Policy: Analysis, Processes, and Current Issues* (Belmont, Calif.: Wadsworth, 1984); Frank Loewenberg and Ralph Dolgoff, *Ethical Decisions for Social Work Practice,* 2d ed. (Itasca, Ill.: F. E. Peacock, 1985); Mary Macht and Jean Quam, *Social Work: An Introduction* (Columbus, Ohio: Charles E. Merrill, 1986); Thomas M. Meenaghan, Robert O. Washington, and Robert M. Ryan, *Macro Practice in the Human Services: An Introduction to Planning, Administration, Evaluation, and Community Organizing Components of Practice* (New York: The Free Press, 1982); Robert Morris, *Social Policy of the American Welfare State: An Introduction to Policy Analysis* (New York: Harper & Row, 1979); Rex A. Skidmore, Milton G. Thackeray, and O. William Farley, *Introduction to Social Work,* 4th ed. (Englewood

Cliffs, N.J.: Prentice Hall, 1988); Edwin J. Thomas, *Designing Interventions for the Helping Professions* (Beverly Hills, Calif.: Sage Publications, 1984); Gerald Zaltman, Philip Kotler, and Ira Kaufman, eds., *Creating Social Change* (New York: Holt, Rinehart and Winston, 1972); and Charles Zastrow, *Introduction to Social Welfare Institutions: Social Problems, Services, and Current Issues,* 3d ed. (Chicago: Dorsey, 1986).

5. For instance, Brill.
6. Alberta Fuentes, interview with the author, 19 May 1989.
7. Anna Kondratas, interview with the author, 10 May 1989.
8. Stella Schindler, interview with the author 12 May 1989.
9. Bill Hobson, interview with the author 14 April 1989.
10. Marsha Moskowitz, interview with the author 19 April 1989.
11. Boona Cheema, interview with the author 31 July 1989.
12. Pearl Pritchard, interview with the author 4 May 1989.
13. Marcia Carlisle, interview with the author 13 April 1989.
14. Frederick W. Seidl in Macht and Quam, *Social Work* p. vi.
15. Ibid., p. 28.
16. Ibid., p. 29.
17. Ibid., p. 33.
18. Paul H. Ephross and Michael Reisch, "The Ideology of Some Social Welfare Texts," *Social Service Review,* June 1982, pp. 273–291.
19. Ibid., p. 280.
20. Ibid.
21. Leiby, in reviewing this chapter, states a belief that this way of discussing the terms *conservative, liberal,* and *radical*

> has no relation to the historic tradition of political philosophy, in which Burke and Hegel are "conservatives" and Mill and Spencer are "liberals." I think that today a "conservative" is somebody who favors market or consumer-oriented policies over public regulation or provision—vouchers for education or housing or health care, for example. This "neo-conservatism" isn't an ideology, in my opinion, so much as a judgment on the implementation and outcome of many public programs and the limits of collective rationality.

Amen.

22. Stuart Butler, interview with the author, 17 May 1989.
23. Marilyn Miller, interview with the author, 19 April 1989. Alan Berger, a Chicago sociologist, comments that a caseload this size would wear a social worker out fairly fast, unless they were very easy clients to work with. In fact, these Portland families tended not to have serious problems other than lack of permanent housing and a job.
24. Robert Huebner, interview with the author, 17 May 1989.

25. Mike Tretton, interview with the author, 13 April 1989.
26. Spencer Marsh, interview with the author, 17 April 1989.
27. Gisela Bushey, interview with the author, 5 May 1989.

CHAPTER 8   *Homelessness and the American Dream*

1. Snyder took his life in the late sping of 1990.
2. Jean Siri, interview with the author, 2 August 1988.
3. Robert M. Hayes, "Testimony before the Subcommittee on Housing and Community Development of the House Committee on Banking, Finance and Urban Affairs, January 25, 1984" (New York: Coalition for the Homeless, 1984).
4. Alberta Fuentes, interview with the author, 19 May 1989.
5. San Francisco, California, 11–14 April 1989.
6. Terry Teachout, interview with the author, 15 May 1989.
7. Edward C. Banfield, *The Unheavenly City: The Nature and Future of Our Urban Crisis* (Boston: Little & Brown, 1968), p. 239.
8. Marilyn Miller, interview with the author, 19 April 1989.
9. Donald E. Clark, interview with the author, 19 April 1989.
10. Marsha Moskowitz, interview with the author, 19 April 1989.
11. Donald Hendrix, interview with the author, 18 April 1989.
12. Timothy L. Gallagher, interview with the author, 19 April 1989.
13. Gretchen Kaufory, interview with the author, 18 April 1989.
14. *Breaking the Cycle of Homelessness: The Portland Model* (Portland, Ore., Office of the Mayor, rev. September 1988).
15. Ibid., p. 1.
16. Dan Steffey, interview with the author, 17 April 1989.
17. Ibid.
18. For documentation of this trend, see William A. Donohue, *The New Freedom: Individualism and Collectivism in the Social Lives of Americans* (New Brunswick, N.J.: Transaction Publishers, 1990).
19. George F. Will, "Begging, Free Speech, and Civilization," *San Francisco Chronicle*, 1 February 1990.
20. William Kornblum, quoted by William Glaberson, "Hard Life of Urban Dwellers," *San Francisco Chronicle*, 23 February 1990.
21. Ronald J. Oakerson, "Reciprocity: A Bottom-Up View of Political Development," in *Rethinking Institutional Analysis and Development: Issues, Alternatives, and Choices*, ed. Vincent Ostrom et al. (San Francisco: ICS Press, 1988), pp. 143–144.
22. Evelyn C. White, "Death in S.F. Stirs Outcry Over Homeless," *San Francisco Chronicle*, 6 December 1988.
23. Michael McCabe and Thomas G. Keane, "Sidewalk Death Ended a Losing Battle with Alcohol," *San Francisco Chronicle*, 7 December 1988.

24. Stephanie Salter, "A Death at Seventh and Market," *San Francisco Examiner,* 11 December 1988.
25. *Oakland Tribune,* 7 February 1990.
26. Ibid.
27. *Tax Burden by Income Class 1986–1987* (Washington, D.C.: Tax Foundation, 1989).
28. William Tucker, *The Excluded Americans: Homelessness and Housing Policies* (Washington, D.C.: Regnery Gateway, 1990).

CHAPTER 9 *Manufacturing a Crisis*

1. Michael Bruce McKuen et al., eds., *More than News: Media Power in Public Affairs* (Beverly Hills, Calif.: Sage Publications, 1981), p. 24.
2. Victoria Rader, *Signal Through the Flames: Mitch Snyder and America's Homeless* (Kansas City, Mo.: Sheed and Ward, 1986), pp. 66–67.
3. Ibid., p. 75.
4. Ibid., p. 80.
5. Ibid.
6. Ibid., p. 113.
7. Ibid., p. 115.
8. Ibid.
9. Ibid., pp. 118–119.
10. Ibid., p. 101.
11. Ibid., p. 109.
12. Ibid., p. 121.
13. Ibid.
14. Ibid.
15. Edward Jay Epstein, *News from Nowhere,* (New York: Vintage Books, 1984) p. 219.
16. David Brinkley in *T.V.Guide,* 1 April 1964, quoted in Edith Ephron, *The News Twisters* (New York: Manor Books, 1974), p. 6.
17. Ephron, *The News Twisters,* p. 8.
18. S. Robert Lichter, Stanley Rothman, and Linda S. Lichter, *The Media Elite* (Bethesda, Md.: Adler & Adler, 1986), p. 20.
19. Ibid., pp. 28–30.
20. Ibid., pp. 30–31.
21. Nick Thimmesch, ed., *A Liberal Media Elite?* (Washington, D.C.: American Enterprise Institute, 1985), p. 16.
22. Ibid., p. 20.
23. Aaron Wildavsky, "The Media's Liberal Egalitarianism," *Public Interest,* Summer 1987, pp. 94–104.
24. Ephron, *The News Twisters,* p. 182.

25. Irving Kristol in George F. Will, ed., *The Press, Politics and Popular Government* (Washington, D.C.: American Enterprise Institute, 1972), p. 50.
26. Ibid., p. 52.
27. Ibid., p. 50.
28. Edith Ephron, *The Apocalyptics: Cancer and the Big Lie* (New York: Simon and Schuster, 1984), p. 9.
29. Robert L. Bartley, "The Press: Adversary, Surrogate Sovereign, or Both?" in Will, ed., *The Press*, p. 22.
30. Peter L. Berger, *The Capitalist Revolution* (New York: Basic Books, 1986) p. 66, n. 32.
31. Unpublished manuscript.
32. Lichter, Rothman, Lichter, *The Media Elite*, p. 29.
33. Ephron, *The News Twisters*, p. 175.
34. Paul H. Weaver in Will, ed., *The Press*, p. 38.
35. *New York Times*, 2 September 1991.
36. Epstein, *News from Nowhere*, p. 270.
37. Ibid., p. 163.
38. Ibid., p. 144.
39. Axel Madsen, *60 Minutes: The Power and the Politics of America's Most Popular TV News Show* (New York: Dodd Mead and Company, 1984), p. 45.
40. Epstein, *News from Nowhere*, p. 58.
41. Ibid., p. 172.
42. Ibid., p. 228.
43. Ibid., p. 140.
44. Ibid., p. 233.
45. Jerry Mildner, interview with the author, 16 May 1989.
46. Epstein, *News from Nowhere*, p. 220.
47. Irving Kristol, *Reflections of a Neoconservative* (New York: Basic Books, 1983), p. 27.
48. Lichter, Rothman, Lichter, *The Media Elite*, p. 22.
49. I compare national television with the local newspapers because these are the principal substantial daily sources of news for most people in America.
50. "The Visible Poor: Media Coverage of the Homeless 1986–1989," *Media Monitor* (Washington, D.C.: Center for Media and Public Affairs, March 1989), p. 6.
51. Ibid., pp. 3–4.
52. Ibid., p. 3.

CHAPTER 10   *America Unraveling*

1. Alan Sutherland, interview with the author, 16 May 1989.

2. Charles H. Cooley, *Social Organization,* reprinted in Edgar A. Schuler et al., eds., *Outside Readings in Sociology* (New York: Thomas Y. Crowell Company, 1952), pp. 23–31.

3. Ibid.

4. George Herbert Mead, *Mind, Self and Society* (Chicago: University of Chicago Press, 1934). This book, the classic Mead text, is a compilation from lectures and articles produced by Mead several decades earlier.

5. For an authoritative description of this process, see Theodore R. Sarbin and Vernon L. Allen, "Social Role as a Functional Unit," in *Handbook of Social Psychology,* 2d ed., Gardner Lindzey and Elliot Aronson, eds. (Reading, Mass.: Addison-Wesley, 1968), vol. 1, pp. 497–506.

6. Alexis de Tocqueville, *Democracy in America,* ed. Phillips Bradley (New York: Alfred A. Knopf, 1945), vol. 2, p. 98. Vol. 1 originally published 1835; vol. 2 1840.

7. Robert Nisbet, *The Quest for Community: A Study in the Ethics of Order and Freedom* (San Francisco: ICS Press, 1990), p. 48. Originally published 1953.

8. These studies reported in Bryce J. Christensen, "Imperiled Infants: A Legitimate Concern," *Family in America,* January 1991, p. 4.

9. David E. Hayes-Bautista, "Latina Health Indicators and the Under-class Model: From Paradox to New Policy Models," University of California, Los Angeles, Chicano Studies Research Center, prepublication manuscript, 18 October 1990, p. 5.

10. Ibid., p. 11.

11. Ibid., p. 6.

12. Ibid., pp. 16–18.

13. Ibid., p. 21. Franz Schurmann, professor of history and sociology at the University of California, Berkeley, asks the question, "Which would better help America's underclasses to survive: fewer children or stronger social fabrics?" He answers, "Fewer children would give mothers a better chance of getting work outside the home, assuming jobs are available. But stronger social fabrics would give children a more nurturing human environment in which to grow up." "Alternative to Limiting Population of Planet: Family Survival a Key to Helping Third World," *San Francisco Chronicle,* 5 June 1991.

14. Hayes-Bautista, "Latina Health Indicators," pp. 4–6.

15. Ibid., pp. 24–26.

16. Ibid., p. 27.

17. Lisandro Perez, telephone conversation with the author, 19 April 1991.

18. Amitai Etzioni, *An Immodest Agenda: Rebuilding America Before the Twenty-First Century* (New York: McGraw Hill, 1984), p. 3.

19. Ibid.
20. William A. Donohue, *The New Freedom: Individualism and Collectivism in the Lives of Americans* (New Brunswick, N.J.: Transaction Publishers, 1990), p. 20.
21. Etzioni, *Immodest Agenda,* p. 111.
22. Donohue, *The New Freedom,* p. 156.
23. Ibid., p. 224.
24. Ibid.
25. Ibid., p. 156, citing Herbert G. Gutman, *The Black Family in Slavery and Freedom, 1750–1925.*
26. Barbara Bunn McCullough, "Homelessness and the Mental Health System," Ph.D. diss., Wright Institute Graduate School of Psychology, 1988, p. 185.
27. For instance, see Richard B. Freeman and Harry J. Holzer, "Young Blacks and Jobs—What We Now Know," *Public Interest,* Winter 1985, pp. 27–28. The authors point out that it is not possible to "declare conclusively" that going to church is an important variable by itself, or whether it is just "a good kid/bad kid indicator." But the fact that in their research, churchgoing and other family factors "have *different* effects on aspects of youth behavior . . . suggests some independent causal role for the church, or as the old fashioned might put it, that church-going builds character."
28. Richard Ek, "For Married Couples Only" *San Francisco Chronicle,* 20 May 1990.
29. Martha Fleetwood, interview with the author, 25 April 1990.
30. Donohue, *The New Freedom,* p. 9.
31. Ibid.
32. Sarah Ferguson, "Us Against Them," *San Francisco Chronicle,* 6 May 1990.
33. William Tucker, *The Excluded Americans: Homelessness and Housing Policies* (Washington, D.C.: Regnery Gateway, 1990), p. 95.
34. Donohue, *The New Freedom,* p. 227
35. Martha Fleetwood, "Homelessness: A Guide to Local Legal Action," *San Francisco Barrister Law Journal,* April 1989.
36. Peter L. Berger, "Worldly Wisdom, Christian Foolishness" *First Things,* August/September 1990, p. 21. Quoted at greater length in Chapter 5.
37. See, for example, Randy Diamond, "Cities Turning Heartless on the Homeless," *San Francisco Chronicle,* 10 December 1990.

CHAPTER 11 *Building Self-Governance*

1. Charles Murray, "How to Win the War on Drugs," *New Republic,* 21 May 1990, p. 21.

2. Ibid.
3. William A. Donohue, *The New Freedom: Individualism and Collectivism in the Lives of Americans* (New Brunswick, N.J.: Transaction Publishers, 1990), p. 240.
4. David T. Ellwood and Lawrence H. Summers, "Poverty in America: Is Welfare the Answer or the Problem?" in *Fighting Poverty: What Works and What Doesn't*, ed. Sheldon H. Danziger and Daniel H. Weinberg (Cambridge, Mass.: Harvard University Press, 1986), p. 98.
5. David T. Ellwood has suggested basing the amount added though the EITC on half the difference between the parent's or parents' hourly wages and $6 per hour.
6. The State of Hawaii has found a way to require employers, no matter how small, to insure all their employees. One of the features that makes it work is that the insurance has deductibles and does not cover some of the things expensive plans do. The problem is that when employers are saddled with additional expenses, they eliminate jobs to meet them. More public employment jobs would likely be needed to carry out the policy I am suggesting if such health insurance were to be required of private companies.
7. William Tucker, *The Excluded Americans: Homelessness and Housing Policies* (Washington, D.C.: Regnery Gateway, 1990).
8. Murray, "How to Win the War on Drugs," p. 24.
9. Ibid.
10. Ibid., pp. 24–25.
11. Ibid., p. 25.
12. James Patterson and Peter Kim, *The Day America Told the Truth: What People Really Believe About Everything that Really Matters* (New York: Prentice Hall, 1991). Authors interviewed by David Gelman, *Newsweek*, 6 May 1991, p. 63.
13. Editorial, *New Republic*, 10 June 1991, p. 8.
14. E. J. Dionne, Jr., *Why Americans Hate Politics* (New York: Simon and Schuster, 1991), p. 332.
15. Ibid., p. 338.
16. Ibid., p. 332.
17. Ibid., p. 338.
18. Daniel P. Moynihan, *Family and Nation* (New York: Harcourt Brace Jovanovich, 1986), p. 190.
19. Dionne, *Why Americans Hate Politics*, p. 335.

Index

Acupuncture program for substance abusers, 66

ADAMHA. *See* Alcohol, Drug Abuse, and Mental Health Administration (ADAMHA)

ADATSA. *See* Alcohol and Drug Addiction Treatment Support Act (ADATSA), Washington State

Addiction
  as disorder, 83
  proposed public policy for, 83

Agnos, Art, 12, 208–9

Aid to Families with Dependent Children (AFDC)
  decline in number of recipients, 219
  effect of resources of, 93
  homeless families receiving, 14
  increase in single-parent families under, 100–101
  proposals to end, 110
  as a right, 258

Aid to the Disabled, 29

Alcohol, Drug Abuse, and Mental Health Administration (ADAMHA), 74, 77, 83

Alcohol and Drug Addiction Treatment Support Act

(ADATSA), Washington State, 60–65, 81

Alcoholics
  services in Portland, Ore., for, 65
  services in Seattle for, 57–59, 61–62, 64–67, 214–15

Alcoholics Anonymous, 58, 65, 77, 83

Alcoholism
  among homeless, 9–11, 21, 58–59
  among homeless women, 10–11

Allen, John, 77–78

American Psychiatric Association (APA)
  task force study of, 31–32, 42, 44

American Psychiatric Association (APA) report, 31–32

Anderson, Martin, 117–18

Antabuse, 71, 77

Antihomelessness act (proposed), 148–49

APA. *See* American Psychiatric Association (APA)

Armat, Virginia C., 31, 32–34, 42–43, 46–47

Association of Bay Area Governments (ABAG), 128

323

The Anderson Foundation

The publication of this book was made possible in part by a grant from the Anderson Foundation, a charitable organization located in La Jolla, California. The foundation was created in 1968 by Arnold C. Anderson to help the needy elderly. Mr. Anderson had observed their condition while serving as a Red Cross volunteer driving indigent patients to receive medical treatment, and upon retirement he established the foundation to provide good housing for them. The foundation's projects include the construction of a fourteen-story apartment building for two hundred elderly tenants. The foundation is now headed by Kenneth E. Anderson.